MW01050873

DEBUNKED?

DEBUNKED?

An auditor reviews the 2020 election—
and the lessons learned

JOSEPH N. FRIED, CPA

DEBUNKED?

FIRST EDITION

Copyright 2022 Joseph N. Fried

All rights reserved. No part of this book may be reproduced in any form or by any electronic or mechanical means, including information storage and retrieval systems, without permission in writing from the publisher, except by a reviewer, who may quote brief passages in a review.

ISBN: 978-1-64572-075-1 (paperback)
ISBN: 978-1-64572-076-8 (ebook)

For inquiries about volume orders, please contact:

Republic Book Publishers

27 West 20th Street

Suite 1103

New York NY 10011

editor@republicbookpublishers.com

Published in the United States by Republic Book Publishers

Distributed by Independent Publishers Group

www.ipgbook.com

Book designed by Mark Karis

Printed in the United States of America

FOR NINA

My wife, advisor, and best friend for over 50 years

FOR DAVID

Our thoughtful, perceptive, and successful son

AND FOR

The many people fighting for election integrity and transparency

CONTENTS

PREFACE

ANALYZING ELECTION ISSUES IS NOT AN ATTACK ON DEMOCRACY

In November 2020, fifty separate state presidential elections were held, and in each case the state election officials "certified" the winner after they performed an "audit" of the vote tally. As an experienced financial auditor, it is apparent to me that those terms, *certified* and *audit*, mean very little in the world of elections, politics, and journalism.

After the election, some states and counties re-counted ballots, and others performed limited audit-type procedures, but none performed a complete and full audit. The Maricopa County (Ariz.) audit was the most complete but, even there, auditors were blocked from performing the two very most vital audit procedures: voter canvassing (knocking on doors) and signature verification.[1] This begs the question: What would happen if state election results were subjected to the rigorous standards of the typical certified public audit (*i.e.,* a *real* audit) of a business or nonprofit organization? Would the results change? Would they still be "certified" or would the auditors issue *disclaimers of opinion*, which are given in the business world when the information is not sufficient to support a certified opinion?

ELECTIONS HAVE CHANGED—REAL AUDITS ARE NEEDED

Things have changed in recent years. Many states are automatically mailing ballots or ballot applications to everyone on voter registration lists—lists that often include millions

---

1   Cyber Ninjas, "Maricopa County Forensic Election Audit, v. II," Arizona State Senate, September 24, 2021, 6, https://www.azsenaterepublicans.com/_files/ugd/2f3470_1ec91dd80a024d5d8612c5490de1c460.pdf.

of people who are not interested in voting, who have already moved away, or who are found in urns or cemeteries. If voting-by-mail continues, it will be essential for states to have *independent* accountants conduct audits (real ones), commencing immediately after elections. This is particularly true for states that use *signatures* as the sole means of identification. And if mail-in ballots become the prevailing practice, the U.S. government may need to make legal or constitutional changes to extend the time between the date of a presidential election and the certification of the election winner. For many states, the so-called election "audits" of today are woefully inadequate.

ILLOGICAL STANDARDS
In the United States, our election audit decisions are made ass-backward. Let me explain with an analogy.

Sweet & Chewy
Ace Accountants are auditing the Sweet & Chewy Candy Company, which makes candy bars in several plants throughout the country. For years, the gross profit of the company has been between 51 and 52 percent, but this year, after management relaxed some of its accounting control policies, the profit sank to just 41 percent. Stockholders are concerned.

"We need to expand audit procedures," proclaimed the independent auditors. "It will take us much more time and documentation to figure out what happened. We have to test more transactions."

To this, company officials objected, saying that the auditors had *no proof* that there were irregularities. Besides, extensive audit procedures were not used in the past, and the certified financial statements were needed immediately. According to these officials, the auditors would have to "certify" without more time or testing.

Question: Who has to prove what, and to whom? Do the auditors have to *prove* fraud in order to acquire more information from the company? Or is the burden now with the company, which must give the auditors the additional information that is needed to explain the sharp drop in profits?

The answer is obvious (at least to any auditor). The company *must* allow expanded testing: Otherwise, the statements cannot be certified. That should be the only choice the company has. It should also be the only choice given to election administrators.

Presently, it does not seem to matter how many unexplained election anomalies exist. It does not matter how sloppy the records are, whether ballots are printed on ten different types of paper, whether chain of custody logs are kept, whether voters provide identification or their signatures are matched to registration records. The losing candidate gets no more than a simple re-counting of ballots—by the very same people who managed the election. To get more than that he must somehow, *prove* fraud. Without that proof, he can't have a real audit.

Any effort to conduct a genuine audit or investigation will be blocked by the presumptive winner (whether Democrat or Republican), by his/her political and media supporters, by disinterested courts, and by a severe lack of time. The election winner may even call a real audit "an attack on democracy." But, should a simple recounting of ballots be sufficient for certification—even where there are significant, unexplained questions and anomalies?

Whether you like him or hate him, the bellicose protestations of Donald J. Trump brought much scrutiny (where election news is not censored) to the election process and to the last-minute legal changes made prior to the election. That scrutiny led to numerous questions about election issues. Here are a few of those issues:

- the integrity of voter registration lists

- the security of ballots sent through the mail

- signature verification standards and other types of identification

- chain of custody documentation for ballots

- computer security

- bipartisan oversight of the process

- the use of unguarded "drop boxes"

- the use of private funding of the election process

- the real-time sharing of election data with political organizations

- the failure of some state administrators to adhere to the law

- disparate treatment of voters by different county administrators within a state

As I write this book, I will consider each swing state's 2020 election as if I have been asked to conduct an audit and render a certification opinion. Of course, I won't have access to most documents or to any voting equipment, so the arm-chair examinations I conduct will be general in nature. My "audits" will simply analyze the major claims of fraud or irregularity, the credibility of those claims, the available evidence, and the *threshold* audit standards and concepts that the states applied, or should have applied, relative to those claims.

> Here is the standard I will use to reach my conclusions: If there are unresolved, credible allegations of irregularities, and they are of such magnitude that the election results could change, then the certification should not have been made. I will apply that standard to each of six swing states, and will itemize the specific arguments supporting my final conclusions at the end of each of the separate state sections. This analysis will be made without regard to political, legal, or practical considerations, such as timing and resources. Changes to the 2020 election may not be legally possible or even desirable. If that is the case, please consider this book to be a contribution to the historical record.

Regarding the quality of the audit *evidence*, my judgments will be based on general audit standards and requirements derived from decades of experience as an auditor and CPA who has professionally conducted and reviewed hundreds of audits, including the audit work of many other CPA firms. However, I do not represent or speak on behalf of any organization, including the American Institute of Certified Public Accountants, of which I am a member.

In my research for this book I will respectfully consider all significant issues and arguments, *no matter which side makes them.* However, the conclusions reached may not sit well with many—especially on the left side of politics. Mainstream media and "big tech" have claimed that *any* questioning of the 2020 election is "an attack on democracy." And due to widespread censorship (under the guise of preventing the spread of misinformation), many people are unaware of certain facts, arguments, and theories.

For example, forty or fifty hours of election integrity hearings were held by several state legislative bodies shortly after the election. The hearings included presentations by data scientists, statisticians, cyber experts, employees of election departments, and numerous eyewitnesses who worked as poll watchers and challengers. An immediate and complete ban was imposed on the hearings by *all* major media outlets, including CBS, NBC, ABC, MSNBC, CNN, Facebook ("Meta"), YouTube, and Twitter. That censorship is the real attack on democracy. In the long run, it is not effective (I hope) because censorship doesn't eliminate dissent: It delays it, and forces it underground.

Although I will strive to be objective, there will be many pointed observations, opinions, and conclusions in the book, and I won't pull my punches! And, with regard to some in mainstream media and "big-tech," I am definitely *not* objective. The censorship that is prevalent today, and the common alliance that seems to exist between much of media and government, are disgraceful threats to the principles set forth in the U.S. Constitution.

The endeavor starts without preconceived notions except for one: It is unlikely that the most extreme points of view are valid. I doubt that claims of irregularities are completely baseless, and I also doubt that either candidate won the election by a landslide. But we shall see!

PART I

THE AUDIT PROCESS

1

INTRODUCTION

In the summer of 2021, Wisconsin performed an audit of the 2020 presidential election. However, two Wisconsin jurisdictions, the City of Madison and Milwaukee County, refused to give the auditors physical access to the ballot certificates and many other election records, after citing guidance received from the Biden administration. The withheld ballots comprised about 19 percent of all state ballots (620,000 of 3.3 million).

The auditors disregarded the omitted ballots, and they examined only the ballots they were allowed to see. Based upon this limited review, the auditors concluded that Wisconsin did a very good job of managing the election, and that Joe Biden won it. Wisconsin legislators and the mainstream media celebrated the findings.[1]

> A. The audit results confirm that Joe Biden won the state of Wisconsin.
>
> B. It was appropriate and helpful for the Biden administration to get involved.
>
> C. Auditing fewer ballots is a good way to save time and money.
>
> D. The audit report might make very good toilet paper.

---

1   Legislative Audit Bureau, "Elections Administration," State of Wisconsin, October 2021, 7, https://legis.wisconsin.gov/lab/media/3288/21-19full.pdf.

The answer is obvious. All audits, whether of election systems, construction companies, the United Way, or a donut shop, involve certain simple but important concepts that must be followed. The most fundamental concept is illustrated by the multiple choice exercise above: In a true audit, the auditee does not determine the items to be tested. If documents are withheld from the auditor (who must be independent) there should be an excellent reason. And if the withheld documents are important to the work of the independent auditors, a disclaimer of opinion must be issued. In such cases, the auditor's report should indicate that, due to the withholding of significant information, no opinion (no conclusion or certification) can be issued.

This is just common sense, and it pertains to all types of investigative work. For example, if the police have a warrant to search your home for an illegal gun, the police expect to search ALL of your home. They won't be happy if you say, "Search wherever you want, but not in this room."

The above illustration is not fictitious: It is based on undisputed facts. During an audit of Wisconsin's election, which was conducted by a quasi-governmental group called the "Legislative Audit Bureau," auditors were told they could not have physical access to about 19 percent of the ballot certificates from two regions (Madison City and Milwaukee County). Nevertheless, politicians and journalists claimed the audit report was proof that the election was generally accurate and fair. It is troubling.[2]

Oh, by the way, did I mention that one of the Madison wards (Madison 124) supposedly increased its voter turnout (2016 to 2020) by 1,285 percent?[3] I wonder if that had anything to do with the refusal of Madison City to show its ballot certificates. For more discussion of the "Madison Miracle," see page 219.

Auditing standards involve math, risk assessments, analytical procedures, statistics, and testing. For an election, the auditor should use those tools to determine who received the highest number of *valid* votes.

A simple recounting of ballots by an election department does not, by itself, preclude the need for an auditor's determination. Likewise, the auditor's assessment cannot be invalidated by a court decision rendered on procedural grounds. I realize that the

---

2   No legal or rational reason for the withholding of records was given. The clerks of Madison and Milwaukee simply said that the federal government expected them to maintain the records and, therefore, they would not let others handle those records. They apparently overlooked the fact that the federal government wants records withheld so that, if there is a question, auditors can examine those records. If no one gets to see the records, we might as well throw them out right away!

3   Will Flanders, Kyle Koenen, Rick Esenberg, Noah Diekemper & Miranda Spindt, A Review of the 2020 Election," *Wisconsin Institute for Law and Liberty*, (December 2021): 78, https://will-law.org/wp-content/uploads/2021/11/2021ElectionReviewStudy.pdf.

auditor won't have the final word in this matter, but she may be the only one who can fairly and accurately determine who *really* won the election.

Audit standards are important, so I recommend that you read the following brief, albeit boring, overview. It involves simple concepts that will be cited throughout the book.

But . . . if you find it too boring, just skip to Part II on page 17.

2

KEY CONCEPTS FOR ALL AUDITS

AUDITOR INDEPENDENCE

Self-audits by election officials are not sufficient to confirm the results of an election. The people who plan and run an election should never be the people who later "certify" their own work. On this simple point, many people are confused. For example, while the Cyber Ninjas[1] were attempting to conduct a real audit of the election in Maricopa County (Ariz.), how often did we hear that the election results had already been confirmed by multiple "audits"? However, those audits could not possibly confirm the validity of the election because they were performed and circumscribed by the same people who ran the election.

The Maricopa County Elections Department had a vested interest in confirming the accuracy and efficiency of the election it had managed. After all, a bad audit report could jeopardize election department jobs. Besides, those weren't audits at all: They were merely recounts.

There is another risk: Even an independent auditor can buckle in the face of resistance from the auditee. As cited on page 3, the Wisconsin auditors were independent— ostensibly. However, they succumbed to the resistance of Madison and Milwaukee County (who refused to fully cooperate), and in so doing they damaged the validity of their audit results.

---

1   Cyber Ninjas were a private group contracted by the Arizona Senate to conduct an audit of the 2020 presidential election held in Maricopa County.

RISK ASSESSMENT

After establishing his or her audit independence, the auditor performs a risk assessment for the organization or system. The assessment is broken into two main components: inherent (or unavoidable) risk, and internal control risk—the risk that controls established by management (the election department) are poorly designed and/or not being followed.

> ### *The murky distinction between inherent and internal control risk*
> Before proceeding, it is worth noting that there is no clear line separating inherent from internal control risk. Generally speaking, inherent risks are those that an organization is stuck with, whereas internal control risks can be controlled. Sometimes, it is hard to tell one type of risk from another. For example, the Michigan Secretary of State decided to mail ballot applications to 7.7 million Michiganders, even though most recipients (more than 4 million) would not use the applications. In the hands of political operatives, those extra applications could be used to obtain tens of thousands of illegal ballots. Was the action taken by the Secretary unavoidable because of the COVID pandemic? Or was that action indicative of the administration's failure to adhere to the internal controls set forth in the legislative code or regulations?

Inherent (or unavoidable) risk assessment

There are many potential risk factors in the environment of an organization or system. These factors, which may exist outside of the election administration offices, are likely to increase risk by creating ambiguity and/or the need for individual judgments. Here are just a few examples. Along with other risk factors, they are analyzed in Part II and/or in sections on specific states:

- A county may have purchased complicated computers with many features that are not clearly understood by election staff. If safeguards are not in place, data files may be removed or altered due to errors, inappropriate use of flash drives, or hacking.

- Some states made last-minute legislative or administrative changes that added complexity to the election. Election employees had limited time to learn the new laws or rules.

- Several states mailed out millions of unsolicited ballots, and this greatly increased inherent risk. This was especially true where ballot mailing was tied to obsolete registration lists.

- Believe it or not, in some states it is legal to pay people to "harvest" votes. While you're watching "90 Day Fiancé," a political operative may knock on your door and ask to file an election ballot on your behalf. In some states he may even offer "guidance" or he may sign the ballot paperwork as a witness. Perhaps he will visit your mom's nursing home to help her "understand" how to cast her vote. Even in states where harvesting is illegal, harvesting can and often does take place. (See the brewing Georgia scandal on page 109.)

- A billionaire tech CEO may decide to influence an election by giving millions of dollars to help voters, but only in certain geographical areas, and only with "strings attached" (e.g., changing the way ballots are processed). In exchange for millions of dollars of funding, some county election administrators may give special access to important election data. (See what Zuckerberg's money bought in Wisconsin, on page 221.)

Inherent risk is also increased if signature verifications are used in place of objective forms of identification, such as your last four Social Security digits or your drivers license number. Signature verification may be useful as a secondary means of identification, but it should never be the only form of identification because it is too subjective. Today, many polling stations use electronic signature pads, which make signature recognition even more difficult and subjective.

QUESTION TO CONSIDER: PLEASE READ THIS AND SELECT BEST ANSWER

In September 2021, the Cyber Ninjas (representing the Arizona State Senate) presented the preliminary results of their audit of the 2020 election in Maricopa County. The auditors were blocked (sued in court) from conducting a standard review of signatures. However, they figured out a clever way to elicit a little bit of useful signature-related data.

As part of the presentation, Dr. Shiva Ayyadurai ("Dr. Shiva"), an MIT-educated pattern recognition expert, reported on his test of the *legibility* of a random sampling of 200 signatures on ballot envelopes received from voters four weeks *prior* to the election versus four days *after* the election. What were the findings of Dr. Shiva and his team?[2]

---

2   Dr. Shiva Ayyadurai, "Pattern Recognition Classification of Early Voting Ballot Return Envelope Images for Signature Presence Detection," EchoMail, Inc., September 2021, 93–94, https://c692f527-da75-4c86-b5d1-8b3d5d4d5b43.filesusr.com/ugd/2f3470_05deb65815ab4d4b83938d71bc53459b.pdf.

A. Most signatures were legible, no matter when received.

B. Most signatures were *not* legible, no matter when received.

C. There was no discernable pattern.

D. 97 percent of signatures received *before* the election were legible, versus only 3 percent of signatures received *after* the election.

The correct answer is letter D: Almost all signatures received before Election Day could be discerned, while almost none of the signatures on ballot documents received after Election Day could be discerned. If Dr. Shiva's work is accurate (and it must be confirmed independently with a much larger sample), this might be a serious indication that ballot "harvesters" were rushing to submit ballots after the election, and did not have time to carefully forge signatures on the ballot envelopes.

Evidence for a courtroom? Probably not. Evidence for an auditor? Yes! This type of anomaly cries out for additional auditing: Specifically, it indicates the need for a review of a large, statistically valid sample of signatures. It may also suggest the need for door-to-door canvassing of a random sample of voters (to ask them if they really voted). In an ideal world, those audit procedures would take place before the election results are certified.

> *Special note: Dr. Shiva later conducted a larger test of signatures in Maricopa County, Arizona. A massive percentage of signatures were determined to be highly questionable. See page 97.*

Thus far we have discussed a few of the inherent risk factors that have known causes. But inherent risk is also evidenced by trends and statistical anomalies for which causes cannot be readily determined. Here are some of the statistically unlikely events (risk factors) from the 2020 election. Trump supporters must wonder how he lost the Electoral College vote despite these statistics:

- Trump won the "bellwether" states of Ohio and Florida. Winning those states has meant winning the national election for nearly sixty years.[3] He also won eighteen of nineteen bellwether counties. Those have been predictive of the national winner for nearly forty years.[4]

- Trump won Ohio, Iowa, and North Carolina. The winner of those three states has successful won the presidency, without exception, since 1898.[5]

- Trump gained votes (more than 10 million) relative to the previous election, yet he lost. It is the first time that happened in nearly 150 years.[6]

- Biden garnered a record number of votes despite consistently trailing Trump in measures of voter enthusiasm. He even shattered Obama's popular vote totals. The highest popular vote total for Obama was 66.9 million in 2008, versus over 81 million for Biden.[7]

- Trump won 94 percent of the primary vote, which is an indication of supporter enthusiasm. No incumbent who has received 75 percent or more of the primary vote has ever lost the national election.[8]

- "Donald Trump was pretty much the only incumbent president in U.S. history to lose his re-election while his own party gained seats in the House of Representatives."[9]

---

3   J.B. Shurk, "5 More Ways Joe Biden Magically Outperformed Election Norms,"*Federalist*, November 23, 2020, https://thefederalist.com/2020/11/23/5-more-ways-joe-biden-magically-outperformed-election-norms/.

4   Petr Svab, "Bellwether Counties Went Overwhelmingly for Trump in 2020," *Epoch Times*, November 17, 2020, https://www.theepochtimes.com/bellwether-counties-went-overwhelmingly-for-trump-in-2020_3579578.html.

5   Doug Wade, "Video interview of Seth Keshel," *PureSocialTV*, January 1, 2021, https://www.youtube.com/watch?v=xXMW9VNMPT4.

6   J.B. Shurk, "5 More Ways Joe Biden Magically Outperformed Election Norms," November 23, 2020.

7   Ibid.

8   Ibid.

9   Randy DeSoto, "History Stands Against the Idea of Incumbent President Losing but His Party Gaining House Seats," *Western Journal*, November 13, 2020, https://www.westernjournal.com/history-stands-idea-incumbent-president-losing-party-gaining-house-seats/.

- Non-polling metrics include registration trends, primary election votes, voter enthusiasm, the number of small donors, social media followers, lawn signs, campaign merchandise signs, and individuals betting on each candidate. Per Patrick Basham, "Every non-polling metric forecast Trump's re-election, and these non-polling metrics have historically had a 100 percent record in indicating who will be president—until 2020."[10]

- There were hard-to-believe voting percentages—primarily in the swing states. Steve Cortes reported that there was an 84 percent turnout rate in Milwaukee, while Cleveland, a city with comparable demographics, had a turnout rate of only 51 percent.[11] Statewide, more than 89 percent of Wisconsin's registered voters cast ballots. And, get a load of this: Over 70 percent of Wisconsin nursing homes (66 of the 91 that were tested) had *turnout rates of 100 percent!* (See page 209.)

In themselves, the anomalies listed above do not constitute proof of election irregularities. Don't bother taking them to a judge because she won't be impressed. However, the auditor must consider these factors in judging inherent risk and in planning the extent of his or her audit procedures. Again, the audit work should take place before the election is certified.

To summarize, we assess inherent (unavoidable) risk by considering all risks in the environment—the ones with known causes and the anomalies without known causes.

Internal control risk assessment

All organizations, including state and local election systems, must have well-designed internal control policies and procedures (IC). For a typical for-profit business, a few of the policies and procedures might be these:

- Require two people to sign checks for amounts greater than $5,000.

- Require the internal accountant to reconcile the cash accounts frequently.

- Require department supervisors to approve all expenditure requests.

---

10   Patrick Basham, "Was the Election Stolen?" *Chronicles*, October 2021, https://democracyinstitute.org/wp-content/uploads/2021/10/Chronicles-October-2021-Bidens-Inexplicable-Victory.pdf.

11   Steve Cortes, "The statistical case against Biden's win," *Real Clear Politics*, November 10, 2020, https://www.realclearpolitics.com/2020/11/10/the_statistical_case_against_bidens_win_528969.html#!.

The internal controls of an election system vary from county to county and state to state, but the internal control policies and procedures might include these:

- Update voter registration lists frequently, and reconcile them to other databases.

- Keep an accurate log of all requests for ballots and make sure the voter requesting the ballot is on the registration list.

- Review ballot applications to ensure all required information has been given.

- Use at least two people, selected by two different political parties, to empty drop boxes, and maintain chain of custody records that tell who emptied the box, how many ballots were removed, and when.

- Restrict access to computers and data tabulators, and maintain individual passwords.

- Print all ballots on one type of paper that resists photocopying.

- Keep the ballots and ballot paper in secure and locked locations. Maintain good records.

- Ensure that ballot processing can be observed at close range by people from all political parties.

- Where a signature is ambiguous, request the voter to follow up with more objective identification.

An evaluation of the IC system usually involves flowcharting the various systems used to issue, authorize, and document transactions, and it includes an assessment of management competence and integrity. Of course, management must fully cooperate with the independent auditors. In the real world, failure to assist auditors could lead to dismissal. Unfortunately, in the world of elections, resistance is sometimes celebrated!

QUESTION TO CONSIDER: PLEASE READ THIS AND SELECT BEST ANSWER

On behalf of the Arizona State Senate, Cyber Ninjas performed an audit of the presidential election conducted by Maricopa County. Which statement is true?

> A. Maricopa County would not let the auditors use its facilities, so all computers, equipment, ballots, and other documentation had to be relocated.
>
> B. Officials with the County refused to answer most of the auditors' questions.
>
> C. Officials with the County refused to furnish routers, electronic file and application logs, and other items, in defiance of a court-approved subpoena.[12]
>
> D. All of the above are true.

The correct answer is D. Although the Arizona Senate's right to conduct an audit was affirmed legally, the Maricopa County Elections Department fought the audit in every way possible.[13] The result was an incomplete audit, a delay of many months, and the extra expenditure of millions of dollars.

PLAN THE AUDIT STRATEGY

Assuming that the organization has a well-designed IC system, test it to ensure that people are adhering to the system. If they are, testing of transactions can be reduced. In other words, fewer ballots and voters and documents need to be tested. If the election department does not rigorously adhere to internal control policies and procedures, the auditor should plan extensive testing of transactions.[14]

Think: Where is fraud most likely?

Doug Logan, the CEO of Cyber Ninjas (the firm that performed the Maricopa County audit) made a very astute comment during a public presentation in December 2021. He said (paraphrasing liberally) it is relatively easy to spot fraudulent changes made

---

12 Electronic file and application logs are commonly called "Splunk logs." Splunk is a widely-used software platform used to monitor and analyze machine-generated data.

13 Maricopa County is merely a subdivision of the state, and as such it is, effectively, mid-level management.

14 Auditors call this "substantive" testing.

after a vote is already cast. But, if someone gains access to the voter rolls, and he casts a real ballot (acquired in some fraudulent way), that is very hard to detect. Logan is right, and it is a factor that an auditor would want to consider in planning his or her audit procedures. In the planning stage, the auditor must devise an appropriate strategy to deal with anticipated types of irregularity.

Canvassing: the new election audit tool

Many times throughout this book you will find reference to "canvassing" and to "knocking on doors." I am an evangelist on this subject because it is clear to me that ONLY door-to-door canvassing can detect the fraud produced by misuse of harvested ballots that lack identification requirements. Standard audit procedures that apply to election office procedures and documentation are important, and they are certainly better than simple re-counts. However, conventional audit techniques will not be enough in this age of mail-in ballots.

Without the slightest question, states that simply mail ballots or ballot applications to everyone on out-of-date registration lists, without requiring identification, will have a certain level of fraud—perhaps lots of fraud. There is only one good way to detect that fraud: through door-to-door canvassing of a statistical sample of absentee or mail-in voters. Very soon after the election, they must be asked whether they voted and the means by which they voted.

Telephone calls will not work! Fraudsters and people who have already moved out of state will answer their cell phones and may give disingenuous answers. You might think you are talking to someone in Nevada but he is actually in California, and has been there for months or years.

A team of professional pollsters or independent auditors could canvass a sample of voters in just a week or two, and they would obtain bullet-proof evidence of fraud, if there is any.

MATERIALITY APPLIED TO FINDINGS

Two types of materiality

What amount of election irregularity (or fraud) is material enough to impact election results? For the auditor, the materiality is of two types: There is overall materiality, which is a relatively large number, and there is performance or systemic materiality, which can be a very small number. If a candidate loses an election by 20,000 votes, a few irregularities involving three or four votes may seem insignificant. However, if those three or four votes are part of a systemic scheme, they must be taken seriously and investigated. One way to investigate is by means of testing.

QUESTION TO CONSIDER: PLEASE READ THIS AND SELECT BEST ANSWER

In the small town of Elmwood, only three people were arrested, prosecuted, and convicted of the crime of shoplifting during the month of May.

> A. Elmwood is lucky to have so little shoplifting.
>
> B. There probably have been hundreds of shoplifting incidents in Elmwood.
>
> C. When businesses complain about shoplifting, they are exaggerating.
>
> D. None of the above is true.

The correct answer is B: Elmwood has probably had hundreds of shoplifting incidents. Under questioning, apprehended shoplifters have estimated that they steal about fifty times before they are caught and, if they are caught, they are turned over to the police only 50 percent of the time.[15] What happens then? Only a small fraction of the shoplifters turned over to the police are actually prosecuted and convicted. The rest might get a citation or fine.

This is the point: If we were to judge the rate of shoplifting by the conviction rate we would be off by a factor of hundreds. The town of Elmwood may have had 300, 400, or 500 cases of shoplifting. (If Elmwood is in California we might be off by a factor of thousands, because shoplifters are rarely prosecuted there.)

Similarly, we must exercise care when assessing the amount of election crime. Like the shoplifter, the election fraudster must first be caught, and that is not likely if there are mail-in ballots and weak identification laws. If the election fraudster is caught, he will probably not be prosecuted and convicted. Thus, a few convictions for election fraud might be the figurative tip of an iceberg.

---

15   Bill Turner, "Exactly What Is a Shoplifter and How Much Do You Know?" *Loss Prevention Magazine*, March 13, 2018, https://losspreventionmedia.com/exactly-what-is-a-shoplifter-and-how-much-do-you-know/.

A real case in Florida

In 2021, the Public Interest Legal Foundation asked several Florida counties how many referrals they made to prosecutors for potential election law violations during or just before the 2020 election. There were 156 *referrals*, and the counties making the most referrals to law enforcement were Broward, Miami-Dade, and Palm Beach. Those referrals involved double voting, vote-by-mail violations, and noncitizen registration and/or voting. Of the 156 cases, how many were prosecuted? *Zero!* Why was that? Well, it could be due to a shortage of law enforcement and prosecutorial manpower, or it could be that big cities have very ideological prosecutors who don't believe these are serious crimes worthy of their time and resources.[16]

TEST TRANSACTIONS

As noted, the amount of required transactional testing depends on the quality of the internal control policies and procedures. Even where internal controls are well-designed and vigorously enforced, some testing of transactions is usually required. In many cases, statistical sampling is used to select items for testing, while in other cases, the selection of transactions is based on auditor judgment.

The testing should be two-fold. There is the testing of relationships (analytical testing). For example, can the log of ballots mailed out be reconciled to the log of ballots received, or can a machine-count of received ballots be reconciled to the number of ballots in boxes?

The second type of transactional testing is of specific documents to determine that they exist, are authentic, and properly authorized, completed, and submitted. For an election, the documents might include ballots and ballot envelopes, ballot applications, chain of custody records, email, and other internet correspondence. A special type of testing might be needed in an election: the canvassing of voters. (See the box on page 14.)

AUDIT CONCEPTS SPECIFIC TO ELECTIONS

You will be happy to know that the general auditing overview is complete. There are additional audit considerations—specific to elections—in Appendix A on page 284.

---

16   On April 25, 2022, Florida Governor Ron DeSantis signed legislation establishing a 15-member police force dedicated to the investigation of potential election law violations. The legislation gives the Governor the authority to assign an additional 10 election law officers, as needed. Democrats in and out of mainstream media vehemently opposed the legislation.

PART II

CONTROVERSIAL ELECTION ISSUES, GENERALLY

3

THE MAJOR ISSUES OF THE 2020 ELECTION

Before and after the election, many Trump supporters had great concern over perceived fraud or irregularities. These perceptions primarily applied to swing states, and they inflamed tensions between Trump and Biden supporters.

Much of the controversy centered on procedural changes made by state administrators just before the election—ostensibly due to concern over the spread of COVID19. Many of those changes were contrary to the literal wording of state law, so legal challenges ensued. In fighting the changes, the Trump campaign had little success in state or federal courts—usually due to process arguments, such as lack of standing, jurisdiction, mootness, or laches. (For more detail concerning the nature of dismissals, see page 279.) These legal issues are mostly beyond the scope of this book; however, some of the key law and administrative changes are included in the separate state sections in Part III.

THE FBI HELPS HUNTER

Ironically, the biggest political story of the 2020 election was unknown to many Americans until after the election. It involved an alleged payoff to Joe Biden from Chinese businessmen, via his son, Hunter. The *New York Post* broke the story based on an analysis of the files in one of Hunter's laptop computers, and based upon allegations made by one of Hunter's former business partners, Tony Bobulinski. Following the lead of Twitter, mainstream media immediately suppressed the story.

The Republican National Committee (RNC) filed a complaint with the Federal Election Commission (FEC), arguing that the coordinated actions of big tech and mainstream media amounted to a "prohibited corporate in-kind contribution" to the

Biden campaign. In September 2021 the FEC ruled against the RNC, stating that Twitter was following its "hacked" information policy—sort of.

The FEC explained: "It remains unclear whether the materials were hacked under the meaning of Twitter's policy." Nevertheless, the FEC was persuaded to rule in Twitter's favor after Twitter's head of Site Integrity, Yoel Roth, argued that the company was suppressing the story due to the guidance it received from federal authorities, namely, the FBI.

This is what Roth stated in an affidavit presented to the FEC:

> Federal law enforcement agencies communicated that they expected 'hack-and-leak operations' by state actors might occur in the period shortly before the 2020 presidential election . . . . I also learned in these meetings that there were rumors that a hack-and-leak operation would involve Hunter Biden.

How could "federal law enforcement" possibly believe that this was hacked information? The FBI had one of the laptops for at least 10 months prior to the election, so there was plenty of time to verify its authenticity. It appears likely that the FBI was spreading disinformation to Twitter, in a scheme to help Joe Biden win the election.

OTHER CONTROVERSIAL ISSUES

Here are the many issues that created controversy and tension in the months just before and after the election. They affected most of the swing states.

- The hyperbolic rhetoric of Donald J. Trump on page 21

- The Dominion computer wizard who guaranteed Trump's loss on page 22

- Mail-in ballots on page 28

- Harvested ballots on page 32

- Dr. Halderman and Mr. Hyde-Halderman on page 38 and page 42

- Mathematical anomalies on page 44

- Low mail-in ballot rejection rates on page 49

- Ballot dumps? on page 50

- Ballot counting stopped in the middle of the night on page 51

- Crazy high turn-out rates? on page 52

- Crazy high registration rates? on page 54

- The Kraken is drowning on page 55

- The Smartest Man in the Room on page 58

- Mike Lindell on page 61

- Hundreds of Statements and Sworn Affidavits on page 61 and 151

- Billionaire drop boxes on page 64

- Alleged ballot shredding on page 65

As you can see, there were allegations concerning several issues that led people to question the results of the election. Here is a summary of each. Many of the issues are further analyzed in the separate sections on swing states.

THE HYPERBOLIC RHETORIC OF DONALD J. TRUMP
We fight like hell, and if you don't fight like hell, you're not going to have a country anymore.

—PRESIDENT DONALD J. TRUMP

Donald Trump made several hyperbolic statements that inflamed the electorate. Sometimes his statements were backed up with shaky sources and little more than gut instinct. For example, what is the evidence that shows he won the popular vote, nationwide?

The above notwithstanding, Trump's protestations do not disturb me, and they were no more anti-democratic than the Russia dossier hoax, Stacy Abrams' ongoing complaints about the Georgia gubernatorial election, or President Biden's declaration that the next election will be unfair if there is no national election legislation.

In addition, many of Trump's claims may be true; and it is vital that America considers all issues impacting election integrity. Trump's hyperbolic bombast may be hard to take, but he has kept alive an issue that mainstream media wanted to kill at birth.

In an Op-Ed in the *Wall Street Journal*, newspaper publisher Conrad Black lamented Trump's "inability to resist indulging in his 'constructive hyperbole.'" But Black also said:

> It is vitally important that President Trump continue to impugn the election result and that his complaint continues to attract a respectable amount of credence so that it cannot be airily rejected as sour grapes.[1]

I completely agree. Where Trump makes a factual misstatement, fire back. But when he raises a valid concern, check it out, investigate it, research it, report it, and repair it, if appropriate.

THE DOMINION COMPUTER WIZARD WHO GUARANTEED TRUMP'S LOSS
Don't worry about the election. Trump's not gonna win. I made f**king sure of that!

According to former tech CEO, Joe Oltmann, those words were spoken by Eric Coomer, a former VP of Product Strategy and Security for Dominion Voting Systems, a company that maintains voting machines in several U.S. states.[2]

Oltmann, the founder and leader of a conservative civic organization, had been receiving much hate and vitriol from several journalists, and the tech-savvy CEO suspected they might be affiliated with the radical organization known as Antifa. Oltmann decided to electronically infiltrate Antifa using his hi-tech cyber skills, and in September 2020 he found a way to listen-in on what he describes as an Antifa conference. In an interview recorded on video by Michelle Malkin, Oltmann described what he heard:[3]

> I got on this call, and in this call you hear all this "fascist, fascist, fascist, fascist," all this stuff that's going on . . . and so I listened for a while and then somebody named Eric came on and started, started talking . . . and so as he starts to talk, someone says, "Who's Eric?" and then someone answers: "Eric is the Dominion guy."
>
> [Eric] keeps speaking and then someone interrupts and says "What we gonna do if f**king Trump wins?" And uh he responds with, and I'm going to paraphrase because obviously I didn't write exactly what he wrote uh is "Don't worry about the election. Trump is not going to win. I made f**king sure of that" [sic].

1　Conrad Black, "The Wall Street Journal's Shabby Rebuttal of Trump Settles Nothing," *The Ohio Star* (November 3, 2021), https://theohiostar.com/2021/11/03/commentary-the-wall-street-journals-shabby-rebuttal-of-trump-settles-nothing/.

2　Until just after the election, Coomer had been listed on the web as an officer of Dominion. However, after the election controversies emerged, his name was removed.

3　Michelle Malkin, "Video interview of Joe Oltmann," MalkinLive, November 13, 2020, https://m.facebook.com/therightmichellemalkin/videos/2336616753141046/?refsrc=deprecated&_rdr.

By Googling the key words, *Eric, Dominion*, and *Denver Colorado* (where the call took place), Joe Oltmann "came up with this gentleman named Eric Coomer," but at first he could not believe he had the right guy.

The Eric Coomer who was revealed through the Google search had an executive position with Dominion, owned Dominion stock and key patents, and had a Ph.D. in nuclear physics. From those credentials it didn't make sense to Oltmann that this guy was Antifa Eric. So, Oltmann set the matter aside, and forgot all about it until several weeks later—after the November election. That is when someone sent him an article about election problems in Georgia.

As Joe Oltmann read the article, the names "Dominion" and "Eric Coomer" popped out and rang a bell. After some serious research, Oltmann discovered that Dominion "Eric" was the "single cog on the wheel that has his name in every state." Oltmann pressed deeper by gaining access to Coomer's private Facebook account (legally, he claims). That is when he learned that the crazy Antifa Eric and the Eric Coomer of Dominion had to be one and the same.[4]

What you are about to learn is shocking, but it is more than credible: Dominion's Eric Coomer has confirmed just about all of it. Apparently, Eric Coomer is a desperate, vitriolic hate-monger, and it is frightening to think that this computer wizard physicist was in charge of the security aspects of Dominion's voting machines, which were used in more than one swing state. Coomer is best described via his own social media postings, which are reflected in screenshots obtained by Oltmann—shortly before Coomer had them all (over eighty) removed. Since the screenshots are difficult to read, transcripts are provided:

Transcription of July 21, 2016 Facebook posting by Eric Coomer:

If you are planning to vote for that autocratic, narcissistic, fascist ass-hat blowhard and his christian jihadist VP pic, UNFRIEND ME NOW! NO, I'm not joking. . . . Only an absolute F**KING IDIOT could ever vote for that wind-bag f**k-tard FASCIST RACIST F**K! No bullshit. I don't give a damn if you're friend, family, or random acquaintance. Pull the lever, mark an oval, touch a screen for that carnival barker. UNFRIEND ME NOW. I have no desire whatsoever to ever interact with you.

---

4   Eric Coomer, Ph.D. v. Donald J. Trump for President, Inc, et al., 2020cv34319 (District Court, Denver County, Colorado, 2020), Video deposition of Eric Coomer @ 2:50:50. A video recording of the Coomer deposition is here: https://rumble.com/vnmezh-eric-coomer-deposition.html.

Here is a transcription of a July 9, 2017 posting:

Ah . . . Texas . . . The land of racists, idiots, and mysoginists. In two hours I've heard, "what's wrong wif hav'n a ralationship with another powr'ful kuntry (Russia)?" I luuuv trump", "goddamn Wimmen jus' dun know hor' ta liss'n", "ya know darling, you're pretty, wish I didn't have to tip you. Them robots is comin" [sic].[5]

Call the Secret Service
In normal times, the Secret Service might be interested in Figure 1:[6]

FIGURE 1: A THREAT?

Dead Prez - Cop Shot (HQ)

In September 2021, Eric Coomer filed a defamation lawsuit against Oltmann, Donald J. Trump for President, Inc., Rudy Giuliani, Sidney Powell, and several news journalists and news organizations. The defendants deposed Eric Coomer on September 23, 2021, at which time he made several surprising statements, under oath. For example, he claimed that he does not know what "Prez" means in his "Dead Prez" posting.[7]

Another Coomer posting (not displayed here) is captioned: "Oi polloi, pigs for slaughter." When deposed, Coomer claimed (under oath) that he was not sure if pigs referred to the police or to real pigs in a slaughter house.[8]

5   Michelle Malkin, "Video interview of Joe Oltmann," November 13, 2020.

6   Ibid.

7   Eric Coomer, Ph.D. v. Donald J. Trump for President, Inc, et al., 2020cv34319 (District Court, Denver County, Colorado, 2020), Video deposition of Eric Coomer, 82.

8   Ibid., 80–81.

In the deposition, Coomer was asked if it was appropriate for an executive in his fifties to post something that says, "F**K the U.S.A." His response was that he was only forty-nine when he posted it. When asked if he thinks "the cops are "motherf**king villains," Coomer replied, "In certain aspects, yes."[9]

Coomer's testimony revealed that he had lied in a December 8, 2020 *Denver Post* Op-Ed, where he stated that he had no social media accounts, and "these individuals are impersonating me." Coomer also stated: "I want to be very clear: I have no connection to the Antifa movement." That was also a lie, as revealed by one of his social media posts, which follows.[10]

Coomer, the oxymoronic Antifa spokesman
Eric Coomer issued a statement from Antifa, to tell the world that there is no such thing! In his posting, below, he either makes an Antifa statement or reposts one (not clear which). He addresses the statement to "Mr. Trump" (Figure 2).[11]

FIGURE 2: A MESSAGE FROM *ANTIFA*
(THE ORGANIZATION THAT DOES NOT EXIST)

Eric Coomer
June 2 ·

In case you didn't know:

"Antifa" has made a statement:

TO: ALL MEDIA

PUBLIC STATEMENT FROM "ANTIFA" IN RESPONSE TO THE THREATS ISSUED BY UNITED STATES PRESIDENT DONALD J. TRUMP

Dear Mr. Trump:

Let us be perfectly clear:

"Antifa" isn't an organization. There's no membership, no meetings, no dues, no rules, no leaders, no structure. It is, literally, an idea and nothing more. Even the claim of this author to represent "Antifa" is one made unilaterally for the purposes of this communication and nothing more; there is no governing body nor trademark owner to dispute the author's right to represent "AntiFa."

"Antifa" is a neologism constructed from a contraction of the phrase "anti-fascist." The truth is, there's no such thing as being "anti-Fascist." Either you are a decent human being with a conscience, or you are a fascist.

9   Ibid., 88.

10 Staff, "In deposition, former Dominion VP Coomer admitted company shared his leftist views," *WorldTribune.com*, October 13, 2021, https://www.worldtribune.com/in-deposition-former-dominion-vp-coomer-admitted-company-shared-his-leftist-views/.

11 Ray Pearson, "The Anti-Trump Dominion CEO Eric Coomer Who Wrote An Antifa Manifesto On His Facebook Page . . ." *YourNews.com*, November 28, 2020.

Eric Coomer, at risk of arrest, as shown on police body cam. Image courtesy of Gateway Pundit.[12]

From all of these postings and from the responses made in his deposition, it is crystal clear that Eric Coomer has warm feelings for the "nonexistent" Antifa.[13] For this reason, it is very likely that this former Dominion executive was, indeed, the voice heard by Joe Oltmann in the Antifa conference call. And there is more.

In his deposition Coomer does not dispute that Oltmann made a Google search for his name (and for the words, Dominion and Denver), just as Joe Oltmann told Michelle Malkin in her video interview. That was on September 26, 2020—well before the election and before Trump's resultant loss. If Oltmann had not heard the words Eric and Dominion in a conversation, why would he be searching for those words in September 2020?[14]

Actually, Antifa Eric admits to just about everything—except for this: He denies saying: "Don't worry about the election. Trump's not gonna win. I made f**king sure of that!" He also denies doing anything to alter the election results. But can we take his words at face value? After all, to admit it might be admitting to treason, as the word is commonly (if not legally) understood.

---

12   Coomer seems to tell falsehoods very easily. As evidence, see this 15-minute video, where he lies to police regarding an accident he had with his truck. He finally confesses after being placed in handcuffs. https://www.worldtribune.com/who-is-eric-coomer-part-ii-bizarre-arrest-video-of-dominion-voting-exec-in-colorado/.

13   FBI chief, Christopher Wray, has said there is no such organization as Antifa. Apparently, Eric Coomer agrees, and yet he issued a statement on behalf of the nonexistent organization?

14   Eric Coomer, Ph.D. v. Donald J. Trump for President, Inc, et al., Video deposition, 100–101.

As part of his defamation lawsuit, Coomer's attorneys deposed Attorney Sidney Powell, one of the defendants. While being deposed, Powell was pressed to explain how Eric Coomer rigged the election. She responded:[15]

- "I know he holds patents on multiple parts of the Dominion/Smartmatic system."

- "I know he absolutely loathed and despised and viewed as inhuman President Trump."

- "I know what Mr. Oltmann said from his affidavit and his interview with Michelle Malkin."

- "I know the results of the election were mathematically impossible."

- "I know that experts have discussed the ability to manipulate the Dominion machines."

- "I know that as recently as March 2020, the democrats were screaming to the rooftops about the manipulability—we'll get that word—the ability to manipulate the vote in the Dominion machines."

- "There's a video called 'Kill Chain,' and of course I had seen the letters from Carolyn Maloney and, I believe, Elizabeth Warren and other—Amy Klobuchar—about the problems with the voting machines."

- "And then we had, you know, the 970 pages of evidence about all of it" [evidence Powell used in her state lawsuits].[16]

As I am not an attorney, I can't say if Powell's arguments are legally persuasive. However, as an auditor, I see things in her statement that would increase inherent audit risk. Here's how:

Coomer corruption is possible
It is obvious that Eric Coomer hated Donald Trump, and it seems probable (to me) that he made the statements described by Oltmann. He definitely had the technical

---

15   Eric Coomer, Ph.D. v. Donald J. Trump for President, Inc, et al., 2020cv34319 (District Court, Denver County, Colorado, 2020), Exhibit K-1, Sidney Powell Deposition, 11.

16   Ibid., 90–93.

27

knowledge required to alter Dominion machines, he reportedly had access to at least some of the machines on or before Election Day, and he apparently had lots of Antifa friends who could be used to harvest ballots to be used as "backfill" (i.e., to make sure the paper ballot count would match the altered machine totals).

J. Alex Halderman, a cyber expert, stated that Dominion machines can be made to manipulate QR codes to switch votes (page 42). Presumably, that is a security weakness that Dominion's head of machine security (Coomer) would also know about.

In addition, two cyber experts found that Dominion's "Trusted Build" update program caused the deletion of Mesa County, Colorado's election database, and the possible cover-up of file tampering. This happened in two consecutive elections. See page 261. We know about Mesa because that is the one (and probably only) place where a backup copy of the database was made (by a whistleblower) just prior to Dominion's "Trusted Build" update.

For these reasons, an auditor would have to conclude that alterations to election data by Coomer cannot be ruled out without extensive testing.

However, none of this proves that Coomer tried to alter the election, or that he was even capable of altering it. Perhaps, he was just making a boastful statement, designed to impress his Antifa friends. It isn't proof, but it is a significant audit risk factor that should be considered as the election results of each state are evaluated.

MAIL-IN BALLOTS

People are getting inundated with ballots, they'll be showered with ballots.

—PRESIDENT DONALD J. TRUMP

Trump said he does not oppose the use of absentee ballots, when they are limited to people requesting them. However, he railed against the blanket mailing of ballots to all registered voters, including voters who did not request ballots. As stated by CBS News in May 2020:

> President Trump has repeatedly criticized mail-in voting in recent days, insisting it leads to voter fraud. On Tuesday, Twitter included a fact check along with one of the president's tweets for the first time, including a link where readers could "get the facts about mail-in ballots" after the president tweeted there is "NO WAY (ZERO!)" that Mail-in Ballots will be anything less than substantially fraudulent."[17]

---

17   Kathryn Watson, "Trump Ramps Up Attacks Against Mail-In Voting," *CBS News* (May 27, 2020), https://www.cbsnews.com/news/trump-vote-by-mail-attacks/.

In its fact check, added as part of its "civic integrity policy," Twitter said:

These claims are unsubstantiated, according to CNN, *Washington Post* and others. Experts say mail-in ballots are very rarely linked to voter fraud.[18]

Twitter cited media outlets—CNN and the *Washington Post*—as voting authorities but did not cite the much more authoritative 2005 report from the Commission on Federal Election Reform. That report, authored by former President Jimmy Carter and former Secretary of State James Baker, does not state that "mail-in ballots are very rarely linked to voter fraud." It says precisely the opposite: "Absentee ballots remain the largest source of potential voter fraud." That is the viewpoint that Twitter decided to censor. The Carter-Baker report added:

Blank ballots mailed to the wrong address or to large residential buildings might get intercepted. Citizens who vote at home, at nursing homes, at the workplace, or in church are more susceptible to pressure, overt and subtle, or to intimidation. Vote buying schemes are far more difficult to detect when citizens vote by mail.[19]

The Commissioners said that, if absentee ballots are to be mailed out, it is important for the states to strengthen voter registration lists and prohibit third parties from handling the ballots. Unfortunately, for the 2020 election this advice was completely ignored in some states. Their elections were run poorly in several ways: They had mail-in ballots, obsolete voter registration lists, they allowed ballot harvesting, and in most cases did not require meaningful voter identification. All the concerns of the Carter-Baker report applied—plus, there were now unmonitored drop boxes. Perhaps Twitter needs to put a fact check on the Carter-Baker report. It obviously violates Twitter's lofty and high-minded "civic integrity policy."

According to economist and educator John R. Lott, Jr., most of Europe does not even allow the use of absentee ballots:

[M]any European countries have much stricter voting rules to prevent fraud. For example, 74 percent entirely ban absentee voting for citizens who live in their country. Another 6 percent allow it, but have very restrictive rules, such as limiting it to those in the military or are in a hospital, [sic] and they require evidence for this. Another 15 percent allow

---

18   Twitter.com, May 27, 2020, https://twitter.com/i/events/1265330601034256384 (accessed November 1, 2021).

19   "Building Confidence in U.S. Elections," Commission on Federal Election Reform (September 2005), https://ucdenver. instructure.com/courses/3034/files/378056?module_item_id=188418, 46.

absentee ballots but require that one present a photo voter ID to acquire it. 35 percent of European countries ban entirely absentee ballots for even those living outside their country [emphasis as written].[20]

On this matter, Trump was absolutely correct: When mail-in ballots are sent to everyone, they are an invitation for fraudulent activities. This is especially true if registration lists are not kept current. I feel confident that 90 percent of audit CPAs would quietly share this sentiment (quietly, because CPAs tend to avoid controversy). In the 2020 election, the use of mail-in ballots contributed to a climate of concern among many voters.

These eight states (and Washington, DC) automatically mail ballots or applications to all eligible voters, whether requested or not: California, Colorado, Hawaii, Nevada, Oregon, Utah, Vermont, and Washington[21]

Although Michigan's Code does not include the automatic mailing of ballot applications, the Michigan Secretary of State mass-mailed them anyway, and a Michigan appeals court supported her action, due to concerns over COVID. That made absolutely no sense, of course, since the normal ways to request a ballot application in Michigan—using the internet, the postal service, or your cell phone—did not involve COVID exposure.

Nevada was the only swing state that automatically mailed out ballots (not just applications) to every voter in the November 2020 election. That state began mailing out ballots to all registered voters just before the election, in August 2020. All other states in the nation (aside from the eight listed) allow at least some distribution of ballots via mail; however, they require the voter to request the ballot—either with a specified reason or without a reason.

A related problem: "Unknown ballots"
Since 2012, the Public Interest Legal Foundation (PILF) has been tracking the status of ballots sent to voters through the mail. By reviewing state election statistics, PILF determined that, in the 2020 election, 1.1 million ballots were undeliverable and 560,000 were rejected. A bigger problem was the "unknown ballot." There were nearly 15 million of those. What does "unknown" mean. Here is the answer from J. Christian Adams, who is President of PILF:

---

20   John R. Lott, Jr., "Trump's Senate Trial Rests on the Claim that He Lied About Vote Fraud, He Didn't," *TownHall* (February 10, 2021), https://townhall.com/columnists/johnrlottjr/2021/02/10/untitled-n2584494.

21   Ballotpedia.org, n.d., https://ballotpedia.org/All-mail_voting (accessed November 17, 2021).

This means there is a wide variety of things that can happen to a ballot in the "unknown" column. A ballot can be put in the wrong mailbox and land in an unfriendly neighbor's trash. It can be thrown out with your unpaid bills. It can be left outside for the wind to carry the last mile (like seen in Nevada in 2020). Election officials simply do not know what happened. Unknown ballots are the greatest blind spot in the American electoral system.[22]

Besides the possibilities listed by Adams, I will give you another one: Some of the unknown ballots will become *known* ballots—but submitted by the wrong person. After they are harvested by paid fraudsters, they will be forged and put into unguarded voter drop boxes.

ID needed for in-person voting, but not mail-in voting?
It is hard to believe, but most states are more likely to require identification for in-person voting than for mail-in voting. Check out Appendix B on page 288, where eleven states are listed, along with key aspects of their voting laws. Of those states, the majority require no more than a signature for mail-in voting.

QUESTION TO CONSIDER: PLEASE READ THIS AND SELECT BEST ANSWER

You moved to your apartment in Nevada a few months ago, just before an election. Your requested ballot is in the mail box along with three other ballots (presumably addressed to prior tenants). To complete a ballot, no identification is required, other than a signature. You sign all four ballots (each with the preprinted name) and put them in the local, unmonitored drop box. Which answer describes the most likely outcome?

> A. Election workers can't tell that the signatures are phony, so nothing happens. The ballots are processed and the votes are tabulated. You feel great because you got to vote four times for your favorite candidate.
>
> B. The election workers spot the phony signatures and remove the ballots; however, they don't refer the matter to county prosecutors because they, and the prosecutors, are overwhelmed with work.

---

22 J. Christian Adams, "Nearly 15 Million Mail Ballots Went Unaccounted for in the 2020 Election," *Public Interest Legal Foundation* (August 2021): https://publicinterestlegal.org/featured/nearly-15-million-mail-ballots-went-unaccounted-for-in-2020-election/.

> C. Officials from the county knock on your door and ask if you signed those three extra ballots. You claim that you didn't, and the officials decide that they have no way of proving that you did.
>
> D. You are arrested and prosecuted, and sentenced to five years of hard labor.

The correct answer is A. It is likely that the ballots will be processed, and it is exceedingly unlikely that you will be caught and convicted, or that your crime will show up as a statistic. Forged signatures are often too subjective to detect, and almost always too subjective to use as the basis for a criminal case.

HARVESTED BALLOTS

All states have bans on electioneering in and near polling places. In contrast, there are no prohibitions on electioneering in voters' homes.

—HANS VON SPAKOVSKY, THE HERITAGE FOUNDATION[23]

The problem of electioneering, identified by Hans von Spakovsky, is just one of the problems associated with the harvesting of mail-in ballots.[24] Does it make sense to prohibit political operatives from getting within one or two hundred feet of a voter standing in line at a polling station, but allow the operative to visit the voter at his home, where he can talk, argue, persuade, and offer free coupons for say—pizza?

Harvesting can produce significant fraud that is very hard to detect unless there are strong voter identification requirements and/or post-election canvass operations (knocking on doors to see if people really voted). A harvester is usually a political operative, or someone paid by a political operative, who rounds up ballots and mails them to the election center, or places them in voter drop boxes. Often, he gives the ballots to a political organization, where they are "reviewed" prior to distribution. The harvester is often paid "by the piece," which means there is a big incentive to get ballots, from wherever they may be.

---

23 Hans A. von Spakovsky, "Four Stolen Elections: The Vulnerabilities of Absentee and Mail-In Ballots," *The Heritage Foundation: Legal Memorandum 268* (July 16, 2020): 2.

24 Harvesting is the act of gathering up ballots to deliver to voting centers. Some are obtained legally, while others may be obtained by means of intimidation, trickery, or bribes. Also, some ballots are retrieved from trash cans, county dumps or dishonest mail carriers.

Supermarket analogy

To find out what can go wrong with harvesting we need only look at the massive and long-time problem of supermarket coupons. The way they are supposed to work is this: Everyone getting a newspaper (I am going back in time to when there were such things) gets manufacturer coupons in the supplements. Think of the coupons as ballots mailed to every registered voter.

The coupons are supposed to be used by the newspaper recipient but an unscrupulous grocery store owner might pay "harvesters" to get the coupons out of the newspapers while they're in the store waiting to be sold, on driveways waiting to be picked up, or in mail boxes. The owner of the grocery store then submits the "harvested" coupons to the manufacturer, claiming (falsely) they were used by customers. It has been a huge problem for decades and still is. In total, coupon scandal fraud costs manufacturers hundreds of millions of dollars.[25]

Think about the above analogy and ask yourself if mail-in ballots are more secure than supermarket coupons. Ballots (or applications) can be taken from mail boxes by mail carriers, who would know exactly who has moved out, who is on vacation, or who has died. An unscrupulous carrier might get significant money for each ballot he sells to an operative. Other harvesters might cruise around neighborhoods, plucking the ballots (or applications) from mail boxes before the residents get home from work. Perhaps, someone working at the city trash dump will pull unused ballots from garbage (and there would be plenty of them). The price paid for these harvested ballots could be very high if the election is closely contested, and there are only a few days left to change the outcome.

It appears that, for the 2020 election, a massive, multistate harvesting ring may have been uncovered. Before we discuss that case, however, let's see exactly what harvesting involves, from the perspective of an expert.

How to harvest ballots – an Expert's guide

Jon Levine, writing for the *New York Post*, interviewed a "top Democratic operative . . . who says voter fraud, especially with mail-in ballots, is no myth. And he knows this because he's been doing it, on a grand scale, for decades."[26] Levine wrote this on August

---

25   AP, "Grocery store owner accused of stealing $307K in coupon scam," *WKYT News*, February 13, 2019, https://www.wkyt.com/content/news/Grocery-store-owner-accused-of-stealing-307K-in-coupon-scam-505800621.html.

26   Jon Levine, "Master at fixing mail-in ballots," *New York Post*, August 29, 2020, https://nypost.com/2020/08/29/political-insider-explains-voter-fraud-with-mail-in-ballots/?fbclid=IwAR0VkQ3jH6apcvyEiVkN7qKvHHMdinLiTN0Ca6seyhOo3S6HkXnJEWlzXv8.

29, 2020, before the subject of election fraud became verboten in the United States.

The identity and work experience of this particular ballot harvester are known to Levine, but anonymous in print, for obvious reasons. The "consultant" claimed to have worked for various campaigns, had "led teams of fraudsters and mentored at least 20 operatives in New Jersey, New York, and Pennsylvania—a critical 2020 swing state."[27]

The harvester described his methodology with regard to New Jersey ballots:

- The blank mail-in ballot is delivered to a registered voter in a large envelope. Inside the envelope is a return envelope, a certificate of mail-in voter, and the ballot itself.

- For New Jersey, the ballot itself has no special security features, so he simply makes copies of it.

- On the other hand, the envelope is too complicated to copy. He has to get them from real voters.

- His operatives go door to door, telling the voters they will mail the (sealed) envelopes with the ballots, on their behalf as a public service.

- The final steps are to steam the envelope open and put a new, counterfeit ballot in.

Care is taken to disperse the harvested ballots into several mail boxes to avoid suspicion. In the interview, the expert expressed his professional displeasure with the sloppy harvesting operation in Patterson, New Jersey, where the fraudsters got caught because they stuffed 900 ballots in just three mailboxes.

Isn't it good to see a true professional who takes pride in his work?

Mail carriers are not angels

The operative said that some postal workers get in on the scam. "You have a postman who is a rabid anti-Trump guy and he's working in Bedminster or some Republican stronghold. . . . He can take those [filled-out] ballots, and knowing 95 percent are going to a Republican, he can just throw those in the garbage."[28] Here are some other tips from the harvesting expert:

---

27   Ibid.

28   Ibid.

- Some mail carriers worked directly within his "work crews."

- Nursing homes can be "a gold mine of votes." In some cases a nurse would be one of his paid operatives.

- Homeless people were a reliable source of cheap ballots.

- He knew of one guy who paid $50 for a single ballot. (Inflation is impacting everyone!)[29]

So now, if you need a little spare cash, you know how to get it. You also know that mail carriers are not Boy Scouts.

In recent years the United States Postal Service has inadvertently made harvesting even easier by moving in the direction of mail box clusters rather than individual curb-side delivery. In fact, clusters are required for almost all new addresses. The cluster of mailboxes is often in a location that is out-of-sight of residences.

Here is the problem with clusters: In a survey of 5,000 households in 2015, the USPS Inspector General (IG) found that people seem to pay less attention to mail in central mail settings, and are more likely to throw it away. For example, the IG found that 11 percent of people responded to promotional ads that were delivered directly to their home mailbox, while only 3 percent responded when the promotion was received at a clustered box. (Perhaps they did not even get the promotional ads, if they were "harvested" in some sort of coupon scheme.)

If people react this same way with election notifications and ballots, it will give political operatives more unused ballots to harvest. And, it is less likely that they will be caught pilfering mail from those less-visible, centralized settings.

Fortunately, there are some things that can be done to minimize the risk of harvest fraud. Preferably, each state will make it explicitly illegal, with stiff penalties. If that is not done, it becomes imperative for the state to update voter registration rolls frequently (nearly continuously), and to purge from the rolls people who have not recently voted. Finally, there must be strong voter ID requirements, and that means more than just signatures.

Republican Harvesting: The McCrae Dowless case
A serious case of ballot harvesting was discovered in North Carolina in 2019. Leslie McCrae Dowless was a harvester working for Mark Harris, the Republican candidate

---

29   Ibid.

in the 9th Congressional District race. The stepdaughter of Dowless admitted that she filled out blank or incomplete ballots to help Republican candidates, including Harris. Although preliminary results showed that Harris won the election by about 900 votes, the North Carolina State Board of Elections refused to certify the election once the Dowless operation was discovered.[30]

ALERT: MASSIVE BALLOT HARVESTING DISCOVERED BY TRACKING CELL PHONE PINGS

A conservative organization named True the Vote (TTV) found an innovative way to detect ballot harvesting. In August 2021, the entity's president, Catherine Engelbrecht, said that the organization had spent months acquiring twenty-seven terabytes of geospatial and temporal data, including trillions of cell phone "pings" in certain areas of Georgia, Arizona, Michigan, Pennsylvania, and Wisconsin. In addition, in the state of Georgia the organization acquired video images of some drop box locations. A TTV document states:

> We are building out video stories and have compiled videos of individuals stuffing ballot drop boxes with stacks of ballots, individuals depositing ballots in multiple drop boxes, unauthorized coordination between government workers engaged in the exchange of ballots, and several other tranches of video that capture unusual patterns such as the wearing of gloves to deposit ballots, taking pictures of ballot deposits, etc.[31]

TTV says it took its information to the FBI and to the Georgia governor. Until recently, however, no actions were taken. Things changed in January 2022 when a possible whistleblower stepped forward and made startling revelations.

The person, identified as John Doe, allegedly said he or she participated in an extensive ballot harvesting scheme during the November 2020 election and the January 5, 2021 runoff elections, and was paid $10 per harvested ballot. He/she would collect ballots from voters in certain neighborhoods and from nongovernmental organizations, which claim to be nonpartisan but are very active, politically.

Author and film maker, Dinesh D'Souza, made a film about this multistate scandal, called *2,000 Mules*. In that movie, Engelbrecht and her associate, Gregg Phillips, provided these estimates of harvested ballots for 5 states:

---

30   Hans A. von Spakovsky, "Four Stolen Elections: The Vulnerabilities of Absentee and Mail-In Ballots," *The Heritage Foundation: Legal Memorandum 268* (July 16, 2020): 14.

31   Matthew Boyle, "True the Vote conducting massive voter fraud investigation," *Breitbart*, August 24, 2021, https://www.breitbart.com/politics/2021/08/24/exclusive-true-the-vote-conducting-massive-clandestine-voter-fraud-investigation/.

TABLE 1: ESTIMATED NUMBER OF ILLEGALLY HARVESTED BALLOTS

State	No. of Mules	Average no. of visits to drop boxes	Estimated harvested ballots Minimum	Maximum
Michigan	500	50	125,000	225,000
Wisconsin	100	28	14,000	83,000
Georgia	250	24	30,000	90,000
Arizona	200	20	20,000	200,000
Pennsylvania	1100	50	210,000	275,000

The trailer for the film can be seen here: https://rumble.com/vtlq96-explosive-new-surveillance-footage-of-ballot-drop-boxes.html. The premiere was in early May, 2022, with 600 showings nationwide.

This is a major scandal that could affect multiple states, especially those that tightly restrict ballots harvesting. Swing states that restrict or ban harvesting include Arizona, Georgia, Michigan, and Pennsylvania. Even in states like Wisconsin, where there are no specific laws pertaining to ballot harvesting, the practice would be illegal if the ballots were delivered improperly, or obtained through bribes, coercion, or theft. According to Engelbrecht, legal investigations have commenced in Georgia and Arizona.

Fact checkers rush to discredit
Mainstream media has put out several fact checks in an apparent attempt to discredit the movie. They correctly point out that there is not much video evidence. Wisconsin simply ignored its own law, and did not make videos of its drop boxes. Other states quickly destroyed their videos (possibly in violation of federal law). Arizona had video recordings of one box, but the imagery was useless.

Fact checkers also claim that the cell phone geotracking data is simply too imprecise to support the conclusions reached. For example, a Reuters fact check cited research (from 2020) indicating that, at best, location error would vary from 6.6 to 33 feet.[32]

However, TTV's lead cyber expert disputes these fact checkers. In a presentation before the Arizona Senate on May 31, 2022, Phillips indicated that TTV could locate mules with an accuracy of plus or minus 39 inches. It did this by combining "three different types of signals," purchased from brokers "that catalogue them from different devices." He asserted that the fact check claims of 40 foot accuracy are "just crazy."[33]

32 "Reuters Fact Check," *Reuters.com*, May 27, 2022, https://www.reuters.com/article/factcheck-usa-mules-idUSL2N2XJ0OQ.

33 "Bombshell Testimony from True the Vote at Arizona Joint Legislative Hearing," *True the Vote.org*, June 1, 2022, https://www.truethevote.org/bombshell-testimony-from-true-the-vote/.

In addition, the fact checkers generally ignore other evidence that supports the harvesting claims:

- Why were these visits to drop boxes mostly at night?

- Why did people take selfies while holding up the ballots in front of the drop boxes?

- Why were latex gloves worn until ballots were placed into a box, and immediately discarded afterwards?

- Why did one drop box contain 1952 ballots for a period of time when only 271 people visited the drop box?

- Why did people visit so many drop boxes—sometimes in a single night? Engelbrecht describes one mule who visited 27 drop boxes in 6 counties in one night.

- Are we to believe that TTV simply made up the story of a Georgia whistle-blower who was paid $10 per ballot?

We cannot state with certainty that the TTV quantity estimates are accurate; however, it is clear that at least some ballot harvesting took place. It is just a matter of determining the amount. But that would require investigations that media and most prosecutors do not want.

DR. HALDERMAN AND MR. HYDE-HALDERMAN
Jekyll had more than a father's interest; Hyde had more than a son's indifference.

—ROBERT LEWIS STEVENSON

Apparently, it is possible to have two different people occupy the very same body. I am talking about Dr. J. Alex Halderman, a Ph.D. professor of Computer Science at the University of Michigan. He became a darling of Democrats when he demonstrated, in 2018, how easily election machines can be hacked.

I am also talking about Mr. Hyde-Halderman, the man who, immediately after Trump lost the 2020 election, tersely dismissed the notion that the election could have been hacked. Kind of makes your head spin, but see for yourself.

In a 2018 article titled, "I hacked an election. So can the Russians," this is what Halderman said:

Our highly computerized election infrastructure is vulnerable to sabotage and even to cyber-attacks that could change votes.[34]

In conjunction with the *New York Times*, Dr. Halderman "staged a mock election to demonstrate voting machine vulnerability." Nicole Moore described the experiment in an article written for Michigan Electrical and Computer Engineering:

A row of voting machines purchased on eBay lined Tishman Hall one winter morning. These were archetypes of the very same equipment used today in many states—Georgia, and parts of Indiana, Kansas, Kentucky, Mississippi, Tennessee, Texas, Virginia, Florida and Pennsylvania. Students cast ballots for the "greatest university"—the University of Michigan or Ohio State. Unbeknownst to the voters, the machines had been hacked by a likely culprit: J. Alex Halderman.[35]

The experiment, which included a Dominion machine, was successful: The election was hacked.[36] Afterward, Halderman did not pull his punches:

I'm here to tell you that the electronic voting machines Americans got to solve the problem of voting integrity; they turned out to be an *awful* idea. That's because people like me can hack them all too easily [emphasis added].[37]

In a moment we will visit with Mr. Hyde-Halderman—the other guy. First, however, let's look at some of the articles published by Dr. Halderman, where he describes his belief about election vulnerability. Here is a partial list of the titles, written to the delight of Democrats, who were angry that Trump somehow got elected in 2016:

- "The midterms are already hacked. You just don't know it yet"

- "How to hack an election—and what states should do to prevent fake votes"

---

34 Nicole Casal Moore, "I hacked an election. So can the Russians," *Michigan ECE Electrical and Computer Engineering*, April 9, 2018, https://ece.engin.umich.edu/stories/i-hacked-an-election-so-can-the-russians.

35 Ibid.

36 Jared Harris, Dominion Machines Cover Millions of Voters, But Watch How Easy It Is To Rig One of Them," *Western Journal*, November 13, 2020, https://www.westernjournal.com/dominion-machines-cover-millions-voters-watch-easy-rig-one/. In this article, it is noted that Halderman's demonstration of the vulnerability of election computer machines to hacking included an Accuvote TSX machine manufactured by Dominion.

37 Nicole Casal Moore, "I hacked an election. So can the Russians," April 9, 2018.

- "Security upgrades are too little, too late for 2018 midterms, and race is already on for 2020, experts say"

- "Sounding the alarm on the dangers of electronic voting"

Enter Mr. Hyde-Halderman

Now, let's get the opinion of Mr. Hyde-Halderman, who emerged from the darkness right after the 2020 election. Were things different now because a Republican was complaining about election fraud, rather than a Democrat? Unlike Dr. Halderman, Mr. Hyde-Halderman could not countenance reckless talk about hacking and the dangers of electronic voting.

In his September 2021 declaration supporting the lawsuit of Eric Coomer *against* Donald J. Trump for President, et al., Mr. Hyde-Halderman stated:

> Starting soon after Election Day, I and other leading election security experts publicly stated that we had seen no credible evidence to support emerging conspiracy theories about the election having been rigged.[38]

How soon did the experts complete their thoughtful analyses? Their work was completed on the very same day the election was declared! AP called the election on November 7, and that was the day Mr. Hyde-Halderman posted a thread on Twitter, declaring that the Antrim County, Michigan, mix-up (Trump votes had been assigned to Biden) "almost certainly resulted from human error rather than 'hacking' or fraud." That is a pretty speedy analysis from someone who probably did not even visit Antrim County for several months.[39]

On November 13, 2020, Mr. Hyde-Halderman went on Fox News to declare a clean election. And on November 16, 2020, just nine days after AP declared Biden the winner, Hyde-Halderman and "58 other leading election security specialists called further attention to the implausibility" of such election conspiracy theories.[40] If you are feeling the déjà vu, you may be recalling the fifty-one former intelligence officials who almost immediately knew that Hunter Biden's laptop was Russian disinformation. Of course, they were all wrong.

---

38   Eric Coomer, Ph.D. v. Donald J. Trump for President, Inc, et al., 2020cv34319 (District Court, Denver County, Colorado, 2020), Exhibit O, Declaration of J. Alex Halderman dated September 17, 2021. ¶10

39   Ibid., ¶11.

40   Ibid., ¶13.

To support his legal declaration, Mr. Hyde-Halderman cited the work done by the *New York Times* on November 9 and 10 (just 2 and 3 days after the election was called). These Times election "experts" (probably entry-level, newsroom gofers) contacted election officials in all fifty states and found that no one had seen any evidence of fraud or other irregularities.[41] Of course, asking the election officials to report their own mistakes is a bit like asking Michael Avenatti if he ever cheated one of his clients.

My goodness, how some experts discredit themselves by flip-flopping their positions when the political winds change or by shooting from the hip before they have studied the issues!

A PAPER BALLOT MEANS NO ELECTION FRAUD?

You may wonder why it should be necessary for an expert to wait a few weeks to pass judgment on election integrity. One reason is "paper ballots." You see, Mr. Hyde-Halderman, like so many others, used paper ballots to justify his conclusion about the lack of fraud. In his declaration (supporting Eric Coomer against Trump) he questioned how there could be computer fraud when we use paper ballots to back up the results. It's a good point, and I agree with it. (Of course, it was also a good point in 2018, when Halderman was so very worried about fraud.)

However, if Mr. Hyde-Halderman were in my little accounting office, I would have to ask him one extremely important question: What good are paper ballots if they remain sitting in cardboard boxes in some county warehouse? Here is what you have to do to get any benefit from the paper ballots:

- You have to open the boxes.

- Then you reach into the boxes.

- Now you pull the paper ballots out.

- You have to examine the paper to make sure the ballots have not been copied or printed.

- You reconcile the ballot identifying documents (e.g., envelopes) to registration lists.

- By examining the envelopes, you assess the authenticity of the identification numbers (if they have them) and the signatures.

---

41   Ibid., ¶17.

- If the voter is not required to provide identifying information, a statistically-significant percentage of registered voters must be contacted (canvassed) in person to ensure that their votes were recorded if they voted, and their votes were not recorded if they did not vote.

All of this takes more than a few days, so experts should spare us their wise platitudes and out-of-thin-air "expert" opinions for a respectable period of time—at least a few weeks.

Here is another way to put it: We need genuine audits after most elections. In the Hyde-Halderman declaration there is an interesting comment. He states:

[A]lmost ten months after the election and following numerous audits and investigations, I am still unaware of any credible evidence whatsoever that the 2020 Presidential election outcome was altered by technical manipulation [emphasis added].[42]

But there's the rub. There have not been *"numerous audits and investigations."* When Halderman issued his declaration there was only one completed audit of which I am aware. That audit was in Antrim County, Michigan, and it resulted in a very big adjustment in favor of Trump. A short while after Halderman's declaration, the Cyber Ninjas completed their audit in Maricopa County, Arizona. Those auditors also found significant irregularities, even though the very most vital steps of canvassing, signature matching, and inspection of equipment were all blocked.

DR. HALDERMAN RETURNS, WARNING OF URGENT RISKS WITH DOMINION

Once the 2020 election was in the rearview mirror, Hyde disappeared and the good old doctor reappeared—but not on behalf of Donald Trump or Mike Lindell or any Republican. Instead, Dr. Halderman came back as an advocate in a case favored by Stacie Abrams, who was still brooding about her own loss of the 2018 gubernatorial election in Georgia.

You see, some of the Georgians who voted on Dominion machines in 2018, and touched the name of Stacie Abrams, believe that their votes were incorrectly delivered to Brian Kemp (now the Republican Governor). A lawsuit was filed (Curling v. Raffensperger) and Judge Amy Totenberg granted Halderman something very unusual: full access to a Dominion machine. That is something that Trump and Lindell could only dream about.

---

42   Ibid., ¶20.

THE MAJOR ISSUES OF THE 2020 ELECTION

After examining the machine for twelve weeks, Dr. Halderman issued a 25,000-word report that cites risks so extreme that the Biden administration and Dominion are fighting against its release. For that reason I can't quote from the report, but I can cite some of Halderman's descriptive legal declarations.

In one declaration Dr. Halderman asserts that Georgia's Dominion election machines . . .

> suffer from specific, highly exploitable vulnerabilities that allow attackers to *change votes* despite the state's purported defenses [emphasis added].[43]

In another declaration, Dr. Halderman notes that there are . . .

> numerous security vulnerabilities in Georgia's Dominion ICX BMDs. These include flaws that would allow attackers to install malicious software on the ICX, either with temporary physical access (such as that of voters in the polling place) or remotely from election management systems.
>
> Informing responsible parties about the ICX's vulnerabilities is becoming *more urgent by the day*. Foreign or domestic adversaries who are intent on attacking elections certainly could have already discovered the same problems I did. [emphasis added].[44]

> *Author's note: If "Foreign or domestic adversaries" could have known of the problem, is it possible that technical people at Dominion, who helped to design the machines, also knew about it? And did one of those experts at Dominion hate Trump enough to use such information?*

When I give you a description of the specific vulnerability, as reported by the Washington Examiner, I think you will understand just how dangerous this situation is:

> Halderman found that malicious software could be installed in voting touch screens to alter QR codes printed on ballots that are then scanned to record votes, or a hacker could wreak havoc by gaining access to election management system computers, according to court records.[45]

---

43 Donna Curling et al., v. Brad Raffensperger, et al, Civil action no. 1:17-CV-2989-AT (District Court, Northern District of Georgia, Atlanta Division, 2021), Declaration of J. Alex Halderman dated August 2, 2021, ¶7.

44 Ibid., Declaration of J. Alex Halderman dated September 21, 2021, ¶2.

45 Daniel Chaitin, "'Secret report' on alleged voting system vulnerabilities roils Georgia ahead of midterm elections," *Washington Examiner*, March 11, 2022, https://www.washingtonexaminer.com/news/secret-report-on-alleged-voting-system-vulnerabilities-roils-georgia-ahead-of-midterm-elections.

So, you push the button for Biden and the QR code says "Trump"—or vice versa. Of course, this is not a problem at all if you are good at reading "QR" code. I wouldn't know—I took Spanish in high school.

And now, would you like to hear the punch line? After saying all this about those Dominion machines, the very same ones used in the 2020 Georgia election and in several other states, Mr. Hyde-Halderman reappeared one more time to address Republican concerns, and to state that there is no evidence that this vulnerability had anything to do with Trump's loss or, apparently, with the Trump voters who complained that their votes were being switched.[46]

My question is this: How on earth could he know that? If these vulnerabilities are "critical" and "urgent" now, why weren't they then? These are the same machines used in 2020. For more on the cyber vulnerabilities of Dominion machines, be sure to read Don't trust Dominion's "Trusted Build" on page 261.

MATHEMATICAL ANOMALIES

Dr. Shiva

Shiva Ayyadurai ("Dr. Shiva") is a Ph.D. who holds four degrees from MIT and is widely considered to be the inventor of the modern email system or a chief developer of the system. His specialization is pattern recognition, and he has used that knowledge with respect to several aspects of the 2020 presidential election. In three of four Michigan counties analyzed, Shiva identified patterns that may suggest the possibility of fraud. See page 145.

In Pima County, Arizona, Dr. Shiva identified very compelling mathematical relationships that seem to support anonymously-made allegations of election fraud. See his "fishtail" pattern on page 73.

And during the Maricopa County audit, his company, EchoMail, Inc., used pattern recognition to identify blank and inadequate signatures on ballot envelopes. See page 95. You will read a lot about Shiva throughout this book. You can also find more information on his website: https://vashiva.com/about-va-shiva-ayyadurai/.

Edward Solomon

More questions were raised in early 2021, when mathematician Edward Solomon noticed unusual patterns in the ratio of Trump's votes to precinct total votes in Georgia

---

46   Dana Ford, "Fact Check: Trump Votes Were NOT Deleted and Were NOT Switched to Biden," *LeadStories.com*, January 13, 2021, https://leadstories.com/hoax-alert/2021/01/fact-check-trump-votes-were-not-deleted-and-were-not-switched-to-biden.html.

and Pennsylvania. It is a principle of mathematics (the "probability of co-primality") that if there is a large set of randomly chosen pairs of integers, about 61 percent of the pairs should be co-prime. Co-prime numbers are pairs of numbers that do not have any common integer factor between them, other than one. An example of co-prime numbers is the pair, 18 and 35, because no integer, other than 1, can evenly divide both.

In the case of Trump's vote totals in relation to the precinct vote totals, Solomon determined that the expected percentage of co-prime numbers did not materialize: It was much smaller than 61 percent. For example, in areas near Atlanta, Georgia, Solomon found that only 13 percent of 335 Trump-to-precinct ratios were co-prime. To Solomon, this apparent deviation from mathematical principles suggests the possibility that votes were being manipulated.[47]

A possible flaw in the analysis has to do with size and randomness. Is the sample size large enough? Was the selection made randomly?

In addition to the issue of co-prime number ratios, Solomon noticed that many precincts seemed to report the exact same ratios (Biden votes versus Trump votes) several times. For example, there were many batches of ballots where Trump had earned exactly 5.5555 percent of the vote (i.e., one vote for Trump to Biden's eighteen votes).

Several other precincts repeated the number 4.167 (one vote for Trump to Biden's twenty-four votes), and there were other repetitious patterns as well. To Solomon, this is strong evidence of possible vote manipulation; however, other mathematicians have disputed these claims. One expert stated: "That several precincts would show exactly the same vote shares at different times is not at all surprising."[48]

In a response to such critics, Solomon claims that he ran "hundreds of simulations" and could not replicate the unusual results found in certain precincts in Georgia and Pennsylvania.

I am not convinced that Solomon's analysis is strong evidence of fraud, but it is a risk factor that can tell the auditor where she should concentrate analysis and testing.

Benford's Law
This is a tool used by some auditors and government investigators to spot possible thefts, embezzlements, and tax cheats. Of course, like all mathematical approaches, it is merely

47   Edward Solomon, "Geometric Proof for Georgia," Edward Solomon Videos, February 7, 2021, https://rumble.com/vdnfcf-edward-solomon-geometric-proof-for-georgia.html.

48   Philip Stark, Associate Dean of the Division of Mathematical and Physical Sciences at the University of California, as quoted by Angelo Fichera and Saranac Hale Spencer in "OAN Report Features Baseless Assertion of Election Fraud by Algorithm." FactCheck.org, February 11, 2021, https://www.factcheck.org/2021/02/oan-report-features-baseless-assertion-of-election-fraud-by-algorithm/.

a way to spot irregularities that might warrant investigation. In itself, Benford's Law provides no proof, and it is unlikely to win an election-related lawsuit in court. Here is how it works: If there is a large batch of random numbers of considerable range, the distribution of the first digit of those numbers should follow a certain pattern, as shown graphically in Figure 3.

FIGURE 3: BENFORD'S LAW SHOWN GRAPHICALLY

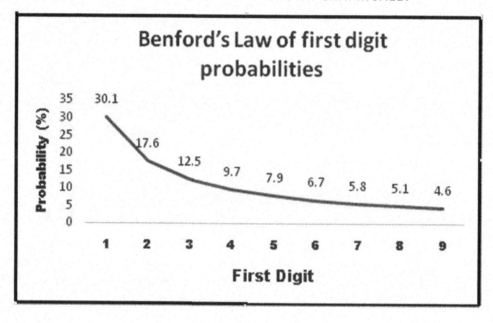

In other words, the number "1" should appear many more times than the number "8" or the number "9." If the pattern does not hold up, it sometimes means that a dishonest person has added or subtracted a standard amount from the batch of numbers. For example, an embezzler may have taken $30 each week from cash, and covered up the theft by adding a $30 phony "expense."

When applied to elections, Benford's Law can be unreliable. After the 2020 election, there were internet postings of Benford's Law graphs for the presidential election in certain cities and counties. In some cases the posted results seemed to strongly suggest fraud. That was true for graphs of the Milwaukee area, two of which are depicted in Figure 4, below.

The lines with the small oval markers show the expected Benford's curve, while the lines with the square markers show the actual results for Trump and Biden. As you can see, Trump's curve lines up fairly well with the expected Benford curve, while Biden's curve does not.

FIGURE 4 AND 4A: BENFORD'S LAW DEPICTED
VISUALLY FOR TRUMP AND BIDEN

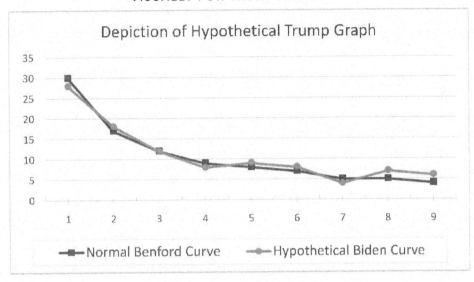

Depiction of Hypothetical Trump Graph

—■—Normal Benford Curve   —●—Hypothetical Biden Curve

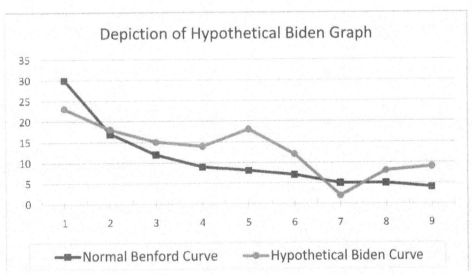

Depiction of Hypothetical Biden Graph

—■—Normal Benford Curve   —●—Hypothetical Biden Curve

This might suggest fraud and, as a matter of fact, I have some concerns about Milwaukee for reasons expressed elsewhere in this book. However, I would hesitate to hang my analysis on Benford because of certain unique characteristics of elections. These unique features are explained by Walter Mebane, a Professor at Cornell:

The basic point is that often precincts are designed to include roughly the same number of voters. If a candidate has roughly the same level of support in all the precincts, which means the candidate's share of the votes is roughly the same in all the precincts, then the vote counts will have the same first digit in all of the precincts. Imagine a situation where all precincts contain about 1,000 voters each, and a candidate has the support of roughly fifty percent of the voters in every precinct. Then most of the precinct vote totals for the candidate will begin with the digits "4" or "5."[49]

For the reasons outlined by Mebane, I think that Benford's Law is too unreliable for application to the Trump-Biden election analysis.

Dr. Douglas G. Frank

Dr. Frank appears to be a gregarious man who easily smiles, like a good-natured uncle. He is also a well-respected chemical engineer, inventor, and educator with about sixty peer-reviewed publications in scientific journals. Frank analyzed the pattern of voting percentages in relationship to voter age, and has done this in many counties within several states.

Frank noticed that each state seems to have a different pattern (voting percentage by age of voter). However, all counties within a given state, whether urban or rural, share the same pattern. For example, the voter turnout rates, by age, for Cuyahoga County are very similar to the voter turnout rates for Coshocton County, which is more rural. Oddly, if you cross the border into neighboring Pennsylvania, the pattern is different, and each Pennsylvania county shares that pattern.

To Dr. Frank, the strange patterns, and the tight fit of his estimates with actual voter turnout, indicate that massive computer power was used to monitor the election in real time: before, during, and after voting. For this reason, he generally supports the claims by Mike Lindell and others, regarding the concept of computer-controlled manipulation of voting equipment during the 2020 election. More information can be found in Part IV, starting on page 248.

Excess Biden votes in Dominion counties?

Ben Turner, formerly the chief actuary of Texas Mutual Workers' Compensation Insurance, runs a fraud detection company in Texas. Although he was very skeptical of the initial claims of 2020 election fraud, his own analysis of election results changed his opinion.

---

49 Walter R. Mebane., Jr., "Election Forensics: Vote Counts and Benford's Law," 2006 Summer Meeting of the Political Methodology Society, UC-Davis, July 20, 2006, http://em.fis.unam.mx/~mochan/elecciones/paperMebane.pdf.

Turner looked at the changes in election results from years 2008 to 2020 for 657 counties that adopted the Dominion voting technology. He found that the adoption of Dominion technology correlated with a 1.55 percentage increase in vote totals for Democrats and a 1.55 percentage decrease for Republicans. In other words, there was a combined change of about 3 percent. Turner reached those results after controlling for several factors, including county population growth, the mix of urban versus rural populations, the total number of votes cast, education level, and immigration rates.

The percentage impact of Dominion decreased somewhat after Turner controlled for more factors, including race, age, and voter preference. In the final analysis, Turner ended up controlling for about 100 factors, and concluded that there was an overall impact of 2.0 to 3.2 percent (Republicans to Democrats).

Although a statistical analysis is not enough to win a court case, Turner believes the results of his analysis justify an audit of the election machines. "If this was a suspected insurance fraud case, the results would warrant a probe."[50]

SUDDENLY, BALLOT REJECTION RATES PLUNGE

Mail-in balloting rejection rates . . . have dramatically shrunk to infinitesimal numbers.

—ERIC MACK, NEWSMAX

When Trump and his supporters claimed that mail-in ballot rejection rates were lower than in past years, self-proclaimed fact checkers immediately labeled their assertions as "false." Although the matter is addressed in the sections for the specific states, some analysis follows here.

In the 2020 presidential election most states rejected a smaller percentage of mail-in ballots than in previous years. Ballotpedia, a nonprofit organization that accumulates election statistics, reports that the average rejection rate for 2020 was .8 percent (.008) for all fifty states. That is down from a rate of 1.0 percent in 2016 and from 1.4 percent in 2018. However, if we separate the six swing states from the other forty-four states we see that the swing states were even less likely to reject ballots. The 2020 rejection rate for the swing states was .617 and the rate for the remaining forty-four states was .823. That is a significant disparity, and it appears to be somewhat suspicious.

So-called fact checkers point out that there were good reasons for the general decline in rejection rates. One reason is that voters mailed their ballots sooner, or used election drop boxes. Therefore, fewer ballots were rejected for being late. And in 2020, more

---

50   Petr Svab, "Fraud Analyst Finds Average of Two to Three Percent Shift in Favor of Biden in Counties That Used Dominion," *Epoch Times*, December 15, 2020, https://www.theepochtimes.com/fraud-analyst-flags-pro-biden-shift-in-counties-that-used-dominion_3619566.html.

states offered voters the opportunity to fix ("cure") ballots. According to one source, thirty-two states had provisions for curing defects—a number that is up from just seventeen states in earlier years.

If these are valid justifications for the decreased rejection rates, there are questionable reasons as well. Unless several poll watchers are mistaken, signatures on ballot envelopes were not always matched to signatures on registration lists or other files. Dr, Judith Burns, a Maricopa County (Ariz.) poll watcher, stated that many of the signatures on envelopes were merely "scribbles." Her testimony, made in respect to the Arizona election, is found on page 76. Also, some of the states claimed to "cure" ballots, when they simply ignored the defects in the ballots.

In Michigan, the Secretary of State, Jocelyn Benson, instructed workers (unlawfully) to "presume" signatures were valid. (See page 140.)

Jessy Jacob, a long-time employee of the City of Detroit, testified that she "was instructed not to look at any of the signatures on the absentee ballots, and was instructed not to compare the signature on the absentee ballot with the signature on file."[51] See page 62.

There were similar claims made about Georgia's signature checking, especially in Fulton County. The Trump people claimed that Georgia's Governor Brian Kemp had eliminated signature matching as a concession to Democrat activist Stacy Abrams. While it is true that the agreement negotiated with Abrams made signature matching extremely difficult, it was not eliminated entirely. (To see just how difficult signature matching became in Georgia, see page 126.)

All of these rejection-related issues are discussed in more detail in some of the separate state sections of this book.

LATE NIGHT BALLOT DUMPS

Shortly after the election several observant people scrutinized the vote updates reported by the *New York Times* (specifically its contractor, EdisonResearch.com/ Election-Polling/). They noted several suspicious "spikes" that seemed hard to explain and seemed beneficial to candidate Biden. Here are some examples that took place on November 4, 2020:

- At 3:50AM (EST) there was an update in Michigan that gave 54,497 votes to Biden and 4,718 votes to Trump.

---

51   John Solomon, "A dozen compelling allegations of voting irregularities in 2020 election," *Just the News*, November 23, 2020, https://justthenews.com/politics-policy/elections/dozen-compelling-pieces-evidence-voting-irregularities-2020-election?amp&__twitter_impression=true.

- At 6:31AM (EST) there was an update in Michigan that gave Joe Biden 141,258 votes while giving only 5,968 votes to Donald Trump.

- At 3:42AM (CST) in Wisconsin, Biden received 143,379 votes while Trump got only 25,163 votes.

- A vote update in Georgia at 1:34AM (EST) showed 136,155 votes for Biden and 29,115 votes for Trump[52]

In themselves these spikes are not evidence of fraud or irregularity. They could be caused by the central processing of mail-in ballots that are subsequently reported in large batches. And in some cases, there were data entry errors that were subsequently reversed. That said, large vote spikes create uncertainty that is best resolved with investigation by independent parties (not the election administrators).

Some of these vote spikes are addressed in the separate state sections. The Georgia spike, described above, was particularly controversial because it came while GOP observers were effectively sent home for the night, and it provided the winning margin for Biden. For now, it suffices to know that Trump supporters were very wary of these spikes, and they do warrant extra scrutiny.

BALLOT COUNTING STOPPED IN THE MIDDLE OF THE NIGHT
All of a sudden everything just stopped.

—PRESIDENT DONALD J. TRUMP

Trump's statement, above, was partly true but exaggerated. Some of the vote counting stopped, but not everywhere and not all at once. And where counting stopped, it is not clear if it signified election cheating. The best overview of this matter may be the reporting by Frank Chung in News.com AU. Here are some of his findings (paraphrased except where shown with quotation marks):[53]

---

52   Tyler O'Neil, "Four Data Dumps in the Witching Hour After the Election Gave Biden Victory. Rand Paul Has Questions," *PJ Media*, November 30, 2020, https://pjmedia.com/election/tyler-o-neil/2020/11/30/fraud-rand-paul-raises-serious-questions-about-suspicious-data-dumps-in-swing-states-n1181098.

53   Frank Chung, "US election: What happened in key battleground states on election night?" *NEWS.com.au*, November 22, 2020, https://www.news.com.au/world/north-america/us-politics/us-election-what-happened-in-key-battleground-states-on-election-night/news-story/2037f4baa76cab7e378fdd468ffe22f1.

- There was the controversial "pipe burst" shut-down at State Farm Arena in Fulton County, Georgia. In reality, there was no pipe burst, and counting stopped only momentarily. GOP and Democrat observers were told that there would be no more counting until morning, so they left. Counting then resumed. While the observers were gone, a large vote spike took place, and it mostly benefited Joe Biden.

- In North Carolina voting stopped during election night, but only when there was a pause in the arrival of ballots (officials claimed).

- "Nevada announced it was done for the night around 2:45AM." Later, officials said "the state had never intended to announce a final result on election night." The state resumed counting as ballots arrived, right up to November 10, 2020.

- At 11:00PM in Pennsylvania, election officials announced that there would be no more reporting of results for the night. That was misinterpreted as meaning that counting stopped, which was not true (according to officials). On the other hand, there were some Pennsylvania counties in which counting did stop. Butler County (near Pittsburgh) stopped counting mail-in ballots at 8:00PM due (allegedly) to mechanical issues with the ballot scanner. And officials in Allegheny County (which includes Pittsburgh) stopped counting around 2:00AM.

- There is no evidence that Wisconsin stopped counting, but it may have seemed that way due to gaps in the reporting of the vote count.

- Michigan did not stop counting, although there was some confused reporting on the issue.

Where stoppages took place it was and is appropriate to make inquiries.

CRAZY HIGH TURN-OUT RATES

In the days following the election, conservative websites printed sensational headlines about sky-high turnout figures in some states—especially Wisconsin and Minnesota. They were both correct and wrong. Wisconsin achieved an extremely high 89.3 percent turnout rate (voters divided by registered voters), while Minnesota had an even higher turnout rate of 91.3 percent.

The "wrong" part of the conservative claims had to do with the inclusion of misleading comparisons to historical turnout rates. Those historical comparison rates were prepared using a different metric (voters divided by the population over the age of 17, rather than voters divided by registered voters).

Figure 5, below, shows the turnout numbers for some key swing states, calculated as total voters divided by total registered voters. The high rates in Minnesota and Wisconsin would cause an auditor to increase testing of the internal controls for those two states and increase testing of transactions (ballot paper and signature authenticity, chain of custody documents, and other administrative documents).

FIGURE 5: VOTER TURNOUT DIVIDED BY REGISTERED VOTERS[54]

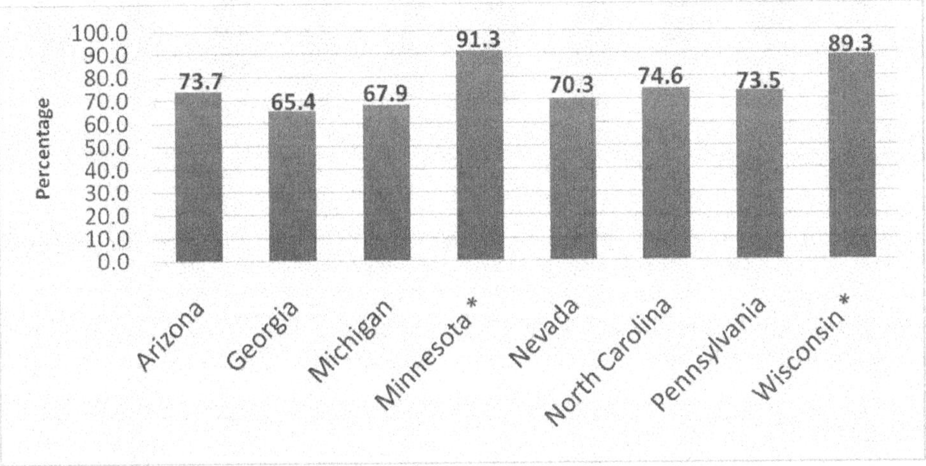

*Unusually high turnout rates

However, there is a different way to look at turnout rates—a better way. The United States Elections Project (USEP) is headed by Michael McDonald, a political science professor at the University of Florida. USEP makes adjustments to the voting-age population to reflect people who are ineligible to vote (e.g., noncitizens and certain prisoners). These adjustments are helpful because ineligible populations are not evenly distributed in the states. The numbers in Figure 6 reflect those adjusted figures, and include 2016 comparison amounts:

---

54   Devon Link, "Claim: Several key states had more ballots cast than registered voters," *USA Today*, November 8, 2020, https://www.usatoday.com/story/news/factcheck/2020/11/08/fact-check-post-argues-states-have-more-votes-than-voters/6191399002/. NOTE: The USAToday fact check had an apparent error with regard to Wisconsin. It reported a 72.3 percent turnout rate but the numbers it provided (3,684,726 registered voters and 3,289,472 ballots cast) imply a rate of 89.3 percent.

FIGURE 6: "VOTING-ELIGIBLE POPULATION" (TURNOUT DIVIDED BY ADJUSTED VOTING-AGE POPULATION)[55]

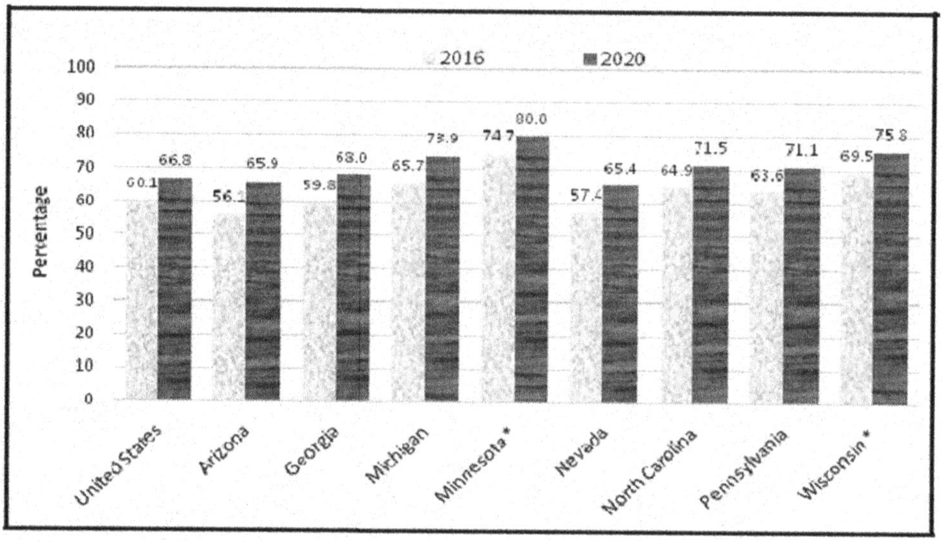

*Using eligible population, highest turnout rates are still in MN and WI.

In Figure 6 we still find that turnout was highest in Wisconsin and Minnesota. However, those 2 states also had very high turnout rates in 2016, so their increases are not particularly high.

The states with the largest increases in voter turnout (2016 to 2020) were Arizona, Georgia, Michigan, Nevada, and Pennsylvania. They were all well above the national increase of 6.7 percent. The increase in the Arizona turnout is of particular concern, as it might relate to an alleged scandal in Pima County, which involves phony or harvested ballots. See page 71.

CRAZY HIGH REGISTRATION RATES?

In October of 2020, the conservative-leaning nonprofit organization known as Judicial Watch (JW), released a comprehensive report on voter registration rates in various counties and states.[56] JW found that 353 counties in 29 different states had registration rates greater than 100 percent of the voting-age population. For example, in the swing state of Michigan, an impossible 105 percent of the population was registered for the 2020

---

55   Michael P. McDonald, "Voter Turnout Data 2016 and 2020," United States Elections Project, February 16, 2022, http://www.electproject.org/home/voter-turnout/voter-turnout-data.

56   "New Judicial Watch Study Finds 353 U.S. Counties in 29 States with Voter Registration Rates Exceeding 100%," *Judicial Watch*, October 16, 2020, https://www.judicialwatch.org/new-jw-study-voter-registration/.

election, according to the Judicial Watch study. Why does it matter? With so many states opting to mail election documents to everyone on their registration lists, whether or not a request is made, the excess registrations mean there will be excess ballots and applications floating everywhere.

Dr. Douglas G. Frank believes that, in some cases, county registration rates were pumped up just before the election in order to create a "credit line," so to speak, of "phantom" voters: dead people, made-up people, or people who had moved away. Some of the ballot applications mailed to the alleged phantoms could have ended up with political operatives.

In states where there is no identification requirement (most states) the operative only has to scribble a signature on the application, get a ballot in the mail, and send it in. If the election office workers question the signature on the ballot envelope (unlikely in most swing states), they may just call the voter (or ballot harvester) on the cell phone number he provided on the application (a meaningless endeavor).

If fraudsters are in a big hurry, there is another way to do this (in theory). A direct change to the vote totals is made in the computer—perhaps on election night or the next day. The bogus vote (generated by the computer) is then paired with a phantom voter name, address, etc. A few weeks after the election, the phantom voter can be entirely removed from the registration records by treating him as being dead (again) or moved away (again). That conceals the crime. See Patrick Colbeck and his theory of the election on page 253. This theory has not been proven.

THE KRAKEN IS DROWNING

Fear the creature that dwells in the darkest depths, the ice-shackled Kraken...

— ERNA GRCIC, *BENEATH THE SURFACE*

Sidney Powell is a tall, dignified-looking woman who became something of a cult figure among Trumpsters. Shortly after the election, Powell unleashed her "Kraken" in four legal cases aimed at overturning or at least modifying the 2020 election results of Arizona, Georgia, Michigan, and Wisconsin.

Now, Powell's Kraken is in trouble because the lawyer made some claims that will be difficult to support. That said, she also made allegations against Dominion that are probably accurate. Let's start by reviewing some of those: the allegations that Dominion machines are flawed and are susceptible to manipulation.

- On January 24, 2020, Texas rejected the Dominion system due to numerous security concerns. The Texas Deputy Secretary of State stated that "[t]he examiner reports raise concerns about whether the Democracy Suite 5.5-A system is suitable for its intended purpose; operates efficiently and accurately; and is safe from fraudulent or unauthorized manipulation."[57]

- The Dominion adjudication system may be conducive to fraud. In a 2016 case (Curling v. Raffensperger) Judge Amy Totenberg of the U.S. District Court for the Northern District of Georgia stated: "There is no question that the default scanner settings used in elections conducted to date on the Dominion system caused certain voter marks to register as blank and therefore prevented some valid votes on hand-marked ballots from being counted."[58]

- Dr. J. Alex Halderman has also reported that Dominion machines are susceptible to serious manipulation. See page 42.

- Two cyber experts reported that Dominion's "Trusted Build" upgrade erased an entire voter database in Mesa County, Colorado, and resulted in the concealment of possible election voting manipulation. See page 261.

- Dominion machines can be connected to the internet, and can be hacked. This is what NBC News reported in early 2020: "The three largest voting manufacturing companies [including Dominion] have acknowledged they all put modems in some of their tabulators and scanners. . . . Those modems connect to cell phone networks, which, in turn, are connected to the internet."[59]

- One of Powell's expert witnesses, Dr. Navid Keshavarz-Nia, declared under oath that there were numerous flaws in the Dominion system, and the company had troubling foreign connections. He declared that the Dominion "ImageCast Precinct optical scanner system was totally hacked in August 2019."[60] More from Keshavarz-Nia is found on page 58.

57 Jose A. Exparza, Deputy Secretary of State, "Report of Review of Dominion Voting Systems Democracy Suite 5.5-A," State of Texas Elections Division, January 24, 2020, 2.

58 US Dominion, Inc. et al. v. Sidney Powell et al., Civil Action 1:21-cv-0040-CJN (District Court, Columbia, 2021), ¶22.

59 Monahan, McFadden, Martinez, "Online and vulnerable: Experts find nearly three dozen U.S. voting systems connected to internet." NBC News, January 10, 2020.

60 Timothy King v. Gretchen Whitmer, 2:20-cv-13134-LVP-RSW (E.D. Michigan, 2020), Declaration of Dr. Navid Keshavarz-Nia, 4.

On the other hand, it's hard to find support for these Kraken allegations:

- Dominion and/or Smartmatic "injected massive quantities" of votes.[61]

- Dominion provides "election insurance. . . . If you put in the Dominion system, you're gonna win – re-elections, no problem at all."[62]

- Powell claimed she has a video of Dominion's founder saying that he could "change a million votes." (Dominion says she has not produced the video.)[63]

- "Another way they [changed votes] was to shave votes. The machines can weight the ballots so Biden votes get a weight of 1.25 count, and Trump votes are reduced to a 0.75 count."[64]

Here is a third category of Kraken claims: those that (as far as I know) may or may not be true:

- Did the Dominion technology originate with Smartmatic and/or Sequoia, and was the technology designed to cheat in foreign elections?[65]

- Did Dominion pay kickbacks to get Georgia officials to sign purchase contracts?[66]

- Is there evidence that Dominion machines shifted votes from Trump to Biden? There is statistical evidence that Biden did better (as much as 3 percent in areas that use Dominion machines). For more information see the separate section: "Excess Biden votes in Dominion Counties," on page 48.[67]

61 Jan Jekielek, "Sidney Powell on Election Lawsuits, Supreme Court Decision, and the Flynn Case," *Epoch Times*, December 13, 2020, https://www.theepochtimes.com/exclusive-sidney-powell-on-election-lawsuits-supreme-court-decision-and-the-flynn-case_3617067.html.

62 Ibid.

63 US Dominion, Inc. et al. v. Sidney Powell et al., Civil Action 1:21-cv-0040-CJN, ¶7.

64 Jan Jekielek, "Sidney Powell on Election Lawsuits, Supreme Court Decision, and the Flynn Case."

65 Tara Subramaniam and Casey Tolan, "Fact-checking Giuliani and the Trump legal team's wild, fact-free press conference," *CNN*, November 20, 2020, https://www.cnn.com/2020/11/19/politics/giuliani-trump-legal-team-press-briefing-fact-check/index.html.

66 US Dominion, Inc. et al. v. Sidney Powell, et al., Rudolph W. Giuliani, and My Pillow, Inc., et. al., Civil Action 1:21-cv-00040, 00213, and 00445 (CJN) (District Court, Columbia, 2021), ¶68.

67 Ibid.

In summary, Sidney Powell raised some valid concerns regarding the potential vulnerability of the Dominion voting systems. However, she probably made claims that she cannot support; and her focus on computer fraud and foreign interference distracted from old fashioned, but solid types of election fraud that were prevalent. For examples of that kind of election fraud, see page 151, which pertains to the Sidney Powell Michigan lawsuit.

Mollie Hemingway made a similar observation in her book, *Rigged*:

> There were also lawyers such as Sidney Powell and Lin Wood, who were pushing unsubstantiated claims of voter system fraud and foreign meddling. Both right-wing activists and the media obsessively focused on their claims at the expense of paying attention to legitimate problems raised by the others.[68]

That said, I would not close the book on the possibility of foreign meddling and/or computer fraud. Proof of that (if it exists) may still be produced if serious audits and cyber investigations take place. Perhaps the gravely wounded Kraken will yet rise from its seaward demise.

THE SMARTEST MAN IN THE ROOM

With respect to a 2020 story about a multi-million dollar fraud case, the *New York Times* said some very nice things about one man, who was instrumental in solving the case:

> "Navid Keshavarz-Nia, those who worked with him said, 'was always the smartest person in the room.' In doing cybersecurity and technical counterintelligence work for the C.I.A., N.S.A. and F.B.I., he had spent decades connecting top-secret dots."[69]

Likewise, the *Washington Monthly* called Keshavarz-Nia a "hero" for unraveling the criminal scheme.[70] I wonder if the *New York Times* and *Washington Monthly* will say nice things about this "hero" in the future.

Keshavarz-Nia has a Bachelor's degree in Electrical and Computer Engineering and a Master's degree in Electronics and Computer Engineering from George Mason

---

68   Mollie Hemingway, *Rigged*, (Washington DC: Regnery, 2021), 292.

69   Andrea Widburg, "The 'smartest man in the room' has joined Sidney Powell's team," *American Thinker*, November 28, 2020, https://www.americanthinker.com/blog/2020/11/the_smartest_man_in_the_room_has_joined_sidney_powells_team.html.

70   Nancy LeTourneau, "The Spy Was a Grifter," *Washington Monthly*, September 17, 2020, https://washingtonmonthly.com/2020/09/17/the-spy-was-a-grifter/.

University. He also has a Ph.D. in Management of Engineering and Technology from CalSouthern University and a Doctoral degree in Education from George Washington University. He is employed by a defense contractor as a chief cyber security engineer and a subject-matter expert in cyber security, and has thirty-five years of experience in performing technical assessment, mathematical modeling, cyber-attack pattern analysis, and security counterintelligence.[71]

Keshavarz-Nia made declarations under oath that supported Sidney Powell in her Michigan lawsuit, and also in her legal problems with Dominion. According to the declaration, Keshavarz-Nia has "performed forensic analysis of electronic voting systems, including the DVS [Dominion] Democracy Suite" and has "conducted ethical hacking to support USIC [United States Intelligence Community] missions."[72]

In the Declaration, Keshavarz-Nia stated:

[There] are tradecrafts used by US intelligence analysts to conduct MITM [man-in-the-middle] attacks on foreign voting systems, including the Dominion Voting System (DVS) Democracy Suite and Systems Software (ES&S) voting machines without leaving an electronic fingerprint. As such, these tools are used by nefarious operators to influence voting systems by covertly accessing DVS and altering the results in real-time and without leaving an electronic fingerprint.[73]

Keshavarz-Nia also declared that he has "studied network communication reports that show DVS [Dominion Voting Systems] data being transferred to Internet Protocol (IP) addresses registered to Scytl [a Spanish software company] in Barcelona, Spain."[74]

A good summary of Dr. Keshavarz-Nia's views regarding elections generally, and Dominion in particular, is presented by Andrea Widburg in the American Thinker:

- "Dominion, ES&S, Scytl, and Smartmatic are all vulnerable to fraud and vote manipulation—and mainstream media reported on these vulnerabilities in the past."

- "Dominion has been used in other countries to 'forge election results.'"

---

71   Timothy King v. Gretchen Whitmer, 2:20-cv-13134-LVP-RSW (E.D. Michigan, 2020), Declaration of Dr. Navid Keshavarz-Nia, 1.

72   Timothy King v. Gretchen Whitmer, 2.

73   Ibid., 1,2.

74   Ibid., 2

- "Dominion's corporate structure is deliberately confusing to hide relationships with Venezuela, China, and Cuba."

- "Dominion's machines are easily hackable."

- "Dominion memory cards with cryptographic key access to the systems were stolen in 2019."[75]

As you might expect, mainstream media and government officials no longer have anything good to say about this man, but one of his critics made a couple of valid points.

The OSET Institute is a nonprofit entity that advocates upgrades to election equipment and software infrastructure, and the development of "open source" systems, where software is transparent and shared by various states and localities. Three of the current or past board members wrote "an analysis of the technical veracity of Navid Keshavarz-Nia's November 25th 2020 Michigan federal lawsuit affidavit."[76]

The OSET officials said Keshavarz-Nia was wrong when he declared, as stated above, that "Dominion memory cards with cryptographic key access to the systems were stolen in 2019." First, the theft took place in 2020, and second, the USB memory hardware belonged to ES&S rather than Dominion.[77] I am not sure that either error is significant.

In addition, the OSET team claimed that the transfer of Dominion data to Scytl in Spain, as observed by Keshavarz-Nia, was not remarkable, since Scytl software is used for unofficial election reporting in addition to vote tabulation.[78] That might be a more significant error: We need more information to know.

Here is my assessment of Dr. Navid Keshavarz-Nia and the criticisms made of his claims. He has made several allegations of fact and opinion that warrant serious investigation. It appears that a couple of his statements may be incorrect or misleading, but the remaining assertions in his declaration, coupled with some of the election anomalies cited elsewhere in this book, could serve as justification for post-election audits conducted in certain key swing states.

Related: In Mesa County, Colorado, two cyber experts examined a copy of an election database that was made just before Dominion implemented its "Trusted Build"

---

75   Andrea Widburg, "The 'smartest man in the room' has joined Sidney Powell's team."

76   Sebes, Perez, and Crowell, "Analysis of Recent Navid Keshavarz-Nia Affidavit," *Oset Institute*, December 2020, https://trustthevote.org/wp-content/uploads/2020/12/04Dec20_Keshavarz-Nia_AffidavitAnalysis.pdf.

77   Ibid., 6.

78   Ibid., 5.

software update. The experts claim the election database had been altered to manipulate votes. Is it possible the Dominion upgrade was implemented for the purpose of concealing the data manipulation? See page 261.

MIKE LINDELL

It was the most corrupt election in U.S. history, and probably in world history

—MIKE LINDELL, CEO, MY PILLOW

By now you have heard of Mike Lindell, the friendly CEO and spokesperson for My Pillow. Perhaps you even bought some of his pillows, using those special half-off promo codes. According to just about every fact checker, Lindell is either a con-man, a dope, or both; and his theories about Chinese computers, hackers, and stolen votes are simply crazy. Well, not so fast. Lindell is no dummy; he picks up ideas like a sponge picks up water (a personal observation).

So, what about the crazy notions? In some ways, they have not been debunked, but considerable skepticism is warranted. This man's theories have created much doubt about the 2020 election results. A full analysis is warranted, and is found in Part IV, starting on page 239.

HUNDREDS OF SWORN AFFIDAVITS – IGNORED!

Trump supposedly had hookers peeing in Obama's bed, so mainstream media spent years reporting and pursuing anonymous tips. In the end, those tips backfired: They led to the indictment of a Hillary Clinton campaign lawyer.[79]

Given the heavy reliance on unsupported and anonymous Russia-Trump collusion allegations, it is puzzling that the media have largely ignored hundreds of on-the-record and under-oath statements from people claiming to have seen election wrongdoing—sometimes in huge quantities. And remember (as noted in the shoplifting example on page 15), for every reported incident there could be a hundred or more that evade detection.

Fortunately, there are a few journalists with credible and consistent standards. One such person is John Solomon, Editor in Chief of Just the News. Back in November 2020,

---

[79] The attorney, Michael Sussmann, was charged with lying to the FBI by denying that he was working on behalf of the Clinton campaign. He was acquitted on May 31, 2022, in a controversial decision by a Washington DC federal jury. FBI agent James Baker had testified that he was "100% confident" the defendant denied acting "on behalf of any particular client." An agent at the Baker-Sussmann meeting (Trisha Anderson) had written notes that indicated he represented "no specific client" (*New York Post*, 5/19/22). In addition, Sussmann had set up the Baker meeting with a text that said he was acting "not on behalf of a client or company" (*New York Post*, 5/18/22). After the acquittal, a juror declared that "There are bigger things . . . than a possible lie to the FBI" (Jonathan Turley, 6/1/22). To some people it appears that jury nullification was in play.

Solomon sifted through what he called a "mountain of evidence" concerning election irregularities. He read reports and affidavits included in private lawsuits pertaining to election 2020.[80]

Here are some of the statements from poll watchers, election employees, and voters. Most of these were from articles and affidavits linked to Solomon's report. Some involve fraudulent behavior; in other cases the behavior is just sloppy and unprofessional. All of the claims constitute risk factors that would probably justify full, or at least partial, auditing.

I urge you to read these statements, which are just a fraction of the total. This is real evidence (not the anonymous type that is sometimes manufactured by politicians):

Affidavit of Jessy Jacob, dated November 7, 2020[81]
Ms. Jacob is a thirty-year veteran employee of the City of Detroit. She worked in the Elections Department headquarters for most of September, spent most of October and part of November at a satellite election location, and was assigned to the TCF Center (a convention center used for processing ballots) on November 4, 2020. Here are some excerpts from her sworn affidavit:

- "On November 4, 2020, I was instructed to improperly pre-date the absentee ballots receive date [sic] that were not in the QVF [Qualified Voter File] as if they had been received on or before November 3, 2020. . . .I estimate that this was done to *thousands of ballots* [emphasis added]."

- "[At the satellite location] I directly observed, on a daily basis, City of Detroit election workers and employees coaching and trying to coach voters to vote for Joe Biden and the Democrat party."

- "During the last two weeks while working at this satellite location, I was specifically *instructed by my supervisor NOT to ask for a driver's license* or any photo I.D when a person was trying to vote [emphasis added]." [Author's note: Under Michigan law, identification is required to vote in person.]

- "[At the TFC Center] I was instructed not to validate any ballots and *not to look for any deficiencies in the ballots* [emphasis added]."

80 John Solomon, "A dozen compelling allegations of voting irregularities in 2020 election," *Just the News*, November 23, 2020, https://justthenews.com/politics-policy/elections/dozen-compelling-pieces-evidence-voting-irregularities-2020-election?amp&__twitter_impression=true.

81 Cheryl A. Costantino v. City of Detroit, Civil Action 2020cv355443 (Circuit Court for the County of Wayne, 2020), Affidavit of Jessy Jacob filed November 7, 2020, 2-3.

- "I was *instructed NOT to look at any of the signatures* on the absentee ballots, and I was instructed not to compare the signature on the absentee ballot with the signature on file [emphasis added]."

Affidavit of Monica Palmer, dated November 18, 2020[82]

- "I am the Chairperson of the Wayne County [Detroit] Board of Canvassers."

- "During [a meeting of the board of Canvassers] I determined that more than 70 percent of Detroit's 134 Absent Voter Counting Boards (AVCB) did not balance and many had no explanation to why they did not balance."

Statements of journalist, Victor Joecks, Las Vegas Review-Journal[83]

- "For months, election officials have told Nevadans not to worry about ballots piling up in apartment trash cans or sent to wrong addresses. 'Discarded mail ballots cannot just be picked up and voted by anyone,' a fact sheet from the secretary of state's office says. 'All mail ballots must be signed on the ballot return envelope. This signature is used to authenticate the voter and confirm that it was actually the voter and not another person who returned the mail ballot.'"

- "I wanted to test that claim by simulating what might happen if someone returned ballots that didn't belong to him or her."

- "Nine people participated in this test. I wrote their names in cursive using my normal handwriting. They then copied my version of their name onto their ballot envelope. This two-step process was necessary to ensure no laws were broken."

- "Eight of the nine ballots went through. In other words, *signature verification had an 89 percent failure rate* in catching mismatched signatures [emphasis added]."

---

82 Monica Palmer, Chairperson of the Wayne County Board of Canvassers, "Affidavit," https://www.scribd.com/document/484955614/Palmer-Affidavit-Wayne-Co-Board-of-Canvassers#from_embed.

83 Victor Joecks, "Clark County election officials accepted my signature – on 8 ballot envelopes," *Las Vegas Review-Journal*, November 12, 2020, https://www.reviewjournal.com/opinion/opinion-columns/victor-joecks/victor-joecks-clark-county-election-officials-accepted-my-signature-on-8-ballot-envelopes-2182390/.

Statement of attorney and Pittsburgh poll watcher David Shestokas
He told Just the News:[84]

- "[Ballot monitors] had no input and no ability to watch anything."

- "All of the folks who were observers for campaigns were maybe 15, 20 feet from many of the tables, in a coral. Other tables may have been 100–150 feet away. We were not allowed to go outside the corral in the one huge room [where processing took place]."

- "As far as I'm concerned, each and every one of those ballots was opened illegally."

There are many more affidavits. Additional examples are found on pages 116 and 151. Do they prove the election was invalid? They do not. However, they absolutely prove the need for full audits, and those have not occurred as of this writing.

Once again, we need to ask why these on-the-record, under-oath statements were less newsworthy than the anonymous (and ultimately discredited) Russia "peeing prostitute" claims.

BILLIONAIRE DROP BOXES
The use of private money—much of it dark money—to fuel election-office policy was the single most revolutionary and effective characteristic of the 2020 election.

—J. CHRISTIAN ADAMS

Mark Zuckerberg and his wife, Priscilla Chan, spent hundreds of millions of dollars before and during the 2020 election in an effort to increase voter participation. The money they spent, through their nonprofit organizations, Center for Tech and Civic Life (CTCL) and Center for Election Innovation and Research (CEIR), was directed towards Democrat voter concentrations in Arizona, Georgia, Michigan, North Carolina, Pennsylvania, Texas, Virginia, and Wisconsin. Most of those states were important to Biden's success in the election.

The money had strings attached, and those strings were "spelled out in great detail" in the grant agreements.[85]

---

84 Daniel Payne, "Pennsylvania poll watcher: 'We literally had no input and no ability to watch anything,'" *Just the News*, November 9, 2020, https://justthenews.com/politics-policy/elections/pennsylvania-poll-watcher-we-literally-had-no-input-and-no-ability-watch.

85 William Doyle, "Mark Zuckerberg spent $419M on nonprofits ahead of 2020 election— and got the Dem vote," *New York Post*, October 13, 2021, https://nypost.com/2021/10/13/mark-zuckerberg-spent-419m-on-nonprofits-ahead-of-2020-election-and-got-out-the-dem-vote/.

The two Zuckerberg organizations were registered as nonprofit 501(c)(3) entities, but they leaned to the left, ideologically. The activities included:

- Adding numerous unguarded, private "drop boxes" in Democrat jurisdictions—the kind that are beloved by ballot harvesters

- Hiring temporary staffing and poll workers to support election office activities

- Interacting with potential voters (voter recruitment)

In a *New York Post* article, William Doyle described the kind of voter "interaction" that took place in the State of Wisconsin:

"CTCL/CEIR funded self-described 'vote navigators' in Wisconsin to 'assist voters, potentially at their front doors, to answer questions, assist in ballot curing . . . and witness absentee ballot signatures.'"[86]

In total, about $420 million was spent by Zuckerberg and Chan in the various swing states. Because the funds were spent in such a way that they heavily favored Democrats over Republicans, CTCL and CEIR were probably in violation of IRS regulations for tax exempt organizations, which state:

[V]oter education or registration activities with evidence of bias that (a) would favor one candidate over another; (b) oppose a candidate in some manner; or (c) have the effect of favoring a candidate or group of candidates, will constitute prohibited participation or intervention.[87]

I doubt the Biden administration plans to investigate these probable violations of IRS regulations. For more information, see the Wisconsin section, starting on page 221, or the Pennsylvania section starting on page 193.

ALLEGED BALLOT SHREDDING

In the aftermath of the election, some people stumbled upon bags of shredded ballots, and they wondered if these were evidence of election fraud. In late November, a

---

86   Ibid.

87   "The Restriction of Political Campaign Intervention by Section 501(c)(3) Tax-Exempt Organizations," Internal Revenue Service, accessed February 16, 2022, https://www.irs.gov/charities-non-profits/charitable-organizations/the-restriction-of-political-campaign-intervention-by-section-501c3-tax-exempt-organizations.

Facebook video showed ballots being destroyed in Georgia's Cobb County.[88] In March, 2021, dumpster divers found a bag of shredded ballots, and a woman posted pictures of the shredded ballots on the internet.

While corruption is always possible, in each case the respective county was able to produce a more likely explanation. For example, they were shredding ballots from a prior election, or sample test ballots, or ballots of deceased voters.

But, there was a case in October 2021 that is a bit more serious. Two Fulton County (Atlanta area) workers were fired after they checked out batches of voter registration forms, and then shredded them. (They were caught on video camera.) About 300 registration forms were involved, and it is not clear if the information can be recovered. It is also not clear if these two workers shredded on a regular basis.[89] Generally speaking, however, it seems that there is a reasonable explanation for most of the shredded ballots found.

88   Trevor Schakohl, "Does this video show ballots being destroyed in Georgia's Cobb County?" *CheckYourFact.com*, November 27, 2020, https://checkyourfact.com/2020/11/27/fact-check-video-ballots-destroyed-georgia-cobb-county/.

89   AP, "Georgia election workers fired, accused of shredding voter applications," *CBS News*, October 12, 2021, https://www.cbsnews.com/news/georgias-election-workers-fired-shredding-voter-applications/.

4

HOW TO INTERPRET THE FINDINGS IN PART II

Nothing in Part II can definitively indicate whether fraud or irregularities took place in the election, or who won or lost. That said, these issues can tell the auditor how much auditing is needed, where it is needed, and the type of auditing that is needed. These matters fall into three categories:

- Up-front risk factors. These might include the disturbed rants of key Dominion VP Eric Coomer, documented vulnerabilities in election machines, and alliances formed between county election workers and billionaire-funded nonprofit organizations.[1]

- Internal control weaknesses. These include out-of-date voter registration lists, the unnecessary mass-mailing of ballots or ballot applications, legalization of ballot harvesting, unguarded drop boxes, the use of multiple types of paper ballots, and the unguarded storage of blank ballots and/or computer storage devices.

- Post-election warning signals. These include historical and mathematical anomalies, very low ballot rejection rates, extremely high voter turnout rates, and several sworn affidavits from poll watchers who allege misconduct.

---

1   If a county believes that mail-in ballots and drop boxes are necessities, these should be considered up-front (inherent) risk factors. If they are not necessities for a fair election, they should be viewed as internal control weakness and should be reduced or eliminated.

The 2020 election began and ended with unusually large risk factors, relative to previous elections. These factors should have been considered by state election administrators as they planned audits of the election results. They were not considered. Election officials simply recounted ballots, and resisted real audits in every case. This had better change, or the United States will lose its democracy.

Part III contains an analysis of each of the six key swing state elections, and an evaluation of the certification decisions made in those states. In formulating the conclusions in Part III, the risk factors of Part II are considered.

PART III

STATE-BY-STATE ANALYSIS

5

ARIZONA

SENATE HEARINGS: 35,000 PHONY BALLOTS?

In a large, somewhat gloomy conference room at the Phoenix Hyatt Regency Hotel, several Republican members of the Arizona Senate gathered on November 30, 2020. They heard a lengthy presentation by Rudy Giuliani, an MIT-trained engineer, an ex-military cyber security expert, a financial analyst, and several others, including upset citizen poll watchers and workers. All expressed concerns about the presidential election that took place on November 3. Before long, they heard a bombshell report—one that has been completely ignored by mainstream media.

An anonymous tip

An explosive allegation was made: In Pima County, thirty-five thousand (35,000) votes had been added to each Democratic candidate in the election, including Joe Biden. The allegation was made anonymously by someone claiming that he or she met with Democrat Pima County election officials on September 10, where a plan to rig the vote was hatched.

The tipster's written words were described and posted at the meeting by a cyber security expert, Retired Army Col. Phil Waldron. According to Waldron, "[The tipster] wanted to remain anonymous, but had enough concern that he wanted to send this to the Criminal Division of the U.S. Department of Justice," which he did.[1] Here are some words from the email of the tipster, as posted at the meeting:[2]

> When I asked how in the world will 35,000 votes be kept hidden from being discovered, it was stated that spread distribution will be embedded across the entire registered-voter range and will not exceed the registered-vote count, and the 35,000 was determined allowable in Pima County, based on our county registered-vote count [sic].
>
> It was also stated that total voter turnout versus total registered voters determine how many votes we can embed.
>
> Maricopa [county] embed total would be substantially higher than Pima's due to embeds being based upon the total number of registered voters.
>
> When I asked if this has been tested and how do we know it works, the answer was yes, and has shown success in Arizona judicial-retention elections since 2014, even undetectable in post-audits because no candidate will spend the kind of funds needed to audit and contact voters to verify votes in the full potential of total registered voters, which is more than 500,000 registered voters.[3]

Journalist Sara A. Carter said she saw the email communication that was sent from the tipster to the DOJ, and this author sent a Freedom of Information (FOIA) request to the DOJ, asking for copies of all communications to and from the department regarding the matter.[4] There has been no response to my request so far, after several months and two inquiries. It is not clear that the federal Department of Justice is investigating the matter, or that it will ever respond to my request—even though the DOJ was required to respond months ago.

The anonymous allegation was cited by the Trump team as a reason to delay certification. In their view, a forensic audit of Pima County was required. However, the allegation did not impress election officials in Pima County, or in Arizona writ large.

---

1   Kristina Wong, "Arizona election integrity hearing witnesses present alleged voting anomalies, irregularities, intimidation," *Breitbart.com*, December 4, 2020, https://www.breitbart.com/2020-election/2020/12/04/arizona-election-integrity-hearing-witnesses-present-alleged-voting-anomalies-irregularities-stories-intimidation/.

2   "Trump Lawyers and Members of Arizona State Legislature Hold Hearing on Election Integrity," *NTD*, November 30, 2020, https://www.youtube.com/watch?v=QfC2T7UpxkI. @1:29:45.

3   Fred Lucas, "4 Takeaways from Arizona's election fraud hearing," *Dailysignal.com*, November 30, 2020, https://www.dailysignal.com/2020/11/30/4-takeaways-from-arizonas-election-fraud-hearing/.

4   Staff, "Arizona witnesses believe election was plagued by fraud, as Trump team fights for investigations," *Saraacarter.com*, December 1, 2020, https://saraacarter.com/arizona-witnesses-believe-election-was-plagued-by-fraud-as-trump-team-fights-for-investigations/.

On that same day, Arizona certified Joe Biden as the winner of the State's eleven electoral votes.

Apparently, this alleged tip was made by someone with knowledge of the election process. The tipster knew it would be necessary to spread the phony votes so that they never exceeded precinct registration numbers. After all, if a candidate's vote totals went too high in any particular precinct, it would be a dead giveaway. And the tipster correctly indicated that the fraud would be virtually undetectable unless voters were contacted after the election. In my judgment, this allegation is very credible, due to the corroborating mathematical evidence, cited below.

THE FRAUD IS CONFIRMED WITH A "FISHTAIL"

Thanks to the efforts of Arizona Representative Mark Finchem and Dr. Shiva Ayyadurai, we can guess which precincts received the phony ballots. Finchem obtained precinct-level voting data for Pima County, the county he represents. These data include, by precinct, the number of people requesting mail-in ballots, the number of people returning the ballots, and the votes for each candidate.[5]

Dr. Shiva, a pattern recognition expert, noticed that Pima County's 2020 election had an extraordinarily high mail-in ballot return rate (about 87 percent), when compared to the national average (71 percent) or the average of other Arizona counties (67.6 percent), depending on the denominator used. Even more interesting was the pattern and distribution of precincts in Pima, when arranged by their mail-in ballot return rates.[6]

Figure 7 is not a Shiva graph, but is presented in a similar manner as one of the graphs in Dr. Shiva's Pima County analysis. Shiva Ayyadurai calls it his "fishtail" graph, for obvious reasons. It reveals a fascinating pattern that may be the key to unlocking fraud in the 2020 election:

---

5   Rachel Alexander, "Citing Precincts with ballot return rate greater than 100 percent, Donald Trump calls to decertify Pima County's 2020 election or hold a new one," *Arizona Sun Times*, October 19, 2021, https://arizonasuntimes.com/2021/10/19/ citing-precincts-with-ballot-return-rate-greater-than-100-percent-donald-trump-calls-to-decertify-pima-countys-2020-election-or-hold-a-new-one/.

6   Shiva Ayyadurai, "The Fish Tail in Pima County. Analysis of Mail-In Ballots Pima County, Arizona," *Vashiva.com*, October 15, 2021, https://vashiva.com/the-fish-tail-in-pima-county-analysis-of-mail-in-ballots-pima-county-arizona/.

FIGURE 7: A ROUGH APPROXIMATION OF A SHIVA "FISHTAIL" GRAPH

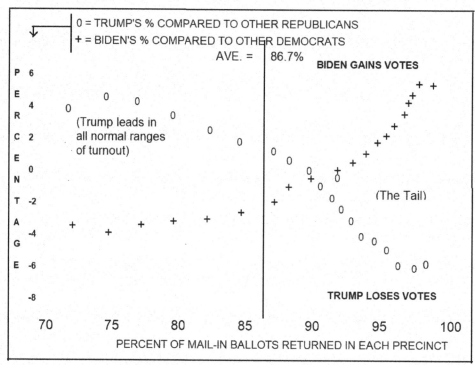

This is an approximation of one of Dr. Shiva's "fishtail" graphs. The head is on the left and the tail is on the right. Plusses represent Biden's vote as a percentage of other Democrats, and circles represent Trump's vote as a percentage of other Republicans.

Be careful when reading the graph. The "x" axis is not a timeline: Rather, this graph displays precinct clusters organized by the percentage of their mail-in ballots returned, with lower return rates on the left and higher return rates on the right. What about the "y" axis? You may think it compares the votes received by Trump in comparison to Biden, but that is not the case. Instead, Trump is compared to Republicans in general, and Biden is compared to Democrats in general.

There may be a temptation to explain Trump's apparent loss by saying he was not as popular as other Republicans. However, this was not necessarily the case. As you can see in Figure 7, Trump had a commanding lead over other Republicans in precincts with average or lower return rates. (And the "average" for Pima—shown with the vertical line—was about 19 percent higher than other Arizona counties.) However, when we move to the right side of the graph, into the super-high (and very unrealistic) return rates of 92 percent to almost 100 percent, Trump starts losing relative to other Republicans, and Biden gains relative to other Democrats.

What does it mean? It is only a theory at this point, but it appears very likely that, in certain Pima precincts, extra ballots were added, and/or were shifted from Trump to Biden. That is what produced such high ballot return rates and caused Biden to win the state. And the ballots were spread widely. Those 8 dots on the right side of the graph, from 92 percent to 100 percent, represent over 140 precincts. Forty of those precincts have virtually impossible return rates of 97 percent or more, according to Dr. Shiva's analysis.[7]

So what is the solution? People need to knock on doors and make inquiries. (Phone calls will not work.) Also, the signatures on envelopes originating from the 140 suspect precincts need to be carefully scrutinized. Are Pima County Officials going to investigate this matter? Of course not! Will Merrick Garland send some agents to check it out? Of course not! But there is some hope. The matter has been referred to Arizona Attorney General Mark Brnovich, and some State legislators believe he is investigating. I hope he has competent accountants on staff who know how to audit this particular matter. Otherwise, there will be no reckoning for this likely fraud.

MULTISTATE BALLOT HARVESTING SCHEME

It appears that there may be a major ballot harvesting scandal in Arizona (and other states). As noted on page 36, an organization named True the Vote (TTV) matched cell phone "ping" location data with video images to detect and map-out ballot harvesting operations. In the movie, *2,000 Mules*, TTV estimated that there were at least 20,000, and as many as 200,000, illegally-cast ballots in Arizona. It is believed that the Arizona Attorney General is investigating these claims, but so far no official statement has been made.

Predictably, media fact checkers have savaged the movie, but don't be misled. The general theory of the movie is credible, and much of the evidence presented is quite strong.

THE SIGNATURES WERE NOT MATCHED—"WHERE IS THE INTEGRITY?"

Linda Brickman, an official with the Maricopa County Republicans, was a volunteer observer at the Maricopa County Tabulation and Election Center. At the Senate hearing at the Hyatt Regency, she claimed that signature matching standards were, effectively, eliminated. Brickman described the process, and its disintegration: At first, signatures on ballot envelopes had to have about fifteen points of similarity with comparison signatures on file. That standard was reduced to three points of similarity, and was eventually reduced to just one point of similarity.

---

7   Ayyadurai, "The Fish tail in Pima County," October 15, 2021.

"Just pass each signature verification through," we were told. This is not the way an election should be run. Where is the integrity?[8]

Brickman also said there were at least thirty different names that were all written with the same handwriting. She said she informed supervisors, who said they would take care of it.

Dr. Burns and the "low confidence" yellow banners
There was more testimony regarding signature matching—and mismatching. At the Arizona Senate's November 30 hearing, Judith Burns, a Maricopa County resident and observer, stated:

> I kept looking at the [computer] screen because it seemed very odd. And in the bottom right-hand corner was a yellow banner, and I got into a position where I could see the yellow banner which said "low confidence." Then I started paying much closer attention to the signatures, thinking this didn't even make sense to me because the signatures on the ballots that were being compared to other signatures didn't even resemble in any way what they were comparing it to. They were completely illegible. They were just scribbles on the ballots.
>
> [T]here were five screeners screening "low confidence" ballots the entire afternoon that I was in there. And I asked [Silvia?] what the low confidence said, and she said not to worry about that, that this was a new program they were testing.[9]

Keep in mind that, if there were five screeners ignoring bad signatures all afternoon, thousands of potentially invalid votes may have been the result—in just one part of one county of Arizona.

> *A journalist EDUCATIONAL ALERT!*
>
> *If you are a journalist reading this, I am talking to you! The testimony of Linda Brickman and Dr. Burns is not proof, but it is EVIDENCE! And when there is evidence, you should not say that claims of fraud are baseless. That word is used when there is no evidence. I have many more tips for you in a special educational section called, "What do they teach in journalism school?" It is on page 281.*

8   Kristina Wong, "Arizona election integrity hearing witnesses present alleged voting anomalies," December 4, 2020.

9   "Trump Lawyers and Members of Arizona State Legislature Hold Hearing on Election Integrity," *NTD*, November 30, 2020, https://www.youtube.com/watch?v=QfC2T7UpxkI, @7:35:00.

SHARPIE-GATE: NOT AS STUPID AS IT SOUNDS

A lawsuit was filed by several Maricopa County voters, claiming that their ballots had been damaged by the use of Sharpie-brand permanent ink markers. The damaged ballots were then entered into the "adjudication" process, during which precinct workers tried to decide the intent of voters.

The Sharpie-related claim was, of course, widely ridiculed and fact checked by mainstream and social media. Facebook labeled the reports as "false," and banned the hashtag, "#sharpiegate" on the platform.[10] On its website, Maricopa County explained that only four types of paper were used for ballots, and they had a special film that prevented Sharpie ink from bleeding through.[11]

A puzzling email

Sharpie-gate certainly sounded like a crazy story, until the leak of a strange email from the Maricopa County Elections Assistant Director, Kelly Dixon. Here is what Dixon wrote on October 22, 2020, about twelve days before Election Day:

> [W]e know you're hearing issues and concerns about the Sharpie Markers. Starting tomorrow, 10/23, and through 11/2, we are asking that Clerks hand voters BALLPOINT PENS rather than markers. We NEED to use Markers on Election Day, but for now and through 11 /2, hand voters a Ballpoint Pen. [The emphasis is Dixon's.][12]

In other words, use ball point pens until Election Day, but on that day, voters "NEED to use Markers."

I had a hard time finding an explanation for this because the entire subject had been mostly censored by mainstream media—of course! I finally found the answer in the AZMirror. The policy had something to do with the drying time of the Sharpie ink. Megan Gilbertson, a spokeswoman for the Maricopa Elections Department, explained:

---

10   Julia Musto, "Arizona voters sue Maricopa County over Sharpie use at polling sites, as officials say votes will count," *Fox News*, November 5, 2020, https://www.foxnews.com/politics/az-voters-file-lawsuit-against-maricopa-county-after-sharpiegate.

11   Tarra Snyder, "AZ audit revelation: Wrong paper was used for ballots, could confirm 'Sharpiegate' according to AZ Sen President," *The Western Journal*, July 15, 2021, https://www.westernjournal.com/az-audit-revelation-wrong-paper-used-ballots-confirm-sharpiegate-according-az-sen-president/.

12   Tom Pappert, "LEAK: Email allegedly from Maricopa Elections Office found issue with Sharpies, said use them on election day anyway," *National File*, November 19, 2020, https://nationalfile.com/leak-email-allegedly-from-maricopa-elections-office-found-issue-with-sharpies-said-use-them-on-election-day-anyway/.

During in-person early voting, voters were given the option to use a ballpoint pen to fill out their ballot because those ballots are placed in a sealed envelope, allowing the ink to dry.[13]

Well, it is not a perfect explanation because Gilbertson said that early voters were given the option of using a ballpoint pen. That may not be true, judging by the words in the Kelly Dixon email. She said: "[W]e are asking that Clerks hand voters BALLPOINT PENS rather than markers [emphasis as written]."[14] Besides, it seems to me that a Sharpie is more likely to bleed than a ballpoint pen. But, that is just my personal impression.

Later, the Cyber Ninja auditors demonstrated that bleeding ink from some Sharpie pens did cause ballots to become unreadable. How did it happen? Contrary to the claims of the Maricopa Elections Department, ten different types of paper were used to print ballots (not just four types), and some of them did not have the required protective film. The use of several types of paper also caused a major internal control risk. As an analogy, consider what would happen if the U.S. Treasury printed $10 bills on various types of paper, of different weight and texture.

To be honest, I am not writing about Sharpie-gate because it was an election game-changer. It was not. However, the claims of the litigants were correct, and the matter illustrates the danger of arrogant journalists making snap judgments and premature fact checks. Journalist, humble thyself!

THE MILITARY LOVES JOE BIDEN

At an Arizona Senate Committee hearing on January 24, 2022, we learned that 95 percent of the 2020 election overseas military vote in Maricopa County was for Joe Biden. That is an amazing percentage, given that the overall county-wide vote was fairly even between Biden and Trump.

Overseas votes are subject to the Uniform Overseas Civilian Absentee Voting Act, commonly referred to as UOCAVA. That Act applies to:

- U.S. uniformed services personnel

- Their families

---

13   Jerod MacDonald-Evoy, "New election conspiracy centers on email from an election official reminding workers of a new policy," *AZMirror*, November 19, 2020, https://www.azmirror.com/blog/new-election-conspiracy-centers-on-email-from-an-election-official-reminding-workers-of-a-new-policy/.

14   Ibid.

- U.S. citizens living abroad

The findings were presented by Paul Harris, a corporate executive who had been asked to conduct the review during the Maricopa County Cyber Ninjas audit. Harris appeared to be almost angry as he noted that all of the ballots were simply print-outs of (presumably) emails or faxes on standard copy paper, and there were unusual aspects to the ballots:[15]

- There was no source documentation and there was no way to identify where any of the "ballots" (sheets of paper) came from.

- There were no chain of custody documents. Harris couldn't determine who processed the ballots, and when.

- The number of ballots was surprising. Paul Harris said that, in the 2016 election, there were only 1,600 UOCAVA ballots, but in 2020 the number jumped to 9,600.

- Harris personally tabulated the votes, and 95 percent went for one candidate. He estimated that it added at least 8,000 votes (net) to the winning candidate, who had (ostensibly) won the State by only a bit over 10,000 votes.

Paul Harris analyzed just one county in Arizona, but there were also lots of UOCAVA votes elsewhere. A witness named Kathleen Alby testified (at the November 30 hearing) that "thousands" of "military faxes" were being processed in Pima County. "At one point that's all that they were processing were the faxed ones." And, like in Maricopa County, it appears there was no chain of custody documentation, according to Alby.[16]

THE BATTLE TO HAVE AN AUDIT OF THE MARICOPA COUNTY ELECTION
On December 15, 2020 a subpoena was sent to the Maricopa County Elections Department. Arizona Senate Republican leaders wanted to conduct an audit of the 2020 presidential election, as held in Maricopa County. They needed all related documents and files, including ballots, ballot envelopes, voter rolls, computers, computer files, routers and other hardware. The Elections Department responded to the Senate

15   Paul Harris testimony, Senate Government Committee SB 1120, Arizona State Legislature, January 24, 2022, https://www.azleg.gov/videoplayer/?eventID=2022011066, @1:53.

16   Kathleen Alby, "Testimony," Arizona Senate Hearing, November 30, 2022, https://www.realclearpolitics.com/video/2020/11/30/watch_live_arizona_state_legislature_holds_public_hearing_on_2020_election.html, @8:32.

subpoena with a lawsuit, stating that the subpoena request was too broad.[17]

Months later, Senate President Karen Fann would state that the Senate had originally offered to conduct the audit jointly with the County Elections Department. Initially, Fann said, the Department seemed to like the offer, but in the end, they refused. In a September 2021 interview with Jordan Conradson, Senate Leader Fann said:

> In fact, we offered to do the entire audit there, I told the supervisors, let's do this together. Let's do it at your facilities, don't move the ballots, keep everything exactly where it is. Let's do this together, and they originally said, "That's a great idea. We'll do it.
>
> And then they went into an executive session and came out and said, now, we're gonna do our own."[18]

And that is exactly what the County did.

The Board decides to audit itself

While waiting for the judge's decision regarding its lawsuit to block the Senate's audit, the County performed its own audit, with a level of thoroughness that is highly questionable. By now you know that this author does not regard self-audits as audits at all. Generally, they are ridiculous.[19]

Perhaps the County thought that auditing itself would satisfy Karen Fann and her Senate colleagues. It did not. Fann felt the County's audit did not go far enough, so she contacted Doug Logan to explore the possibility of having his company, Cyber Ninjas, do the audit for the Senate. This was controversial because Logan had been a Trump supporter.

Database disappears

The results of the self-audit were interesting, to put it kindly. On February 23, 2021, the auditors hired by the County reported that they found no malicious hardware on the voting machines and determined that the machines had not been connected to the internet. But later, in an interview on November 29, 2021, Doug Logan (Cyber Ninjas CEO) questioned the findings and veracity of the County-hired auditors:

---

17   Staff, "How we got here: An Arizona audit timeline," *AZCentral.com*, September 24, 2021, https://www.azcentral.com/story/news/politics/arizona/2021/09/24/arizona-audit-timeline-how-we-got-here/8238674002/.

18   Jordan Conradson, "AZ Senate President Karen Fann on Maricopa County Agreement: 'It's A Huge Win For Us – We Needed Data So We Could Finish the Audit,'" *Gateway Pundit*, September 19, 2021, https://www.thegatewaypundit.com/2021/09/video-az-senate-president-karen-fann-huge-win-us-people-want-audit-finished-got-get-done/.

19   Ibid.

We've known from the beginning those weren't real audits. They weren't looking at anything associated with the election results. And they couldn't because the database was purged before they (EAC vendors) came in. There was nothing for them to look at. . . . That blew my mind because there are literally logs that say—at this time, on this date, they clicked an option that said "purge database."[20]

The County (Elections Department) claimed that removing the database was a normal archival function but Logan pointed out that this kind of purge did not take place after previous elections.[21] And I would add this: If archiving was needed, they should have first discussed the planned archiving with the auditors.

The Cyber Ninjas start

After Maricopa County Superior Court Judge Thomason ruled the legislative subpoenas were valid (on February 26, 2021), the Senate hired Cyber Ninjas to lead its audit. Before starting, Logan made a conciliatory offer to Dominion and to the County:

We actually invited Dominion to watch us when we touched their machines. We told them if you want to make sure we're doing it right, send somebody down. We also notified the County that we were glad to have Dominion watch us. So why didn't they send anybody? They would know it was done right and they would have to attest to it.[22]

Big Tech tries to hinder audit

To perform a complete hand count of over 2 million ballots, Cyber Ninjas would need lots of volunteers, but efforts to recruit them were hindered, allegedly, by the heavy hand of big tech. According to a group calling itself, "ArizonaAudit," their online recruiting form, seeking audit volunteers, was de-platformed by Google: "Because Google chose to censor our form recruiting Volunteer Observers from all parties, we are now using this link: arizonaaudit.wufoo.com/ forms." Later, the new link was also censored. Nevertheless, the Cyber Ninjas were able to get the many volunteers (at least 1,500) that they needed.[23]

---

20 Jovan Pulitzer, "Video interview of Doug Logan," *Cut the Crap*, November 29, 2021,@55:29, https://www.facebook.com/real.jovanhuttonpulitzer/videos/1984527931726020.

21 Ibid, @56:11.

22 Ibid.

23 J.E. Dyer, "Big tech de-platforms Maricopa County election audit recruiting effort," *Liberty Unyielding*, April 16, 2021, https://libertyunyielding.com/2021/04/16/big-tech-de-platforms-maricopa-county-election-audit-recruiting-effort/.

Maricopa Elections Department—the auditee from Hell!

The Maricopa Elections Department engaged in evasive, self-protective actions designed to cripple the audit. In my opinion, the Department declined to work with the Cyber Ninjas and the Senate for several, self-serving reasons:

- If the Elections Department worked with the auditors, it would effectively ratify the accuracy and legitimacy of the final product. The Department did not want that.

- Also, if they worked together, the Department would have to explain to the auditors how calculations were made, and it would have to share the information sources used. In the end, even when the audit was over, many of those information sources were not revealed.

- The Elections Department wanted to stall the entire process just as long as possible. Perhaps it was hoping the audit funds would run out, and the audit would stop. Working with Democrats, the Department fought every subpoena in the courts.

- On the most important items, signature matching and canvassing, the Department never gave in. To block these audit procedures, it recruited friends throughout the Democratic Party, including Arizona Secretary of State Katie Hobbs, and U.S. Attorney General Merrick Garland. Since those two audit steps (canvassing and signature matching) were the only steps likely to find the big fraud items, the Cyber Ninjas were greatly limited.

- The Elections Department refused to let the Cyber Ninjas see the routers or electronic file and application logs after Soros-funded County Sheriff Paul Penzone argued that law enforcement would (somehow) be compromised if auditors were allowed access to the equipment. Supporters of the Cyber Ninjas said the Sheriff's claims were absurd. This created much delay.

Auditors often encounter some resistance during audits, but in this case it was different. Maricopa's intransigence was supported by a lot of cheerleaders—the mainstream media. Diversionary and resistance tactics were applauded.

THE CYBER NINJAS' MARICOPA AUDIT REPORT

"Arizona election audit report confirms Biden victory over Trump," the *New York Post* declared.[24] Dozens of others in the media had similar headlines, but they were mistaken.

The audit results cast doubt on the certification decision that was made, for reasons that are explained later. First, however, let's identify the audit finding that is least important: the fact that the paper ballot count approximately matched the computer totals.

As an auditor, I would be stunned if the number of paper ballots in the boxes didn't approximately add up to the tabulated amounts in the machines. And I would be very surprised if the auditors found Joe Biden with fewer votes than originally announced. It is likely that, from the start, the County had the correct number of ballots in paper and electronic form (but not necessarily the correct number of authentic votes).

Further, I doubt there was significant cheating taking place *within* the Elections Department offices. Any fraud would probably take place before ballots reached the Elections Department. However, if there was fraud inside the Department, the perpetrators had several months to "fix the books."

It is much more likely that fraud, if any, took place in the community at large. After all, this was a unique year—the year of the mail-in ballot. And mail-in ballots make it easy to cheat without detection, and without the inside assistance that normally might be required.

One might ask, if people within the Maricopa County election system were not committing fraud, why did the County Elections Department fight so relentlessly against the audit? The most like reasons are (1) job security of election administrators, (2) political influence from those who liked the election results as they were, and (3) the election officials may genuinely feel they did a pretty good job (and are not necessarily aware of irregularities, if any).

The audit results

Audits can be terrifying events for those responsible for maintaining the system of procedures and documents and equipment in any large institution. Auditors usually find lots of errors—some minor and some large. And all of those errors, even the little ones, make the responsible personnel look bad.

Indeed, the audit report released on September 24, 2021 revealed a large number of irregularities and mistakes. The County responded that most of those revelations were misleading or false. Here's a partial list of claims made by the Ninjas:[25]

24   Samuel Chamberlain, "Arizona election audit confirms Biden victory over Trump," *New York Post*, September 24, 2021, https://nypost.com/2021/09/24/arizona-election-audit-confirms-biden-victory-over-trump/.

25   Cyber Ninjas, "Maricopa County Forensic Election Audit," Arizona State Senate, September 24, 2021, Vol. I, 2-3, https://www.azsenaterepublicans.com/_files/ugd/2f3470_a91b5cd3655445b498f9acc63db35afd.pdf.

- "None of the various systems related to elections had numbers that would balance and agree with each other. In some cases, these differences were significant."

- "There appears to be ... 27, 807 ballots cast from individuals who had moved prior to the election." [In Table 2, below, this number is broken into 3 numbers: 23,344, 2,081, and 2,382.]

- "Files were missing from the Election Management System (EMS) Server."

- "Ballot images 284,412 on the EMS were corrupt or missing." [The County claimed it was able to open the "corrupted" files on its own cloned copy of the hard drive.]

- "Logs appeared to be intentionally rolled over, and all the data in the database related to the 2020 General Election had been fully cleared."

- "On the ballot side, batches were not always clearly delineated, duplicated ballots were missing the required serial numbers, originals were duplicated more than once, and the Auditors were never provided [complete] chain of custody documentation."

- "Maricopa County failed to follow basic cyber security best practices and guidelines from CISA."

- "Software and patch protocols were not followed."

- "Credential management was flawed: unique usernames and passwords were not allocated."

- "Lack of baseline for host and network activity for approved programs, communications protocols and communications devices for voting systems."

Frankly, some of these errors (if they are errors) are probably not that serious, and may be found in election departments around the nation. The more serious issues include the internet connections, the use of shared passwords, and the large-scale deletion of files. Let's give more consideration to those issues.

The County denies there was hacking, saying that the Election Management System

(EMS) is air gapped, without connection to the internet.[26] A subsequent analysis, led by Former Congressman John Shadegg, confirmed that, during the time period October 7 to November 20, 2020, there were no connections to the "public internet," and no evidence of "data deletion, data purging, data overwriting, or other destruction of evidence or obstruction of the audit."[27]

As for the passwords, Maricopa County claims it uses physical safeguards (presumably keys, locked rooms, cabinets, etc.), and those "function similar to how a password functions for credential management and logging system access."[28] That sounds weak to me.

What about the wholesale deletion of files? The Cyber Ninjas claim that the County deliberately deleted a massive number of files, one day before auditing was to begin. The County counters that the files were removed and put into archival storage as a routine procedure.[29] It adds that the archived files were not given to the auditors because archived files were not covered by the subpoena. Apparently, the County thinks that subpoenaed files are no longer subpoenaed files if you remove them and put them into storage. (Anthony Weiner could have used that information.) By the way, this "routine" archiving was not done in previous years, according to the Cyber Ninjas.

The Ninjas also claim that "a user leveraging the EMS admin account remotely logged into the EMS server...and began executing a script..." hundreds of times.[30] According to the Ninjas, this was done deliberating for the purpose of overwriting security logs. The County does not seem to deny that the security logs were deleted, but it claims this was unintentional, and was caused by automated actions initiated by the Dominion software.[31] Whether or not intentional, it appears there was a serious loss of information.

Deep in the weeds!
Now we descend into some minutia that, believe it or not, some people find boring! If you are such a person, you may wish to jump to The County's Unforgivable Error on page 90.

---

26   Staff, "Correction the Record," Maricopa County Elections Department, January 2022, 36, https://recorder.maricopa.gov/justthefacts/pdf/Correcting%20The%20Record%20-%20January%202022%20Report.pdf.

27   John Shadegg, Special Master, "Answers to Senate Questions Regarding Maricopa County Election Network," Agreement between Senate and County, March 23, 2022, https://www.maricopa.gov/DocumentCenter/View/74501/Final-Report-Answers-to-Senate-Questions.

28   Ibid., 51

29   Ibid., 21

30   Cyber Ninjas, "Maricopa County Forensic Election Audit," Vol. III, 86-87.

31   Staff, "Correction the Record," Maricopa County Elections Department, 29-30.

The Cyber Ninjas had several issues of concern regarding ballot and voter numbers, and in the tables that follow we analyze those issues, as well as the County's responses. It is pretty tedious, but in Table 2 you will find a summary of these amounts and issues:

TABLE 2: CYBER NINJAS FINDINGS AND
MARICOPA COUNTY'S RESPONSES[32]

Ninjas Ref. #	Description	# of ballots	See Ref. # below
5.3.1	Ballots mailed from prior address	23,344	a.
5.4.1	More ballots returned by voter than sent	9,041	b.
5.4.2	Voters may have voted in multiple counties	5,295	c.
5.5.1	Official result does not match who voted	3,432	d.
5.5.2	More duplicates than original ballots	2,592	e.
5.5.3	In-person voters who had moved away	2,382	f.
5.5.4	Voters moved out of state after October 5, 2020	2,081	f.
5.5.5	Votes counted in excess of voters who voted	1,551	d.

The basic response of the Maricopa County Elections Department was to say, *take our word for it*, and if you don't understand precisely how we do things in our offices, you must not be expert auditors. In fact, you might be stupid!

This is something auditors are used to. We see the methods and idiosyncrasies of hundreds of organizations. On the other hand, the people within an organization often know of only one system—their own. As a result, they have trouble distinguishing between industry-wide methods and their own particular methods. For example, if a twenty-year veteran employee in the Maricopa Elections Department has always stored computer media in a certain way and in a certain place, he may expect an experienced auditor to know that, without asking. But the auditor probably won't know that because every organization has its own procedures.

The Maricopa Elections Department never worked side-by-side with the auditors to show them its documentary evidence, or to explain exactly how things are done in Maricopa. Rather, the Department stayed away, and read the criticisms made by Cyber Ninjas. Weeks later, the Elections Department responded critically in tweets and media interviews, and mostly with generalities.

---

32   Cyber Ninjas, "Maricopa County Forensic Election Audit," Vol. III, 5.

There may be a lot of truth in the answers provided by the County, but it is impossible to be sure, due to the evasiveness of the organization. The specific responses are footnoted here:

Table 2: Ref. a. 23,344 ballots mailed from prior address.

The Department broke this amount (the 23,344) into 18 smaller numbers. Here are some of the comments made by the County in relation to the largest four portions:[33] [34]

Number	County's response	My comment
7,866 voters with no record of address change	"Cyber Ninjas data showed the voter moved several years or a decade prior to the cutoff. However, our records show the voters' address had changed much more recently. In all instances, the updated address is within Maricopa County."	That is nice to *hear*, but an auditor needs to see the evidence. Maricopa has provided nothing.
5,512 voters with no record of address change	"Maricopa County relies on the *voter attestation* of a move <u>OR</u> a trusted source (like USPS or the NCOA report) when updating voter registration information. These voters were likely incorrectly identified due to the soft matching techniques used by Cyber Ninjas [emphasis added]."	Ninjas also used U.S. Postal Service Change of Address (NCOA), via Melissa. More importantly, the word, "OR," in the County's response probably means it gets the voter's attestation via a cell phone call. That call or text could also go straight to a fraudster (who put his own cell phone number down when he mailed in the ballot).
2,801 voters with no address change.	County gave same response: It relied on *voter attestation* <u>OR</u> a trusted source.	This is not an adequate response to the question raised by the auditors. We still have no idea whether these votes were legal, or illegal.
631 voters with no address change.	County gave same response: It relied on *voter attestation* <u>OR</u> a trusted source.	This is not an adequate response to the question raised by the auditors. We still have no idea whether these votes were legal, or illegal.

33   The above four numbers account for 16,810 voters out of the 23,344 top line number. The balance is found in fourteen smaller amounts, which I didn't bother to analyze.

34   Staff, "Correction the Record," Maricopa County Elections Department, 55.

The use of the "OR" conjunction makes me suspect that the Department just calls the voter to get his/her attestation (a meaningless endeavor).

Table 2: Ref. b. 9,041 more ballots returned than requested by voters. [35]

Number	County's response	My comment
9,041 excess ballots returned	Maricopa County said some ballot envelopes were scanned 2, 3, or even 4 times as employees went back and forth with voters in an effort to "cure" signature or other defects. In addition, there were several "unique" reasons given for the mismatching numbers.	It is important for the auditee to cooperate with the auditor, *while the audit is underway!* Each side (auditor and auditee) added to a different total, and the County asserts that its calculations are the accurate ones. The auditors are gone. Where is the evidence?

Table 2: Ref. c. 5,295 voters may have voted in multiple counties. [36]

Number	County's response	My comment
5,295 people voted in multiple counties	Again, Maricopa County claimed that the Cyber Ninjas used "soft" (unreliable) data sources, rather than the great sources that the Department used.	County administrators should have shown their sources to the auditors *in real time.* We still do not know how many voted illegally.

Table 2: Ref. d. 3,432 votes where official results don't reconcile; 1,551 votes counted in excess of voters [37]

Number	County's response	My comment
3,432 and 1,551	Apparently, this is not a County error. Cyber Ninjas stated: "We've been informed shortly before the release of this report that some of the discrepancies outlined could be due to the protected voter list."	The County should have given the explanation much sooner. Instead, it waited until the Ninjas were only hours away from releasing their report. Was purpose of the delay to make Ninjas look bad?

---

35   Ibid., 67–69.

36   Ibid., 57.

37   Ibid., 65.

Table 2: Ref. e. 2,592 more duplicates than original ballots.[38]

Number	County's response	My comment
2,592 more duplicates than original ballots.	The County's explanation: "It has been reported that during the Cyber Ninjas' hand count, observers noted contractors spilled a box of UOCAVA ballots 'across the Coliseum floor.'"	Ninjas said that only 20 ballots slid onto floor, and they stayed in order and were immediately picked up. This is ridiculous. It should have been resolved, person-to-person during the audit.

Table 2: Ref. f. In-person voters who had moved away; Voters moved out of state after October 5, 2020.[39]

Number	County's response	My comment
2,382 and 2,081 ballots	As it did so often, the Department claimed that Ninjas' data sources were "soft" and unreliable.[152]	The Department never offered to show its wonderful data sources; the Elections Department continues to keep its supporting materials secret.

Let's explore one more audit issue. For the sake of argument, assume that cheating (if any) was taking place within the Maricopa Elections Department. You might ask, "Wouldn't that show up in the count of ballots?" The answer is, "Probably not."

If there was someone inside the Department committing fraud, he/she had lots of opportunity to cover the tracks. This is true because of the sloppy storage procedures of Maricopa County, which make it easy to add or subtract ballots without detection. How sloppy was the storage of ballots? Here is a post-audit description from Doug Logan, the man who spearheaded the Cyber Ninjas audit.

After noting that there were forty-six pallets of ballot boxes, with almost forty boxes on each pallet, Logan said:

All of the boxes [of ballots], except for 52, were sealed just with regular package tape. . . . [The 52 boxes] had tamper-resistant seals on them, but the rest of them [over 1,500] just had regular box tape. When you opened the boxes there was [sic] stacks of ballots on top of stacks of ballots on top of stacks of ballots. . . . A few boxes had random stuff in them too . . . literally trash.[40]

---

38 Staff, "Correction the Record," Maricopa County Elections Department, 85.

39 Ibid., 58.

40 Jovan Pulitzer, Video interview of Doug Logan, November 29, 2021, @30:00 to 32:00, https://www.facebook.com/real. jovanhuttonpulitzer/videos/1984527931726020.

Before addressing the remaining parts of the audit, which are the most important parts, I have one more comment to make regarding the Maricopa County Elections Department: Some people in the County Elections Department need firing.

The county's unforgivable error
County officials made a few forgivable errors—except for one that is unforgivable. In every way imaginable, they refused to cooperate with the Cyber Ninjas. As a result, they wasted tremendous amounts of time and taxpayer funds. In addition, there are no meaningful audit results because meaningful evidence was not presented to the auditors. County resistance was manifested in several ways:

- Multiple lawsuits to impede the audit

- The refusal to turn over access codes and equipment

- Forcing the auditors to spend millions of dollars to move equipment

- Refusing to provide the auditors with access to routers because that could impede law enforcement? (Are you kidding?)

- Failure to answer many basic questions except via snarky tweets

- Failure to give access to source information

- Mobilizing forces to block signature verification

- Mobilizing forces to prevent voter canvassing

Election officials had every right to "push back" where the Ninjas made demands that seemed unreasonable. However, they should have invited the auditors into County facilities where they could work side-by-side, share information, and answer questions quickly and efficiently.

Absolutely disgraceful!

THE UNOFFICIAL, AND MOST IMPORTANT, MARICOPA AUDIT REPORTS
The detailed audit issues described above are important, and require resolution, but in the grand scheme of things, they are a side-show. The big fish in Maricopa County were caught by Liz Harris and Dr. Shiva.

As noted in the Preface, the Cyber Ninjas were blocked from physically contacting people (canvassing) to see if those who voted according the documentation, actually exist and actually voted. Of course, the Ninjas were not going to ask people *who* they voted for—just *if* they voted, and whether it was in person or via mail.

Apparently, the limited canvassing plans of the Cyber Ninjas put the County in a panic, and this resulted in multiple threats to the auditors and to the Arizona Senate. Democrats in the U.S. Congress and the Biden Justice Department warned that canvassing operations could be construed as "voter intimidation."[41] This seems a bit odd, since polling organizations routinely contact voters, in advance of an election, and they even ask questions about party affiliation and who the person plans to vote for. The Ninjas were just going to ask whether the respondent voted, and by what means.

Maloney and Raskin take charge
Congresswoman Carolyn Maloney and Congressman Jamie Raskin sent a threatening letter to Cyber Ninjas, expressing concern over the planned canvassing and concerning several other matters. They were particularly disturbed by the Ninja's embrace of "election conspiracy theories." As a result, they demanded lots and lots of documents, including all communications with:

- Former President Trump

- Any Trump administration official

- Any formal or informal representative of President Trump's presidential campaign, legal team, or political action committee

- Any representative of Voices and Votes, Fight Back, America Project, or any other funder of the Maricopa County audit

- Rudy Giuliani or any of his agents or representatives

- Sidney Powell

- Lin Wood

---

41   Ben Giles, "In response to Justice Dept., Arizona Senate says plan to canvass voters is on hold," *NPR*, May 7, 2021, https://www.npr.org/2021/05/07/994945179/in-response-to-justice-dept-arizona-senate-says-plan-to-canvass-voters-is-on-hol.

- Patrick Byrne

- Michael Flynn

- Michael Lindell

The two Congress people warned the Ninjas that their Committee "has broad authority to investigate 'any matter' at 'any time'...."[42] Well, the threats worked, and the Ninjas abandoned their plan. The audit procedure most likely to uncover fraud, was abandoned.

Enter Liz Harris

Real estate broker, Liz Harris, had made an unsuccessful effort to run for the Arizona House of Representatives in the 2020 election. Her first, and relatively modest, canvassing efforts were revealed at the Arizona Senate hearing held on November 30, 2020. Subsequently, Harris recruited many volunteers who spent hundreds of hours visiting the homes of nearly 12,000 residents in Maricopa County. In her Canvass Overview, Harris describes the results of these canvassing efforts as "nothing short of earth-shattering." They are.

The Harris team had a standard pitch they gave to residents. If the resident answered the door, the canvass volunteer would "identify themselves as private citizens conducting voluntary election integrity research" and ask if the person at the door would mind answering a few questions. After verifying the resident's name and after establishing that they were in the County database, these questions would be asked for each registered voter at the address:[43]

- What method do you use to vote?

- How many ballots did you receive in the mail for yourself?

- How many ballots did you receive for person(s) who do not live here?

---

42 Representatives Maloney and Raskin, "Letter to Doug Logan, CEO of Cyber Ninjas," House of Representatives, July 14, 2021, https://oversight.house.gov/sites/democrats.oversight.house.gov/files/2021-07-14.CBM%20JR%20to%20Logan-Cyber%20Ninjas%20re%20Arizona%20Election%20Audit.pdf.

43 Liz Harris, "Election 2020 Grassroots Canvass Report," Maricopa County Canvass, September 8, 2021, 6, https://canvass50.com/wp-content/uploads/2021/09/Maricopa-County-Canvass-Report-Final-090821.pdf.

- What did you do with any extra ballots received?

- How many registered voters are there supposed to be at this address?

- Total number of registered voters who voted in the November 2020 election?

The answers were keyed into a database for later analysis. Here is a summary of the findings, taken from Liz Harris' "Executive Summary" dated September 8, 2021:

Of 11,708 attempted voter contacts, interviews yielded data on 4,570 registered voters. These results are shown in Table 3, by precinct. Harris says that sworn affidavits can be produced to back up these results.

TABLE 3: ATTEMPTED CONTACTS AND SUCCESSFUL INTERVIEWS[44]

>>>>>>Precinct>>>>>	Warn-er	Dunbar	Wag-goner	Ritten-house	County wide	Total
# Registered homes visited	7228	1692	943	991	854	11708
# Registered voters from which data gathered	2699	637	566	315	353	4570

TABLE 4: RESPONDENT VOTED BUT MARICOPA HAS NOT RECORDED IT[45]

>>>>>>Precinct>>>>>	Warn er	Dunbar	Wag-goner	Ritten-house	County wide	Total
Per Maricopa, did not vote	714	134	43	35	38	964
Per respondent, he/she did vote	249	50	13	9	9	330
Potential error %	34.9	37.3	30.2	25.7	23.7	34.2

---

44   Liz Harris, "Election 2020 Grassroots Canvass Report," 6.

45   Ibid., 7.

TABLE 5 MARICOPA RECORDED THE VOTE BUT VOTER IS UNKNOWN[46]

>>>>>>Precinct>>>>>	Warner	Dunbar	Wag-goner	Ritten-house	County wide	Total
Voters registered at home of interviewee	1985	503	523	280	315	3606
Mail-in voters registered at home of interviewee	1547	276	564	239	271	2897
Registered mail-in voter unknown or moved pre 10/1	90	11	29	12	22	164
Potential error %	5.82	3.99	5.14	5.02	8.12	5.66

Interpretation of Table 4: Of the 4,570 registered voters contacted by Harris, 964 did not vote, according to Maricopa County records. However, 34.2 percent of her sample (330) said he or she did, in fact, vote. By extrapolating the results to the total number of non-voting registered voters (505,709, per Maricopa County), Harris estimates, with a 95 percent confidence level, that somewhere between 165,500 and 180,600 people may have voted without being recorded.

The above analysis notwithstanding, I am a bit skeptical of the results displayed in Table 4 because I believe some people may have said they voted to avoid the embarrassment of admitting that they did not vote. Also, it is not a randomly-selected sample, and that could have an impact.

Interpretation of Table 5: Of the 4,570 registered voters contacted by Harris, 2,897 were mail-in voters who voted in the election, per Maricopa County. However, 5.7 percent of these people were either unknown, or known to have moved out of the residence pre-October, 2020. And, as Liz Harris notes, election mail cannot be legally forwarded. By extrapolating the results to the approximate total of mail-in voters in the 2020 election (in Maricopa County), Harris estimates that between 70,844 and 121,933 people who supposedly voted by mail, were not the ones who actually voted.

Again, there is reason to be skeptical. It is possible some people managed to pick up their mail or have a friend forward their mail (even the part that is not supposed to be forwarded). The 164 number is small, and could be affected by interview errors, or confusion on the part of respondents. And like the Table 4 results, the Table 5 sample is not random. That said, the 5.7 percent results obtained by Liz Harris could be very significant because, if just one percent is accurate, it could be enough to change the election results.

46   Ibid., 8.

In conclusion, these error estimates are not conclusive, but they are troubling. They could reflect sampling error or a method error on the part of Maricopa County. But there is also the possibility of fraud.

The estimated error shown in Table 4 could reflect ballots systematically excluded from processing. The Table 5 estimated error could reflect ballot harvesting, where ballots are, essentially stolen. They may be pulled out of mail boxes, collected by unscrupulous mail carriers (and sold), or pulled out of trash. The Arizona Attorney General needs to follow up on these results, which reinforce the findings of True the Vote. (See page 75) Harris says that sworn affidavits, confirming the survey work, are available.

QUESTION TO CONSIDER: PLEASE READ THIS AND SELECT BEST ANSWER

After reading about the 5.7 percent potential error rate, shown in the Harris canvassing report, Maricopa County became very concerned. It asked Harris for a list of the voters she visited so that some of them could be contacted by the County. The plan was to determine if the 5.7 percent estimated error rate was correct. Officials were determined to ensure that the election was fair.

> A. The narrative about Maricopa County is true.
>
> B. The narrative about Maricopa County is false.

The answer is "B." I don't think the County Elections Department has the slightest interest in proving that it may have tabulated fraudulent votes, and it is receiving no pressure to do canvassing from mainstream media. Even if the County wanted to do it, the Biden administration and Representatives Maloney and Raskin would most likely try to block the effort.

DR. SHIVA'S BLANK SIGNATURE TEST FOR MARICOPA COUNTY

As noted, Democrats filed a lawsuit arguing that the Arizona Senate's auditors could not legally verify the authenticity of signatures on ballot documentation. As a result, the Senate agreed to abandon the signature-verification project. However, a pattern recognition expert, Dr. Shiva Ayyadurai ("Dr. Shiva"), was commissioned to analyze the signature region on Early Voting Ballot (EVB) envelopes, for the purpose of classifying the signature area as:

1. Blank   2. Likely blank   3. Scribble, or   4. Signature

In a ninety-nine-page, detailed report issued by his company, EchoMail, Inc., Dr. Shiva starts with an explanation of the normal process for signature verification. Here are the first few steps in the process:[47]

- Each EVB return envelope has a code, unique to the voter.

- The signature on the envelope is reviewed by a County employee.

- Reviewers are trained to look at "27 different points of comparison (slopes, pen drops, etc.)."

That is how it is supposed to work; however, the Senate Liaison to the County election audit, Ken Bennett, claimed that the twenty-seven-point comparison requirement was dropped. Here is the statement Bennett made:

We've literally been told by people who worked in that process for Maricopa County that the standard at the beginning was quite reasonable and high. But they got so far behind, we've been told that they went to the people on that team, 40-some people, and said, "OK, reduce it to 10" and then to five and then one [point of comparison]. And then we're told, and I can hardly believe that this might have been the case, but it needs to be verified. We're told they finally told them, *"Let everything go through, including blank signature boxes."* If that happened, that is a terrible failure [emphasis added].[48]

Bennett's statement directly confirms the observation of Linda Brickman, the volunteer observer at the Maricopa County Tabulation and Election Center. She claimed she was told: "Just pass each signature verification through." (See page 75)

If Bennett and Brickman are accurate, the verification of signatures was completely abandoned, and this would explain the very significant and serious findings in Dr. Shiva's report. Here are a few highlights from those findings:

---

47 Shiva Ayyadurai, "Pattern Recognition Classification of Early Voting Ballot (EVB) Return Envelope Images for Signature Presence Detection," EchoMail, Inc., September 24, 2021, 24, https://c692f527-da75-4c86-b5d1-8b3d5d4d5b43.filesusr. com/ugd/2f3470_05deb65815ab4d4b83938d71bc53459b.pdf.

48 Jay Greenberg, "Arizona County Skipped Signature Verification Requirement on Mail-In Ballots: Auditor," *NeonNettle. com*, June 23, 2021, https://neonnettle.com/news/15686-arizona-county-skipped-signature-verification-requirement-on-mail-in-ballots-auditor.

- The use of mail-in voting in Maricopa County increased by 52.6 percent from 2016 to 2020; yet signature rejections decreased by 59.7 percent.[49]

- The county found only 587 "bad signatures." Dr. Shiva was not permitted to review signatures, but he found 2,580 "scribbles," which comprised just a few light dots and dashes. Thus, his scribbles were 4.4 times greater in number than all of the bad signatures found by the county.[50]

- The county failed to identify at least 464 completely blank EVB envelopes.[51]

So, 2,580 scribbles and 464 more complete blanks were missed by the Maricopa County signature process. That is over 3,000 potentially bad ballots identified by Shiva Ayyadurai, without even reviewing the actual signatures on the other 1,900,000 (approx.) EVB envelopes.

There is a possibility that some of the envelopes had signatures in unauthorized locations (although voters were told to keep signatures within one location on the envelope). Also, the decline in rejections from 2016 to 2020 could be partly due to so-called ballot curing. However, a rigorous review is needed. For more on rejection rates see page 49.

The State knew or should have known, when it certified the election, that many signatures in Maricopa County (probably tens of thousands) were not checked. We know they were not checked based on the statements heard by Ken Bennett, based on the observations of poll watchers, and based on the analysis of Dr. Shiva. At the least, this means that a few thousand illegal ballots were probably counted.

However, it might be much worse. If ballot harvesters knew that the signature verification process was being relaxed, or even eliminated, it was like an invitation for them to jam the system with phony ballots.

UP TO 204,000 BALLOT ENVELOPES HAVE PHONY SIGNATURES

In January, 2022, long after the Cyber Ninjas were done with the Maricopa County audit, Dr. Shiva Ayyadurai conducted a signature verification pilot study, commissioned by the Arizona State Senate. The study was performed by three expert forensic document examiners and three novice reviewers. Each examiner and each reviewer analyzed

---

49   Shiva Ayyadurai, "Pattern Recognition Classification of Early Voting Ballot (EVB) Return Envelope Images for Signature Presence Detection," 31.

50   Ibid., 87

51   Ibid.

the signatures on 499 early voting mail-in ballot envelopes from the 2020 election held in Maricopa County.[52,53]

Based on their review, ALL SIX agreed that 60 of the ballot envelopes, out of the 499 envelopes, had signatures that did not match verified records.[54] In other words, 12 percent of the signatures were mismatches.

> *Think about it: Three expert forensic document examiners and three other reviewers unanimously agreed that 12 percent of the signatures appeared to be phonies. If we apply that percentage to the entire mail-in voting population of Maricopa County, it means there could be 204,000 phony ballots in an election decided by about 10,400 votes!*

Someone might say, "Wait a minute! All of those ballots could have been 'cured!'" However, that is unlikely for a very simple reason: Many were probably forgeries! How would you cure those—by having the forger confirm his illegal signature?

Unfortunately, that is exactly what some election departments do. They simply call the cell phone number listed on the ballot application, and the voter (or fraudster in some cases) confirms the signature. Pathetic! (Note: In some states, applicants can list any phone number they want on the application.)

By the way, even if 90 percent of the questionable ballots were "cured" (an impossibility), we'd still have a problem. The remaining 10 percent is easily enough to alter the Arizona election results.

THE ARIZONA ATTORNEY GENERAL'S INTERIM REPORT ON MARICOPA

In April, 2022, Attorney General (AG) Mark Brnovich issued a brief "Interim Report" on election failures and potential misconduct in the 2020 election in Maricopa County, Arizona. He prefaced his report by stating that his team of investigators found "instances of election fraud by individuals who have been or will be prosecuted." He would not comment on that further because, he said, the investigations are ongoing, and his office is "limited in what we can disclose."[55]

---

52 Natalia Mittelstadt, "Arizona Senate study finds 200k ballots counted in 2020 with mismatched signatures," *Just the News*, February 27, 2022, https://justthenews.com/politics-policy/elections/maricopa-countys-200k-mail-ballots-mismatched-signatures-not-cured-2020.

53 Shiva Ayyadurai, "Scientific Study Reveals Maricopa Counted 200,000+ Ballots With Mismatched Signatures Without Review ('Curing')," Vashiva.com, January 14, 2022, https://vashiva.com/scientific-study-reveals-maricopa-counted-200000-ballots-with-mismatched-signatures/.

54 There were many more ballot envelopes where 4 or 5 reviewers thought the signatures were questionable.

55 AG Mark Brnovich, "Interim Report – Maricopa County November 3, 2020 General Election," Office of the Attorney General of the State of Arizona, April 6, 2022, 1, https://justthenews.com/sites/default/files/2022-04/2022-04-06%20Fann%20letter.pdf.

The Interim Report is divided into four main areas: Part one concerns the "combative and/or litigious approach." of Maricopa County in responding to requests for information. For example, it took the county nearly four months to make its first response to the AG's request for documents, and that response omitted much of the information needed. (I guess some people never learn.)[56]

Part two pertains to "serious vulnerabilities" concerning inadequate signature matching, and Part three concerns early ballot drop boxes (primarily chain of custody issues). Part four addresses $8 million of private money and "... serious concerns regarding the legality of certain expenditures" of that money.[57]

The County released a statement that was dismissive in tone—as if these areas of vulnerability are inconsequential. In reality any one of the three last areas (2, 3, or 4), on its own, could have altered the outcome of this election.

THE ANALYSIS BY DR. DOUGLAS FRANK

As mentioned starting on page 48, Dr. Douglas Frank has precisely predicted the voter turnout, by age, for most or all counties in several states. To do this, Frank creates a "6th order polynomial key," which he then applies to every county in a given state. That key, however, cannot be used in other states – a fact that makes voting results appear to be artificial.

In the case of Arizona, Dr. Frank's analysis led him to conclude that ballot stuffing took place in the 2020 election. He said there were "tell-tale behaviors" that "strongly suggest" that computer algorithms were operating.

Frank's conclusion meshes with Liz Harris' Maricopa County canvassing results, where 5.7 percent of people surveyed voted, but did not know they had voted. It also fits well with Dr. Shiva's findings in Pima County, where an alleged 35,000 ballots may have been stuffed into several precincts.

A possible weakness of his analysis is exposed by some of Frank's other work. He also found high correlations in non-swing states, such as Montana, where Trump won by 16 percent, and in Washington state, where Biden won by 19 percent. Were non-swing state elections also manipulated? If so, why?

The Arizona analysis of Dr. Douglas Frank is found here: https://electionfraud20. org/dr-frank-reports/arizona/.

---

56   Ibid., 2-3.

57   Ibid., 4-8.

BEWARE THE "FEDERAL-ONLY" VOTER

In response to a 2017 lawsuit by the League of United Latin American Citizens (LULAC), Arizona signed a consent decree in which it agreed that either voter registration form (state or federal) could be used, without proof of citizenship, by any person wanting to vote in a federal election. Since the signing of that decree, there has been a big surge in the number of federal-only voters.

According to AMAC,[58] Arizona had 1,700 "federal-only" voters in 2018 but by the 2020 election the number swelled to 11,600. In all cases, these were people who could not or would not provide evidence of citizenship.[59]

It is reasonable to assume than many, if not most, "federal-only" voters are not legal citizens. Based on 2018 information, it is also likely that most are Democrats. For that year the Arizona Secretary of State reported that, among federal-only voters, registered Democrats were about 3.5 times more numerous than registered Republicans. If we apply that ratio to the 2020 results, that would produce a net illegal benefit of about 4,300 votes for Joe Biden.[60]

Currently, an Arizona voter registration form (state or federal) cannot require proof of citizenship for voting in federal elections; however, Arizona Governor Doug Ducey wants to require documentary proof of citizenship for all future elections. On March 30, 2022, Ducey signed legislation requiring all Arizonans to provide documented proof of citizenship to vote in future elections—federal or state. Sponsors of the legislation are hopeful that the more conservative U.S. Supreme Court will now give support to states that wish to require this documentation.[61]

NO CHAIN OF CUSTODY FOR 740,000 BALLOTS?

A group calling itself "Verity Vote," performed what appears to be a careful analysis of drop box chain of custody records from the 2020 election in Maricopa County. The findings in the report are stunning. If they are verified, the report (on its own) would justify decertification of the election for the entire state.

Verity Vote describes itself as:

58 AMAC is the Association of Mature American Citizens.

59 Staff, "AMAC Joins Coalition to Support Safeguarding Arizona's Voter Registration Process," *The Association of Mature American Citizens*, March 21, 2022, https://amac.us/amac-joins-coalition-to-support-safeguarding-arizonas-voter-registration-process/.

60 Jeremy Duda, "Few voters use federal-only ballots," *AZ Mirror*, January 9, 2019, https://www.azmirror.com/blog/few-voters-use-federal-only-ballots/.

61 Garrett Archer, "Governor signs bill restricting federal-only voters," *ABC15.com*, March 30, 2022, https://www.abc15.com/news/local-news/governor-signs-bill-putting-further-restrictions-on-federal-only-voters.

a group of capable investigators who've provided investigation and intelligence training to large corporations and government agencies, performed supply chain audits, along with published scientists and engineers.[62]

The group's website includes contact information, such as address, telephone number, and email, but no individual names are given—presumably to avoid harassment from those who prefer censorship over debate.

The Verity Vote process
Arizona requires that an "Early Voting Ballot Transport Statement" (EVBTS) be completed every time there is retrieval from a ballot drop box. Verity Vote submitted several Arizona Public Record Requests to obtain all available EVBTs forms, and it verified that it had been given all of them—a total of 1895 forms. However, more than 80 percent of the forms (1514 of 1895) lack ballot counts, a clear violation of the "Elections Procedures Manual" (EPM). In addition, 48 of the forms lack one or both of the required signatures, which should represent people with at least two different party preferences. Compliance with the EPM is mandatory under Arizona ARS Title 16-452.

62   "Election Integrity Research," Verity Vote, accessed March 25, 2022, https://verityvote.us/.

FIGURE 8: AN EVBTS WITH NO BALLOT COUNT AND ONLY 1 SIGNATURE

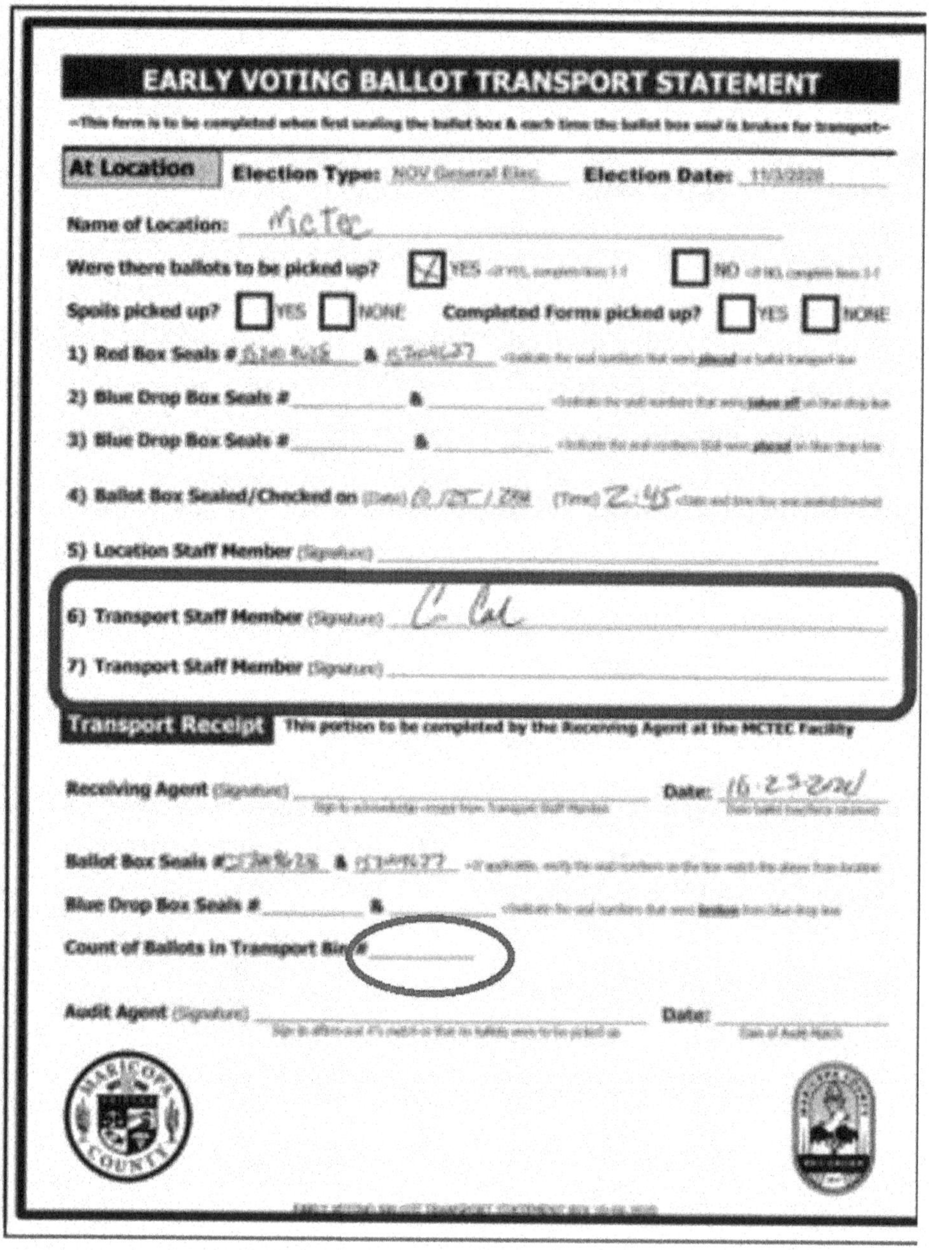

EARLY VOTING BALLOT TRANSPORT STATEMENT

~This form is to be completed when first sealing the ballot box & each time the ballot box seal is broken for transport~

At Location — Election Type: NOV General Elec — Election Date: 11/3/2020

Name of Location: McTec

Were there ballots to be picked up? [x] YES [ ] NO

Spoils picked up? [ ] YES [ ] NONE — Completed Forms picked up? [ ] YES [ ] NONE

1) Red Box Seals #

2) Blue Drop Box Seals # ____ & ____

3) Blue Drop Box Seals # ____ & ____

4) Ballot Box Sealed/Checked on (Date) (Time) 2:45

5) Location Staff Member (Signature)

6) Transport Staff Member (Signature)

7) Transport Staff Member (Signature)

Transport Receipt — This portion to be completed by the Receiving Agent at the MCTEC Facility

Receiving Agent (Signature) ____ Date:

Ballot Box Seals # ____ & ____

Blue Drop Box Seals # ____ & ____

Count of Ballots in Transport Bin # ____

Audit Agent (Signature) ____ Date: ____

This failure to comply with the EPM, required by law, means that anyone could have added a few hundred or even several thousand extra ballots in this election, which was decided by only 10,400 votes.

This is the procedure used by Verity Vote to estimate that 740,000 ballots have no chain of custody documentation, whatever:

- It examined all early voting ballot transport forms and added up quantities on the form, no matter where the quantities were written, and regardless of defects on the form. That number is 183,406.

- The results were subtracted from Maricopa County's report of total Early Voting ballots accepted at vote centers or drop boxes. That quantity is 923,000.

- The difference between the two numbers is about 740,000—the number of ballots without chain of custody documentation.

Verity Vote has given its information to Karen Fann, Arizona Senate Leader, and has discussed its findings with the office of Arizona Attorney General (AG). The AG included the chain of custody issue in his "Interim Report," however he reported that only 20 percent of ballots (instead of 80 percent) were without chain of custody documents. Verity Vote is aware of this discrepancy, and asserts that the AG's report has likely inverted the 20 percent and 80 percent numbers, due to clerical error. Whether the failure rate is 20 percent or 80 percent it is an amount that vastly exceeds Biden's winning margin.

OPEN ITEMS IN PROCESS

Attorney General investigation

- State officials claim that the Arizona Attorney General is investigating certain findings from the Cyber Ninjas audit and allegations concerning the Pima County fraud allegation. See pages 71 and 80.

WAS CERTIFICATION OF THE ARIZONA ELECTION PREMATURE?

This is not a close call: Certification of the Arizona election was premature for these clear and very important reasons:

- In a January 2022 pilot study, Dr. Shiva asked six reviewers, including three forensic document examiners, to analyze the signatures on a sample of 499 Maricopa County mail-in ballot envelopes. With regard to 60 of the envelopes (12 percent) there was unanimous agreement that the signatures did not match verified signatures. If we extrapolate the 12 percent figure to all Maricopa mail-in ballots, we get an estimate of 204,000 questionable signatures. If only 10 percent of those questionable signatures were found to be invalid, there would still be enough (20,400) to cast doubt on the election certification. This is strong evidence of likely fraud.

- Based on another test performed by Dr. Ayyadurai, during the Cyber Ninjas audit, it appears certain that the County failed to adequately verify signatures on large numbers of ballot envelopes. Ayyadurai was blocked from directly examining the signatures on ballot envelopes, so he totaled the number of envelopes that had "scribbles"—dots and dashes. The number he produced was more than 4 times greater than the total number of bad signatures found by Arizona on 1.9 million ballot envelopes.

- Ken Bennett, the Senate Liaison, said that the signature standard requirements were ignored by the County. According to Bennett, election workers were told: *"Let everything go through, including blank signature boxes." This also corroborates the findings of the signature test (bullet point one).*

- The Pima County fraud allegation (35,000 phony votes given to Democrats), when coupled with Dr. Shiva's analysis of Pima turnout rates, appears to be credible—even likely. However, the U.S. Department of Justice is nonresponsive to FOIA requests related to this topic. The matter has been referred to the Arizona Attorney General for investigation. If the anonymous tip is correct, the certification of the election was premature. Indeed, it would mean that Trump won the State of Arizona—easily.

- There are credible allegations of a large-scale ballot harvesting scheme in Arizona and other states. The investigation involves cell phone "ping" technology, videos, and at least one whistleblower describing the operation in detail. The organization conducting the research, "True the Vote," estimates that there were at least 20,000 illegal (and as many as 200,000), harvested ballots in Arizona.

- The Maricopa error estimate produced by the Liz Harris canvassing effort is significant and troubling. The extrapolated error amount greatly exceeds the margin of Biden's victory. Harris has collected many signed affidavits from people stating that they did not vote in the election, even though the County claims they did vote. It is likely that, in some cases, ballots were "harvested" and filed by fraudsters. Her findings are supported by the True the Vote findings.

- The UOCAVA (overseas) votes are not supported by chain of custody records, are very numerous compared to prior elections, have no identifying information, and are 95 percent for the Democrat candidate, which seems very unusual for overseas military ballots. Alone, UOCAVA votes in just one county could have added 8,000 votes for Biden in an election decided by 10,400 votes. When other counties are considered, UOCAVA vote irregularities—by themselves—could have altered the outcome of the election.

- It appears that there are at least 200,000, and as many as 740,000, ballots for which lawfully required chain of custody records do not exist. If confirmed, this one irregularity, by itself, should lead to decertification of the state election results.

- The conduct of the Maricopa County Elections Department was so evasive and uncooperative that it calls into question the integrity of the department leaders. This is another reason to question the election certification.

The issues cited above produce uncertainty with regard to thousands of votes in amounts that vastly exceed the margin of Biden's ostensible victory in the state (only about 10,400 votes). These matters should be resolved by means of competent investigations. A decision to affirm or rescind the certification should be made, based on the results of the investigations.

AT A MINIMUM, THESE SPECIFIC AREAS OF EXAMINATION ARE NEEDED:

1. Dr. Shiva's pilot signature test of 499 early voting mail ballot envelopes needs to be expanded, and should include several counties in Arizona. Where there are questionable signatures, "voters" should be directly contacted to confirm that they produced the signatures on file. If possible, affidavits should be obtained to confirm their responses.

2. As noted on page 73, there are several precincts that have ridiculously high voter turnout figures. They are located in Pima County, and specific precincts have been identified by Dr. Shiva Ayyadurai. Door-to-door canvassing of these precincts, by professional pollsters or auditors, is essential. This should take place while the Arizona Attorney General investigates the allegation of 35,000 fraudulent votes in those areas.

3. The cell phone "ping" harvesting investigation must be continued and expanded. There are an estimated 20,000 illegally-cast votes (or much more)—enough to invalidate the state's certification of the presidential election. See page 75.

4. The canvassing effort if Liz Harris should be analyzed and, if possible, verified. Harris has the addresses of the homes she contacted. In many cases she has affidavits of people stating they did not vote in the election, even though the county records show otherwise.

5. On a test basis, confirmation letters or emails should be sent to people voting from overseas. These are called UOCAVA (overseas and military) votes. In Maricopa County, Joe Biden received 95 percent of the UOCAVA vote, a rate which appears to be almost impossible. As part of the audit procedures, chain of custody records must be found and tested. If such records do not exist, the votes should be eliminated from the state totals. There are *other Arizona counties* that also have many overseas voters. The UOCAVA ballots and custody records of those counties should also be tested.

6. Extra scrutiny should be given to the ballot envelopes that arrived with deficient chain of custody documentation. Signatures should be checked and a sample of voters should be contacted at their residences.

When these actions are concluded, it may be possible to affirm the certification of the election. However, this is very unlikely.

6

GEORGIA

It takes at least one second to scan a ballot, but there are over 4,000 ballots with precisely the same timestamp—to the second

—GARLAND FAVORITO, PRESIDENT, VOTERGA.ORG

BALLOT EARTHQUAKE: 524,000 PHONY OR UNAUTHENTICATED BALLOTS
Garland Favorito is a mild-mannered senior citizen living in Georgia, but don't be deceived. He has been an election integrity warrior for years, and has a forty-year background in information technology. Favorito has produced solid evidence showing that the 2020 election results in Georgia should not have been certified.

In a long and very detailed press conference, Favorito and other election experts at VoterGA.org (a 501c3 tax exempt entity) itemized fifteen categories of ballot fraud and irregularities found during their analysis of ballot images acquired from Fulton County, Georgia. I urge you to view the press conference, using the link in the footnote (starting at 27:00). The number of "funny" ballots and "impossible" ballots is about forty-five times larger than the Biden margin of victory for Georgia, which was around 11,700. And this is just for Fulton County.

Here are a few of the findings:[1]

1. Although it takes at least one second to scan a ballot, there are over 4,000 ballots with precisely the same timestamp—to the second. Not possible.

---

1   Garland Favorito, "Press Conference," VoterGA.org, March 6, 2022, @27:00 https://rumble.com/vwmwup-VoterGA.org-press-conference-march-7th.html.

2. 16,034 mail-in ballot authentification files (.sha files) were added several days after scanning. This makes no sense because the system should create the .sha files simultaneously with the image files.

3. 17,724 final certified recount presidential votes have no .tif files, which are ballot images. They have no support whatever. This appears to be another impossibility because the image is needed to create a "cast vote record," which is needed to tabulate the vote. About 13,300 of those votes were for Biden, and 4,300 were for Trump.

4. There are no images to support 374,128 "certified" in-person votes, which is a violation of both federal and Georgia law.

5. Regarding mail-in votes, 132,284 ballot images (.tif files) cannot be authenticated due to missing .sha files.[2] As noted, when a ballot image is created, a .sha authentication file is created *simultaneously*, to authenticate the image. Without the .sha file, the authenticity of the ballot image cannot be determined. A similar finding was made as the result of a cyber investigation in Colorado. See page 262.

6. All but two of the early vote tabulator closing tapes for 350,000 votes were unsigned. Thus, there is no chain of custody established for those files.

Those are six of the fifteen categories. The VoterGA.org team found a lot of irregularities, but the press conference ended on a somber tone. VoterGA.org would like to present this information to the Fulton County District Attorney, Fani Willis, but so far, she does not seem to be interested. She is trying to prosecute Trump for pressuring Raffensperger to "find" votes. (See page 110, regarding the President's phone call to the Secretary of State.) Findings of election fraud would completely undermine her case.

Since this was a federal election, the FBI should have a team of cyber experts investigating the Favorito findings. Has anyone seen the FBI lately? (The folks at Mar-a Lago have, but that is another issue.)

---

2   A .sha file is a "secure hash algorithm" file, which uses a hash tag to ensure the authenticity of a file.

BIG BALLOT HARVESTING SCANDAL IS UNFOLDING THROUGHOUT STATE

The VoterGA.org findings fit nicely with the next scandal. You see, when electronic voting records are pumped up, extra paper ballots are needed as "backfill." A Georgia whistleblower has allegedly stepped forward to say that he or she was part of a large ring of Democrat ballot harvesters that operated during the November 2020 election and the January 5, 2021 runoff elections.

Based on analysis of cell phone pings and video evidence, obtained by the organization True the Vote (self-proclaimed election integrity advocates), it is estimated that 242 people made 5,662 ballot drops in Georgia, and produced at least 28,000 illegally-collected votes.[3] In the movie, *2,000 Mules*, True the Vote expressed the results as an approximate range of 30,000 to 90,000 harvested ballots (depending on the definition of "mule"). It is likely that many or most of these votes would be disqualified if it were shown that harvesters intercepted the ballots, used trickery, coercion, bribes, or forgery to get them, or if chain of custody documentation is missing.

No big deal?

It is both amusing and sad to see so-called fact checkers dismissing ballot harvesting as inconsequential. USA Today felt the need to rush out a fact check to assure readers that this is no big deal. It may be election fraud but, according to USA Today, the votes are still perfectly legal.[4] Really? Perhaps the USA Today folks need to read the work of *New York Post* journalist Jon Levine, who interviewed a veteran ballot harvester for an article in the *New York Post*. The harvester's dirty business included steaming open envelopes so that ballots could be replaced. It involved working with paid Post Office mail carriers who gathered up ballots (somehow). And it involved an alliance with nursing home employees who grabbed the ballots from demented residents. It is a dirty business that is illegal in Georgia, and should be illegal everywhere. More from the *New York Post* story is found on page 33.

Raffensperger, the Georgia Secretary of State, has launched an investigation.[5] His first step was to request the Elections Board to grant him subpoena power for the investigation.

3   John Solomon, "Georgia opens investigation into possible illegal ballot harvesting in 2020 election," *Just the News*, January 4, 2022, https://justthenews.com/politics-policy/elections/georgia-opens-investigation-possible-illegal-ballot-harvesting-2020.

4   McKenzie Sadeghi, "Fact Check: Georgia investigation into alleged ballot harvesting is not evidence of election fraud," *USA Today*, January 7, 2022, https://www.yahoo.com/news/fact-check-georgia-investigation-alleged-011359385.html.

5   John Solomon, "Georgia ballot harvesting probe advances as state elections board approves subpoena," *Just the News*, March 20, 2022, https://justthenews.com/politics-policy/elections/georgia-ballot-harvesting-probe-advances-state-elections-board-approves.

That power was granted by the Board in mid-March, 2022, and can be used to obtain all of True the Vote's information, and to compel the testimony of the whistleblower.

Trump and his supporters have expressed skepticism regarding Raffensperger's commitment to a serious investigation. I am also skeptical, but right now, Raffensperger is about the only hope Trump and other Republicans have. Most of the other swing states have Democrat administrations that are unlikely to pursue this matter. And, don't hold your breath waiting for U.S. Attorney General Merrick Garland and other Feds. More information is available on page 36.

THE PRESIDENT'S JANUARY 2 PHONE CALL WITH THE SECRETARY OF STATE

Fellas, I need 11,000 votes. Give me a break. You know, we have that in spades already.

—PRESIDENT TRUMP[6]

The spin is that Trump wanted Brad Raffensperger, the Georgia Secretary of State (the guy in charge of elections) to fabricate out of thin air about 11,000 votes so that Trump would end up winning the state election. That is what the words seem to say until they are considered in context.

Trump started by itemizing the reasons he felt he won Georgia by hundreds of thousands of votes. The emphasis was on Fulton County (Atlanta area), and that is significant. Long after that phone call, it would become clear that Raffensperger did not want anyone to see the Fulton County election records—ever.

Specific claims made by Trump[7]

- "We have at least . . . 250–300,000 ballots [that] were dropped mysteriously into the rolls. Much of that had to do with Fulton County, which hasn't been checked. We think that if you check the signatures – a real check of signatures going back in Fulton County you'll find at least a couple of hundred thousand of forged signatures."

- "Another tremendous number . . . and that's people that went to vote and they were told they can't vote because they've already been voted for."

- "We had; I believe it's about 4,502 voters who voted but who weren't on the voter registration list."

6   "Read the full transcript and listen to Trump's audio call with Georgia secretary of state," *CNN*, January 3, 2021, https://www.cnn.com/2021/01/03/politics/trump-brad-raffensperger-phone-call-transcript/index.html.

7   Ibid.

- "You had 18,325 vacant address voters. The address was vacant and they're not allowed to be counted. That's 18,325."

- "Smaller number—you had 904 who only voted where they had just a P.O., a Post Office box number—and they had a Post Office box number and that's not allowed."

- "We had at least 18,000—that's on tape we had them counted very painstakingly—18,000 voters having to do with Ruby Freeman. She's a vote scammer, a professional vote scammer and hustler."

- "You had out-of-state voters. They voted in Georgia but they were from out of state, of 4,925."

- "You had absentee ballots sent to vacant, they were absentee ballots sent to vacant addresses. They had nothing on them about addresses, that's 2,326."

- "[Y]ou have drop boxes where the box was picked up but not delivered for three days. So all sorts of things could have happened to that box."

Those were the opening comments of Trump, but he went on to also mention 5,000 dead people voting, the shredding of ballots, the possible burning of ballots in Fulton County, and the fact that the GOP won "every single statehouse and we won Congress."

Whether or not Trump had his facts straight is something that can be debated, but the implication that he wanted the fabrication of votes is clearly false. He seemed to genuinely believe that he had those votes already—easily.

Responses from Secretary of State Brad Raffensperger
Mark Meadows brought Raffensperger into the conversation with this statement:

What I'm hopeful for is there ['s] some way that we can we can find some kind of agreement to look at this a little bit more fully. You know the president mentioned Fulton County. But in some of these areas where there seems to be a difference of where the facts seem to lead, and so, Mr. Secretary, I was hopeful that, you know, in the spirit of cooperation and compromise is there something that we can at least have a discussion to look at some of these allegations to find a path forward that's less litigious?[8]

---

8   "Read the full transcript and listen to Trump's audio call with Georgia secretary of state," *CNN.*

Raffensperger's reply seemed to imply that sharing information could weaken Georgia's legal case.

> Well, I listened to what the president has just said. President Trump, we've had several lawsuits and we've had to respond in court to the lawsuits and the contentions. Um, we don't agree that you have won. . . . [T]he challenge that you have is, the data you have is wrong.

Trump then asked one of his attorneys, Cleta Mitchell, to respond. She pleaded for access to the Georgia data.

> We have asked from your office for records that only you have and so we said there is a universe of people who have the same name and same birth year and died. But we don't have the records that you have. And one of the things that we have been suggesting formally and informally for weeks now is for you to make available to use the records that would be necessary.[9]

A long conversation ensued regarding the State Farm Arena and several other matters. Trump brought up Fulton County again, noting that the Secretary of State did a signature check of Cobb County even though the Trump team wanted a signature check of Fulton County. (Fulton County comprises most of Atlanta, while Cobb County is a suburb to the north of Atlanta.)

Raffensperger and his associates disputed every assertion made by the Trump team but never supported their assertions with data, citations to data, or even promises to eventually show data. Instead, they claimed that their information was correct, and it would be presented in court (and not before): "And then it comes before the court," Raffensperger said, "and the court then has to make a determination." But that never happened: So far, no court has issued a ruling on the merits of these claims, or even considered the claims.

As the conversation finally ended, Trump seemed to get a commitment for at least one more meeting—a meeting that would never take place, for the reason outlined in the next section.

Expert witness, Bryan Geels, CPA

A digression: During the Enron scandal, it was frustrating to me that CPAs were rarely interviewed regarding a matter that involved very complex accounting and tax issues.

---

9   Ibid.

After all, that is what we do, and Enron directly involved intricate issues and a huge accounting firm, Arthur Andersen. Instead of CPAs, the media interviewed lawyers, a few professors of accounting (but not CPAs), and loads and loads of instantaneously-expert political pundits.

In the 2020 election disputes, which also involved issues that are auditing related, the same thing happened. We heard a lot from pundits, but rarely from CPAs.

Bryan Geels is a CPA who assisted the Trump legal team with regard to Georgia election issues. In February, 2022, Geels gave a little talk at an event sponsored by VoterGA. org, and he discussed some of his election findings and the treatment he received from the Georgia Secretary of State. Although you can hear and see Geels by using the link in the footnotes, I will quote and summarize some of his conclusions here.[10]

- "Mr. Raffensperger, as a CPA I work in trust for a living. A quality auditor would not have been comfortable expressing any opinion affirming the results with so many unexplained irregularities in the data."

- "We found enough irregularities and illegalities in the data that it would be impossible for anyone to truly know who won the election that was decided by less than 12,000 votes."

- Of "23 analyses [I prepared] there were 10 categories that I placed in a 'vote-should-have-been-rejected' category, which had over 97,000 votes that I believe shouldn't have been counted."[11]

- "I flew out to Georgia to finally sit down with the Secretary of State and collaborate on the issues that I identified in his data and to get more information and context to better interpret what it means."

- "Instead of following through on his agreement to sit down with the president's expert, Team Raffensperger leaked the phone call to the *Washington Post*. I am still left to wonder why."

10   Bryan Geels, "Truth About Georgia Elections, *VoterGA.org*, February 9, 2022, @52:30, https://rumble.com/vuea9f-truth-about-georgia-elections-2-9-22-10-am.html.

11   The entire "Expert Report of Bryan Geels, CPA" in the matter of Trump v. Raffensperger (Fulton County – 2020 cv 343255) can be found here: https://www.scribd.com/document/558503891/Geels.

Regarding Geels's last point, about the "agreement to sit down" together, some people may not realize that the Trump people saw the phone call as an opportunity to finally gain access to Raffensperger's data. Cleta Mitchell, made this point during a TV interview in late January 2022. Said Mitchell:

> That phone call was for the purpose of trying to reach a settlement . . . because we had not had a judge appointed to hear the election contest. . . . We said, well, why don't you bring your evidence and we'll bring our evidence, and let's see who is right. And we had been trying to get them to do that for a couple of weeks.[12]

That information-sharing meeting would have involved Bryan Geels, Trump's numbers man, but it never happened. It was scuttled by the leaking of the phone call.

THE FULTON COUNTY COVER-UP

Later, in that same month of January, Secretary of State Raffensperger appeared on national television to boast about the clean Georgia election. On 60 Minutes he said, "We had safe, secure, honest elections."

However, the secretary had to know that there were serious problems in Fulton County, because a detailed report of problems had already been issued to Raffensperger. John Solomon, journalist with Just the News, obtained a copy of the report. Here is how Solomon described the secretary's 60 Minutes commentary:

> That rosy assessment . . . masked an ugly truth inside his agency's own files: A contractor handpicked to monitor election counting in Fulton County wrote a twenty-nine-page memo back in November outlining the "massive" election integrity failures and mis-management that he witnessed in the Atlanta-area's election centers.
>
> The bombshell report, constructed like a minute-by-minute diary, cited a litany of high-risk problems such as the double-counting of votes, insecure storage of ballots . . ., the mysterious removal of election materials at a vote collection warehouse, and the suspicious movement of . . . ballots on Election Day.[13]

The contractor, Carter Jones, warned of other problems, including a "massive chain of custody problem."

---

12   Cleta Mitchell, "The Real Story with Natalie Harp," *OAN News*, January 23, 2022.

13   J. Solomon and D. Payne, "Georgia investigator's notes reveal 'massive' election integrity problems in Atlanta," *Just the News*, June 19, 2021, https://justthenews.com/politics-policy/elections/ga-investigators-election-day-notes-reveal-chaotic-unsecured-ballot.

Did you notice something? If Raffensperger had the critical report in November, he must have had that report when he had his long telephone conversation with Trump, in January. Perhaps this is why he wouldn't let Trump near the data, and perhaps it is the reason he tested signatures in suburban Cobb County instead of urban Fulton County.

THE STATE FARM ARENA CONTROVERSY

According to some fact checkers the following story is false! But, it is not. State Farm Arena is a large Fulton County facility where ballots were counted for the 2020 election. At around 10:30 in the evening of November 3, 2020, Democrat and Republican poll observers were told, or effectively told, that there would be no more counting of ballots until the next morning. This was confirmed by poll observers in sworn affidavits, and also by a news release by ABC News.

NEW: The election department sent the ballot counters at the State Farm Arena in Atlanta home at 10:30 p.m., Regina Waller, the Fulton County public affairs manager for elections, tells ABC News.

—ABC NEWS POLITICS (@ABCPOLITICS) NOVEMBER 4, 2020[14]

Sometime later, the Trump team obtained video coverage (filmed by Arena security cameras) of the transactions that took place right after observers left. On the video, workers could be seen pulling boxes (described by some as looking like suitcases) from under a large skirted table. The workers proceeded to scan the ballots, and it appeared on video as if some workers scanned the same batch of ballots multiple times.

This went on for about an hour and a half, and there was a large vote spike of 23,487 votes during the processing. Of that amount, Joe Biden was awarded about 23,000 votes (98 percent), and Trump got the remainder of less than 500 votes (2 percent). In an election decided by about 12,000 votes, the spike that took place during the unobserved State Farm Arena processing easily gave the election victory to Joe Biden.[15]

That doesn't prove fraud, of course, but it absolutely proves the need to audit the Fulton County ballots—all of them. This would have to involve checking paper, checking signatures, and knocking on doors to verify voting activity. Yet that did not happen, and it still has not happened as of the time of this writing.

14 Emily Shapiro, "Pipe bursts in Atlanta arena causing 4-hour delay in processing ballots," *ABC NEWS*, November 3, 2020, https://abcnews.go.com/Politics/pipe-bursts-atlanta-arena-causing-hour-delay-processing/story?id=73981348.

15 Peter Svab, "Infographic: What happened in Atlanta on Election Night," *Epoch Times*, December 9, 2020 and April 8, 2021, https://www.theepochtimes.com/what-happened-in-atlanta-on-election-night-2_3607130.html.

WHISTLEBLOWER SUSAN VOYLES, ET AL.

Susan Voyles was employed by Fulton County as an election poll manager, and had about twenty years of experience handling ballots at the time of the election. In November 2020, Voyles signed a sworn affidavit indicating that she observed irregularities while monitoring the ballot count in Fulton County.[16] Effectively, she was a whistleblower against her long-time employer.[17] According to Voyles:

- The first box of ballots she inspected had a blank seal, "signed by no one, and no information had been supplied."

- "Inside the box were stacks of ballots of approximately 100 ballots each."

- "[O]ne batch [of ballots] stood out. It was pristine. There was a difference in the texture of the paper. . . . There was a difference in the feel."

- "There were no markings on the ballots to show where they had come from, or where they had been processed. These stood out."

- "In my 20 years' of experience of handling ballots, I observed that the markings for the candidates on these ballots were unusually uniform, perhaps even with a ballot-marking device. By my estimate in observing these ballots, approximately 98 percent constituted votes for Joseph Biden."

At least five other poll observers signed affidavits swearing they observed irregularities in the mail-in ballots. These affidavits were filed with the Garland Favorito lawsuit. (See below.) The observers believe the ballots had been photocopied, had no creases, were printed on different paper, or had unnatural markings.[18]

There were additional witnesses (besides those filing affidavits). In testimony on December 3, 2020, before a subcommittee of the Georgia Senate Judiciary Committee, Hal Soucie, a poll watcher, confirmed the existence of the pristine ballots mentioned by Susan Voyles. Scott Hall, also a poll watcher, testified that he saw, "over and over," large quantities of ballots at the World Congress Center that appeared to have been machine-produced.[19]

---

16   Lin Wood v. Brad Raffensperger, 1:20-cv-04651-SDG (N.D. Georgia, 2020), Voyles Affidavit.

17   Ibid., 4–5.

18   Garland Favorito v. Mary Carole Cooney, Civil Action: 2020cv343938, (Superior Ct. of Fulton County), 4.

19   William T. Ligon, Chairman, "The Chairman's Report of the Election Law," Study Subcommittee of the Standing Senate Judiciary Committee (Ga.), December 3, 2020, http://www.senatorligon.com/THE_FINAL%20REPORT.PDF.

Again, this testimony does not constitute proof of fraud but it is evidence, and warrants serious investigation. As an auditor I would add this: No one would bother to mix in a few fake ballots in just one box out of thousands of boxes. It wouldn't impact the election. Rather, they would slip a small number of fake ballots in each of many boxes until there were a few thousand fake ballots. That might be enough to flip an election.

After that day, Voyles and her colleagues had no more opportunities to look for fake ballots. The next day they were given just sixty ballots to check, and were then sent home. According to Voyles, the veteran employee of Fulton County, people at the other tables were asked to examine about 3,000 ballots each.[20]

THE GARLAND FAVORITO V. FULTON COUNTY CASE

At the beginning of the Georgia section is a presentation of some of the Fulton County ballot irregularities found by Garland Favorito and his organization, VoterGA.org. Favorito has been an election integrity activist for years and has challenged election authorities many times and in multiple ways.

Mr. Favorito applied serious pressure to Fulton County and state election officials with a lawsuit he filed in late December 2020. During the morning of November 5, 2020, he noticed that Biden's votes seemed to increase by about 20,000, while Trump's decreased by about 1,000. He could not understand why Trump's votes would decrease, so he made an Open Records request with the Fulton County Election Board, inquiring as to how the vote decrease occurred.

When Favorito received no response, he filed a Petition for Declaratory and Injunctive Relief, asserting that Fulton County had, among other things, violated equal protection laws through the uneven administration of election law.[21]

Favorito's civil action was supported with numerous witness affidavits, in addition to that of the previously mentioned, Susan Voyles:[22]

- Robin Hall, a hand count audit monitor, observed 3 boxes containing 100 percent Biden ballots.

- Another hand count audit monitor, Judy Aube, saw 3 boxes with 98 percent of the ballots cast for Biden.

---

20   Lin Wood v. Brad Raffensperger, 1:20-cv-04651-SDG (N.D. Georgia, 2020), Voyles Affidavit, 6.

21   Garland Favorito v. Mary Carole Cooney, Civil Action: 2020cv343938, (Superior Court of Fulton County).

22   Ibid., Affidavits (various).

- Election auditor Barbara Hartman, poll watcher Gordon Rolle, and auditor and poll watcher Sonia Francis-Rolle each noticed ballots that had no creases, as if they were never in the required mailing envelopes.

- Gordon Rolle and Sonia Francis-Rolle also noticed paper that was different than that used for normal ballots, and ballots that appeared to be marked with toner rather than writing implements.

In addition to those witnesses, there was testimony from David Sawyer, forensic accountant and former partner with the huge audit firm, Ernst & Young. He outlined several anomalies. There were "sequence breaks" in the images of ballots, and these breaks suggested some ballots (161 ballots) were missing. There was evidence that some ballots had been scanned twice. This forensic accountant testified that a physical examination of the paper ballots and envelopes was essential.[23]

By March 15, 2021, Favorito seemed to be making legal headway. Henry County Judge Brian Amero conditionally granted Favorito's group (VoterGA.org) the right to unseal and inspect, for evidence of fraud, ballots from the 2020 election. A well-known paper expert, Jovan Pulitzer would conduct an examination. It was rumored (but not confirmed to my knowledge) that the Fulton County Election Board hired top criminal defense attorneys.[24] But then, the audit train got derailed by Secretary of State Raffensperger.[25]

Raffensperger goes into "cover-up mode."
In an effort to thwart Favorito, Raffensperger filed an amicus brief with the court, a document claiming it is illegal to give public access to paper ballots (even though there are no identification markings on ballots). In addition, Raffensperger maintained that "[t]he Elections Code is furthermore clear that it is only authorized elections officials who are legally permitted to verify and tabulate ballots in an election." Apparently, it is the view of the Secretary of State (SoS) that, once election officials "verify and tabulate" ballots in an election, there can be no review. It is final! Indeed, Raffensperger made this anti-democratic viewpoint crystal clear:

---

23   Ibid., Deposition of David Sawyer.

24   Gabriel Keane, "Georgia: Fulton County Election Board Hires Top Criminal Defense Attorneys After Judge Allows 2020 Election Audit," *Nationalfile.com*, May 28, 2021, https://nationalfile.com/georgia-fulton-county-election-board-hires-top-criminal-defense-attorneys-after-judge-allows-2020-election-audit/.

25   Michelle Edwards, "GA SoS Raffensperger: "Only Ballot Images Should be Audited," *UncoverDC*, April 6, 2021, https://uncoverdc.com/2021/04/06/ga-sos-raffensperger-only-ballot-images-should-be-audited/.

The public interest would not be served by allowing Petitioners to undergo an *unlawful fishing expedition* into sealed ballots in their attempt to undermine the results of the general election, when the ballots have already been tabulated, audited, and recounted as provided by law [emphasis added].[26]

According to Favorito, Raffensperger was now engaged in a cover-up. "What concerns us," said Favorito, "is that we have a secretary of state who doesn't believe in election integrity."[27] In the months following the election, Trump argued that there were election irregularities in Georgia, while Raffensperger maintained that Georgia had a clean election. As reported by Sophie Mann in Just the News, "Favorito believes Raffensperger filed his amicus brief because Trump is right, and the secretary of state has something to hide." In other words, the SoS was afraid that an in-depth audit might make him look foolish and negligent.

Judge Amero seemed to largely disregard the Raffensperger amicus brief, although he did leave it up to Fulton County officials to do the scanning of ballots. On May 21, 2021, the judge agreed to unseal the absentee ballots so they could be scanned at high resolution by county officials for use by the plaintiffs. The details would be worked out in a future order.[28]

Flip flop no. 1: Let's have an audit!
Incredibly, Raffensperger took credit for the Amero ruling, even though Judge Amero had ruled against him:

From day one I have encouraged Georgians with concerns about the election in their counties to pursue those claims through legal avenues. Fulton County has a *long-standing history of election mismanagement* that has understandably weakened voters' faith in its system. Allowing this audit provides another layer of transparency and citizen engagement [emphasis added].[29]

---

26   Garland Favorito v. Mary Carole Cooney, Civil Action 2020cv343938 (Superior Court of Fulton Georgia, 2020), Brief of Amicus Curiae Georgia Secretary of State Brad Raffensperger, 7.

27   Sophie Mann, "GA Election Chief Raffensperger in 'cover-up mode,' says plaintiff in Fulton Co. vote fraud case, "*Just the News*, April 8, 2021, https://justthenews.com/politics-policy/elections/w-georgia-sec-state-files-brief-prevent-ga-voter-group-auditing-physical.

28   AP, "Judge agrees to unseal Fulton absentee ballots for audit," *ABC News*, May 21, 2021, https://abcnews.go.com/Politics/wireStory/judge-agrees-unseal-fulton-absentee-ballots-audit-77833150.

29   Ibid.

So, the Georgia Secretary of State, who told Trump that Fulton's election was just fine, who refused to share any information with Trump, and who filed an anti-audit brief with the Amero Court, had an epiphany: He was now concerned about Fulton's mismanagement of the election, and he decided that a "fishing expedition" in Fulton County would be just fine! But the epiphany was short-lived.

Raffensperger had one more flip to flop: a "Hail Mary" play that would stop the audit again!

Flip flop no. 2: Nothing to see here!

As noted, the judge handling the Favorito case, Brian Amero, conditionally ruled that Fulton County would have to provide high-quality ballot images to Favorito and his VoterGA.org organization. The details were to be worked out—probably in the month of October 2021. But in the intervening time, Raffensperger saw an opportunity. He would write another brief, arguing that there were no valid issues to review. On October 12, 2021, the SoS filed this response to the judge's ruling.[30]

On October 12, 2021, just before Judge Amero was to finalize his ruling that would allow inspection of ballots, Raffensperger issued another court filing. He returned to his belief that there was nothing to see here: There was no sign of a problem in Fulton County. You might ask, "What about the several people who swore under oath that they saw?"

- Boxes with 100 percent Biden ballots?

- Boxes with 98 percent Biden ballots?

- Pristine and unfolded ballots that could not have been mailed?

- Ballots printed on different weight paper?

- Ballots with toner marks instead of written marks?

Apparently, those people were mistaken because Raffensperger's employees (without any witnesses) checked the box with the particular number identified by Susan Voyles (Box 5/Batches 28–36), and inside they found no suspicious ballots. These very diligent government workers even checked two or *three* other boxes (out of hundreds), but still

---

30   Garland Favorito v. Alex Wan, Civil Action 2020cv343938 (Superior Court of Fulton Georgia, 2020), Response of the Georgia Secretary of State to the Court's order of September 20, 2021.

found no suspicious ballots.[31] For sure they would have preferred to look in additional boxes, but how many boxes can you check when you only have ten or eleven months to conduct an investigation?

For good measure, Raffensperger's communication to the court said that nothing bad had happened at the State Farm Arena. The SoS made that argument by ignoring certain issues, such as these:

- The SoS did not comment at all on the huge vote spike that took place, although he generally stated that the counting of ballots was appropriate.

- The SoS also did not comment at all on the legality of processing ballots after the observers were told that processing would stop.

Of course, nothing was proven by this investigation, which was performed by Raffensperger's own people, without advance notice, in the sole presence of they, them, and themselves. It was a "self-investigation" performed by acolytes of a man who would likely lose his job if fraud were found. And the same goes for the Fulton County workers who observed the investigation: It was strongly in their interest to find nothing.

Nevertheless, this "Hail Mary" apparently worked. The next day, Judge Amero decided that Favorito did not have the legal standing that the judge thought he had months earlier. Case dismissed![32]

Case dismissed, but Fulton issues keep growing
At this point, Raffensperger was back in bed with Fulton County's election officials. Once again, Raffensperger decided that Fulton County officials did a good enough job, so no audit, no transparency, no investigation was needed. But the Fulton problems kept growing, and the SoS would soon have more headaches.

David Perdue wants to see Fulton County ballots
In December 2021, former U.S. Senate candidate David Perdue and Elizabeth Lennon (a voter) filed a civil action that was expressly "similar and related to" the Favorito case. The filing even requested that the case be heard by the judge who decided the Favorito case, Judge Brian J. Amero. Presumably, the petitioners hoped that, in the view of

---

31   Ibid., 8.

32   Garland Favorito v. Alex Wan, Civil Action 2020cv343938 (Superior Court of Fulton Georgia, 2020), Notice of Appeal, Exhibit A, Order Granting Motion to Dismiss.

Judge Amero, they have the standing that Favorito did not have.[33] Instead, the case was heard—and dismissed in May 2022—by Judge Robert McBurney. Perdue indicates that he plans to appeal. If he does not succeed, it is likely that tens of thousands of suspicious ballots will be destroyed, without meaningful review.

WHY WAS ELECTION CERTIFIED WITH MISSING CHAIN OF CUSTODY DOCUMENTS?

Months after the Georgia Secretary of State certified the state election, hundreds of thousands of drop box chain of custody documents were still missing. Those are the records that can prove if the ballots were properly collected out of drop boxes. It is beyond belief that an election with a 12,600 vote margin was certified without knowing who picked up hundreds of thousands of ballots and from where. For all that Brad Raffensperger knew, thousands of the ballots were printed in someone's basement and added to ballots already taken from drop boxes. Or, perhaps they were genuine ballots harvested from mailboxes and trash cans and then placed into drop boxes.

The Georgia Star News (The Star) was all over the chain of custody story. On March 4, 2021 The Star wrote:

> Four months after the November 3, 2020 presidential election, state and county offi-cials in Georgia have failed to produce chain of custody documents for an estimated 404,691 vote by mail absentee ballots deposited in drop boxes and subsequently deliv-ered to county registrars for counting.[34]

At that point, Fulton was just one of thirty-five counties that had not produced the documents requested by The Star under an Open Records request. By April 8, 2021, things were a bit better. The number of missing chain of custody records dropped to 355,918—still a gigantic number.[35]

By May, 2021, most counties supplied The Star with the missing chain of custody records, but not Fulton County. On May 20, Fulton provided The Star with some

---

33   David A. Perdue and Elizabeth Grace Lennon v. Richard Barron, Fulton County Elections Director et al., Civil Action 2021 cv 357748 (Superior Court of Fulton Georgia, 2020), Petition for Declaratory Judgment and Injunctive Relief for Inspection and Examination of Election Materials.

34   Tiffany Morgan, "Four Months After 2020 Presidential Election in Georgia No Chain of Custody Documents Produced," *Georgia Star News*, March 4, 2021, https://georgiastarnews.com/2021/03/04/four-months-after-2020-presidential-election-in-georgia-no-chain-of-custody-documents-produced-for-404000-absentee-ballots-deposited-in-drop-boxes-fulton-county-one-of-35-scofflaw-counties/.

35   Ibid.

additional records, but there were still 385 missing forms covering 18,901 missing absentee ballots.[36]

"In a stunning admission...," The Star reported, "a Fulton County election official told the Georgia Star News on Wednesday [June 9, 2021] that 'a few forms are missing' and that 'some procedural paperwork may have been misplaced.'"[37]

There were still missing custody records in October—eleven months after the election and about ten months after the election was certified by the Secretary of State. The missing number, as reported by The Star, was 6,995.[38]

Not missing, but improperly completed chain of custody forms
In late January 2022, the nonprofit group, VoterGA.org, announced some preliminary results from a study it performed of incomplete or improperly completed drop box chain of custody forms. It found that 107,000 ballots from the 2020 election were supported with forms that were incomplete or incorrect in one or more ways. Specific violations included:

- Unsigned forms

- Forms with only one signature instead of the required two signatures

- Forms that didn't indicate who received the ballots at the election center

- Forms received after the day of pickup from the drop box

Many of these defective chain of custody forms, especially the unsigned ones, were of very little benefit. Ballots could have been added or subtracted after being taken from the drop boxes.[39]

---

36   Laura Baigert, "Fulton County supplied two different versions of 34 critical chain of custody documents for absentee ballots," *Georgia Star News*, May 20, 2021, https://georgiastarnews.com/2021/05/20/fulton-county-supplied-two-different-versions-of-34-critical-chain-of-custody-documents-for-absentee-ballot-drop-boxes-that-go-back-in-time/.

37   Laura Baigert, "Fulton County election official admits chain of custody documents missing for absentee ballots deposited in drop boxes," *Georgia Star News*, June 14, 2021 https://georgiastarnews.com/2021/06/14/fulton-county-election-official-admits-chain-of-custody-documents-missing-for-2020-absentee-ballots-deposited-in-drop-boxes/.

38   Laura Baigert, "11 Months After 2020 Election Georgia Secretary of State Missing Chain of Custody Documents for 6,995 Absentee Ballots Deposited in Fulton County Drop Boxes," *Georgia Star News*, October 4, 2021, https://georgiastarnews.com/2021/10/04/11-months-after-2020-election-georgia-secretary-of-state-missing-chain-of-custody-documents-for-6995-absentee-ballots-deposited-in-fulton-county-drop-boxes-3/.

39   Chris Butler, "VoterGA.org Presents New Evidence of Election Irregularities Throughout Georgia," *Georgia Star News*, January 22, 2022, https://georgiastarnews.com/2022/01/22/VoterGA.org-presents-new-evidence-of-election-irregularities-throughout-georgia/.

Let's spell it out: The fact that these records were missing or defective means:

- The election should not have been certified.

- Favorito and his organization, VoteGA.org should have been allowed to audit Fulton's ballots.

- Raffensperger knew, or should have known, when talking to Trump on the telephone (January 2), that the chain of custody records were missing.

JOSEPH ROSSI, A PRIVATE CITIZEN, FINDS PROBLEMS THAT ELECTION OFFICIALS MISSED

Imagine this: Raffensperger, his Chief Operating Officer (Gabriel Sterling), and all their helpers couldn't identify any significant problems in Fulton County. Yet, a private citizen, sitting at home in front of a computer, with no special help or resources, found plenty of problems—just by viewing the Secretary of State website. Here is a description of the efforts of Joseph Rossi, as described by Kevin Moncla of uncoverdc.com:

> In January, he [Rossi] began to look into the Georgia election results and soon focused on the Georgia hand-count "audit." Mr. Rossi soon had questions and sought answers from Gabriel Sterling of the Georgia Secretary of State's office. Mr. Rossi's emails to Mr. Sterling went unanswered, as did his questions, but he didn't just give up. Instead, Mr. Rossi called Gabriel Sterling's office every day for twenty-one days. Finally, he sent Sterling a certified email and received confirmation that it was received. In that email, Mr. Rossi wrote, "*Now I know you've read this . . .*" and something to the effect of "*I'm not going away.*"[40]

When Rossi finally got a response from Sterling, he asked him for the batch tally sheets for the Fulton County hand count. A batch might be 100 ballots, and the tally sheet is filled out by the person who hand counts the ballots. On the tally sheet, the vote counter writes in the totals for each candidate.

As reported by Moncla: With "a condescending tone, Mr. Sterling directed Mr. Rossi to the Secretary of State's website for the publicly available batch tally sheets."[41] Using that information, Rossi and some friends determined that about 275,000 ballots

---

40   Kevin Moncla, "Georgia governor validates Rossi findings: discredits hand-count "audit," *uncoverDC.com*, December 1, 2021, https://uncoverdc.com/2021/12/01/georgia-governor-validates-rossi-findings-discredits-hand-count-audit/.

41   Ibid.

were not accounted for on the publicly available tally sheets.

Rossi emailed Sterling, but was again ignored. Perhaps he was too busy doing TV interviews. After another couple of weeks of daily emailing, Rossi finally got a response. There were many missing tally sheets that still needed to be posted to the website.

But there were other problems. Rossi found that the originally posted tally sheets disappeared and were replaced with new ones. Further, there were discrepancies between the totals per the Fulton County tally sheets and the data put online by the Secretary of State.

Once more, Sterling dismissed the findings, saying they were trivial, but Rossi persisted and reached out to the Governor's office. Governor Kemp's staff eventually spent weeks doing their own investigation. The Kemp team agreed with Rossi: There were thirty-six discrepancies (potentially involving many, many ballots). The discrepancies could not be explained away.

On November 17, 2021, Governor Kemp wrote a pointed and terse letter to members of the State Election Board, outlining in detail the Rossi findings. In part, the governor stated:

> The data that exists in public view on the Secretary of State's website of the RLA Report does not inspire confidence. It is sloppy, inconsistent, and presents questions about what processes were used by Fulton County to arrive at the result.[42]

Governor Kemp indicated that the board should take several specific actions to further investigate and resolve the issues, and he added: "This is one issue where I believe this Board must act swiftly." He sent a copy to Brad Raffensperger. Perhaps the Secretary should ask Garland Favorito if he is still willing to conduct an audit—the one that Raffensperger relentlessly blocked.

GEORGIA REJECTION RATES DROP MORE THAN ANY OTHER STATE
In 2016 the overall rejection rate for absentee ballots in Georgia was 6.40 percent. By 2020, that rate dropped to just 0.36 percent. In other words, it declined to about 1/18 of what it used to be. That drop was bigger than that of any other state, and it is very surprising when we consider that many Georgia voters had never used the absentee

42   Margot Cleveland, "Georgia Governor Releases More Evidence that the 2020 Ballots Were Miscounted," *Federalist*, November 24, 2021, https://thefederalist.com/2021/11/24/georgia-governor-releases-more-evidence-that-2020-ballots-were-miscounted/.

voting process before.[43] (First time mail-in voters usually have more difficulty filling out the paper work.)

If the 2016 rejection rate had been applied to the 1.3 million absentee ballots received in 2020, it would have decreased the vote by about 78,000—a big decline in a state where the election was decided by less than 12,000 votes. The dramatic change could signify a lack of diligence in the enforcement of legal and administrative standards, it could be due to an improved ballot "curing" process, or it could be due to weaker signature verification standards. Changes in the curing process and the signature verification standards are directly attributable to a controversial settlement signed by Brad Raffensperger.

The Raffensperger-Democratic Party Settlement

In all likelihood, the former president would attribute the rejection rate decline to the "Settlement" (often misidentified as a "consent decree") made between Secretary of State Raffensperger and the Democratic Party of Georgia. Trump and many other Republicans believe that the Settlement weakened signature verification standards—and without question, it did.

The Settlement required each voter to be promptly notified if and when his or her absentee ballot was found to be deficient. That much was fine. However, the signature standards were, effectively, gutted. The best way to demonstrate this is with a hypothetical example:[44]

> **In Georgia, it was almost impossible to fail a signature test**
>
> Snidely Smith lives in an apartment complex with high turnover rates, and there are several extra ballot applications in the area where mailboxes are kept. Snidely picks up a few of the extra applications—each of which has a pre-printed name and address. He mails the applications to the election center after signing each one. Snidely does not even try to change his normal handwriting.
>
> Under terms of the Settlement, county clerks have to compare Snidely's signature "with the signatures or marks in eNet [on-line registration database] and on the application for the mail-in absentee ballot." That sounds pretty tough, right? The signature must be compared to *two* references: the registration signature and the application signature.

---

43   "Comparison of rejected absentee/mail-in ballots, 2016-2020," *Ballotpedia*, accessed February 10, 2022, https://ballotpedia.org/Election_results,_2020:_Analysis_of_rejected_ballots.

44   Democratic Party of Georgia v. Brad Raffensperger, Civil Action No. 1:19-cv-05028-WMR (United States District Court, Northern District of Georgia, Atlanta Division, 2020) Attachment A, Compromise Settlement Agreement and Release.

However, if the signature matches *either* reference, it must be accepted. So, if Snidely's signatures on the ballot mailing envelopes match the ones he put on the applications, we now have "proof" that the signatures are valid. (Matching the registration signatures is not required.) Since Snidely signed his own application and the applications for the extra ballots, all will be accepted.

Although the signature matching standards were virtually eliminated by the Settlement, some of the decline in rejection rates is probably attributable to stronger efforts to cure defective ballot applications. Regarding this curing process, the Gateway Pundit alleged that illegal curing may have taken place. The conservative website claimed that the Democratic Party deployed "Ballot Rescue Teams" to cure ballots, and in the process, violated Georgia State laws regarding the manner of curing and chain of custody:

In my judgment it is not certain that this process was illegal. It would depend on how it was accomplished. Georgia Code Title 21, §21-2-386 indicates:

> The elector may cure a failure to sign the oath, an invalid signature, or missing information by submitting an affidavit to the board of registrars or absentee ballot clerk along with a copy of one of the forms of identification enumerated in subsection (c) of Code Section 21-2-417 before the close of such period.

If the Ballot Rescue Teams were well trained, they may have been careful to collect properly executed affidavits and identification. Where they may have screwed up, however, is in maintaining proper chain of custody. Ballots handled by political operatives could break those chains.

To sum up, there was a very sharp decrease in ballot rejection rates. Without doubt, much of the decrease was due to weak signature matching standards. In addition, some of the decrease may have been cause by aggressive or even improper curing efforts. Either way, expanded audit procedures are warranted.

By the way, what was the 2020 rejection rate for just the county of Fulton? It was just 0.05 percent, which is about 1/7 of the 2020 statewide rate. And that rate (for Fulton County 2020) was just 1/128 of the 2016 state wide rate.[45] Compared to the rest of us, I guess the residents of Fulton County (i.e., the City of Atlanta) are pretty

---

45   Declan Chin, "A Deep Dive into Absentee Ballot Rejection in the 2020 General Election," *A Project of MIT Election Data and Science Lab*, December 16, 2021, https://elections-blog.mit.edu/articles/deep-dive-absentee-ballot-rejection-2020-general-election.

accurate when it comes to paperwork! There is more discussion of rejection rates on page 49. To gauge the magnitude of the Fulton County rejection rate change, see Figure 9, below.

FIGURE 9: NOTICE HOW ACCURATE THEY BECAME IN FULTON COUNTY

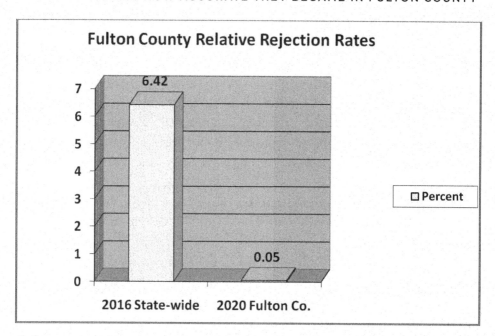

LOOK AHEAD AMERICA FINDS MORE THAN 13,000 ILLEGAL VOTES

In late 2015 and early 2016, Matt Braynard worked with the Trump-for-President Campaign before he was fired, allegedly, for demanding a pay raise. According to the *Washington Post*, Braynard worked for years in Republican polling and data analysis and served as an expert witness in some of the post 2020 election court cases.[46] Presently, Braynard is the executive director of Look Ahead America (LAA), which is a politically active nonprofit organization.

In July 2021, LAA issued "The Georgia Report – Revision A," a report that describes six tranches of potentially illegal ballots in the November 2020 Georgia election. The first three tranches have been analyzed by LAA in depth. Here is a description of those tranches:[47]

46 Ellie Silverman, Rachel Weiner, "Matt Braynard, former Trump aide, nabs spotlight with capitol crusade," *Washington Post*, September 17, 2021, https://www.msn.com/en-us/news/politics/matt-braynard-former-trump-campaign-aide-nabs-spotlight-with-capitol-crusade/ar-AAOz0dA.

47 Matt Braynard, "The Georgia Report – Revision A," *The LAA Research Group*, July 30, 2021, 3, https://14oqrc3mu9t3duv5t3o92h75-wpengine.netdna-ssl.com/wp-content/uploads/LAA_GAReport_Rev_A.pdf, 4.

1. Early and Absentee Ballots Cast in the Names of Voters (EABCINV) registered illegally

2. EABCINV matched to permanent, out-of-state moves in the National Change of Address Database (NCOA)

3. EABCINV matched to Out of State Subsequent Registrations (OOSSR) using our National Voter Database (NVD).

The potentially illegal votes exceed the Biden margin of victory in Georgia. These are LAA's findings with regard to tranches 1 through 3, respectively.

TABLE 6: THREE TRANCHES OF POTENTIALLY ILLEGAL BALLOTS

Tranche	No. of votes
1	1,401
2	10,769
3	857
Total	13,027

It appears that these results were found by means of careful analysis; however, Georgia's election officials would probably dismiss the results by claiming Georgia has better data sources. Because they won't share those sources, and they won't put together their own analyses, I don't believe them.

Let's discuss the largest number produced in "The Georgia Report"—the 10,769 figure in the second tranche. Here is part of the process used by LAA to calculate the amount:

The National Change of Address database is maintained by the US Postal Service. It includes individuals who request to have their mail forwarded and includes the individual's original address, their new, forwarding address, and whether or not it is a permanent or temporary move.[48]

48   Matt Braynard, "The Georgia Report – Revision A," 7.

The entire database of Early and Absentee Ballots Cast in the Names of Voters (EABCINV) was then matched by LAA to the NCOA database. That process yielded a population of 15,700 EABCINV who had filed permanent address changes more than one month prior to the election, and for the purpose of moving out of state.

Although moving out of Georgia permanently will (normally) invalidate a person's right to vote, LAA recognized that there could be exceptions. For example, a person might have moved back into Georgia. To quantify this potential exception, LAA "analyzed a randomized sample from the 15,700 EABCINV-NCOA matches and subjected it to further investigation by using a variety of publicly and semi-publicly available tools to find supplemental evidence they had established residency outside the state." LAA also looked for other reasons the individual might qualify to vote in Georgia, despite moving.

The sample size was 242, and the tools used by LAA "included social media websites including Facebook, LinkedIn, and Instagram, property and tax records, court records, and state driver license databases."[49]

A certain percentage of the sample was found to comprise valid voters (76 of 242). When that percentage was extrapolated to the 15,700 EABCINV-NCOA matches, the estimated number of illegal votes was reduced to 10,769—the amount in tranche 2. With regard to that number, the LAA team has expressed a confidence level of 95 percent with a margin of error of 5.8 percent.[50]

The sample size (242) used to test the validity of the initial number of EABCINV matches (the 15,700 number) is small. In itself, this analysis is not proof of irregularities. But it strongly suggests that additional analysis is needed. Further, there is support for the LAA calculation from another source. See the following.

Another source also finds over 10,000 illegal votes
In the Federalist, Margot Cleveland reported that another individual, Mark Davis, independently calculated an estimate of illegal voters. His calculation method and sources were similar to those used by Braynard's LAA team. So were his results. Mark Davis is the president of Data Productions, Inc. The Federalist characterizes Davis as "an expert in voter data analytics and residency issues."[51]

Like Braynard, Davis obtained the National Change of Address (NCOA) database that identifies people who confirmed moves with the U.S. Post Office. After excluding

---

49   Ibid., 8.

50   Ibid., 8.

51   Margot Cleveland, "New Evidence Indicates Enough Illegal Votes In Georgia to Tip 2020 Results," *Federalist*, July 9, 2021, https://thefederalist.com/2021/07/09/new-evidence-indicates-enough-illegal-votes-in-georgia-to-tip-2020-results/.

those who moved within thirty days of the election, he compared the NCOA information to the voter database provided by the Georgia Secretary of State. He found 35,000 people who, potentially, had voted in a county or state in which they did not live. Such votes would be illegal.

Here is where the Davis approach was different than the LAA approach. Whereas LAA used social media and other information sources to *reduce* its initial estimate of people who voted (illegally) after moving, Davis went in the other direction. He only counted those who, effectively, confirmed their move by updating their voter registration information. That was a gradual process that led to an *increasing* number. By May 2021, more than 10,300 people had already updated their registration information. That made it almost certain that their votes were cast illegally. And, Davis expected that number to grow because many people delay in updating voter registration.[52]

What do team Raffensperger and Sterling think about this? According to the Federalist, "Upon learning of this new development, the Georgia Secretary of State's Office quietly opened an investigation."[53] But Gabriel Sterling, the guy who ignored dozens of communications from Joseph Rossi, was not impressed. To him, "these are normal, everyday Georgians who are just trying to exercise their right to vote in a very weird year."[54]

See no evil, hear no evil, speak no evil! Instead, just use a little virtue signaling to cover up your incompetence!

RAFFENSPERGER'S NEVER-TRUMP SIDE-KICK, GABRIEL STERLING
"This must be about stopping Trump"

—GABRIEL STERLING

It just occurred to me that I haven't discussed Raffensperger's Chief Operating Officer (COO), Gabriel Sterling. The fact that he is a "Never-Trumper" is fine, but he might want to disclose that fact the next time he is spinning election information on 60 Minutes. He has signed tweets with a #Never-Trump signature, and he has written this:

---

52   Ibid.

53   Ibid.

54   Margot Cleveland, "Georgia Voting Official Makes Excuses For Residents Who illegally Voted in 2020," *Federalist*, July 19, 2021, https://thefederalist.com/2021/07/19/georgia-voting-official-makes-excuses-for-residents-who-illegally-voted-in-2020/.

I remind you again, regardless of whoever your candidate is, to stop Trump, you need to vote for Marco Rubio. He is the closest to Trump in the polls here. This must be about stopping Trump.[55]

If Sterling has not been candid about these feelings then he is probably concealing his views so that his criticisms of Trump will have extra impact. We all know people who do that.

I also have a problem with Sterling's many definitive statements about the Georgia election and how absolutely clean it was. Way back on January 4, 2021, in a video presentation recorded on C-Span and elsewhere, the COO made these definitive (and ridiculous) assertions about the 5 million voters in Georgia:[56]

- How many people died before the election? "Potentially two"

- How many registered past the deadline or without being registered? "Zero"

- How many underage voters? "Zero"

- How many voted from nonresidential P.O. Boxes? "Should be zero"

Are we to believe that Gabriel Sterling knew all of this in early January, when there were still hundreds of thousands of chain of custody records missing? And, when none of the election records had been tested in a meaningful way?

Thirteen months after Sterling gave his flippant assessment to the mainstream media, VoterGA.org issued a detailed, point-by-point refutation of the claims of Sterling, including the ones listed above. In each case the sources used by VoterGA.org were identified in its report, linked below. Notice how the VoterGA.org assessments differ from those of Sterling.[57]

---

55   Jim Hoft, "This explains a lot: Corrupt Georgia Elections Official Gabriel Sterling is unhinged #never trumper...," *Gateway Pundit*, December 6, 2020, https://www.thegatewaypundit.com/2020/12/explains-lot-corrupt-georgia-elections-official-gabriel-sterling-unhinged-nevertrumper-tweeted-nasty-attacks-donald-trump/.

56   "Campaign 2020: Georgia Election Security - Gabriel Sterling Press Conference," *C-Span*, January 4, 2021, @ 13:00, 12:45, 12:00, 11:25, and 12:15, https://www.c-span.org/video/?507710-1/georgia-election-official-refutes-president-trumps-voter-fraud-allegations.

57   Garland Favorito and Bob Coovert, "Refutation of Georgia Secretary of State Brad Raffensperger's False Election Claims," *VoterGA.org.*, February 10, 2022, 13-14, https://voterga.org/wp-content/uploads/2022/02/VOTERGA-Raffensperger-Congress-Letter-Refutation.pdf.

- How many people died before the election? ~~"Potentially two"~~ 873

- How many not registered or registered late? ~~"Zero"~~ 4502

- How many underage voters? ~~"Zero"~~ 2,047 (registered below age 17)

- How many voted from nonresidential P.O. Boxes? ~~"Should be zero"~~ 907

Those four categories total to 8,329 potentially illegal votes. They do not include the large number of illegal votes cast by people who moved out of state before the election. As noted, Braynard's estimate is 10,769, and the Mark Davis estimate is 10,300. Those estimates were produced independently, with methods and sources fully revealed. When will the "Never-Trumper" show his methods and sources?

I don't know what Sterling's educational background is; however, I am certain it is not in auditing or accounting. He seems to accept quantified information without checking or confirming it. For an elections officer, that is not an acceptable modus operandi.

Sterling's epic failure in the Rossi matter
Finally, there is Sterling's performance in the Joseph Rossi matter, which is outlined on page 124. Rossi spotted potential errors on the Secretary of State's election website, and he sent numerous emails to Sterling without getting a response. After weeks of daily efforts, Sterling finally responded—dismissively. And even after Rossi described several errors, Sterling did nothing. In the end, the Governor of Georgia had to investigate the matter and present his findings to the State Election Board. It is no wonder that Sterling thinks the election was just fine: He refuses to investigate complaints or to even hear them.

SEVENTY-FOUR GEORGIA COUNTIES HAVE LOST THEIR BALLOT IMAGES
In November 2021, Garland Favorito's nonprofit organization, VoterGA.org, issued a press release indicating that seventy-four Georgia counties could not produce the original November 2020 election ballot images, which they are required to maintain by federal law. In the statement, Favorito stated: "These violations are yet another glaring reason why Georgians cannot trust the Secretary of State's office."[58]

---

58   Natalia Mittelstadt, "Watchdog group says 2020 ballot images destroyed in 74 Georgia counties," *Just the News*, November 10, 2021, https://justthenews.com/politics-policy/elections/74-georgia-counties-unable-produce-original-images-2020-election-ballots.

The ballot images had been requested by VoterGA.org by means of Open Records requests, and were (and are) needed to determine if the vote tally includes fake or forged ballots. It makes you wonder about the competence of Raffensperger and Sterling.

EDWARD SOLOMON'S ANALYSIS CASTS DOUBT ON ELECTION RESULTS

"Attention Dominion and ES&S: Sue me please. I volunteer to be sued!"

—EDWARD SOLOMON, MATHEMATICIAN

Before summarizing the Georgia section, we should consider the work of mathematician, Edward Solomon. As pointed out on page 44, Solomon analyzed election results in the Atlanta, Georgia, area (which is in Fulton County), and he noticed two unusual characteristics of the results.

First, the results show a possible violation of a mathematical principle—the "probability of co-primality." If there is a large set of randomly chosen pairs of integers, about 61 percent of the pairs should be co-prime.[59] For the 335 precincts analyzed by Solomon, when the Trump vote is paired with the total precinct vote, only 13 percent of the relationships are co-prime.[60]

Also, Solomon noticed that many precincts reported the exact same ratio several times (Trump votes versus precinct totals). This is a pattern Solomon could not find or replicate in the results of other elections.

I don't believe the sample sizes are large enough to make these anomalies strong indicators of election irregularities, but they do suggest increased audit risk.

OPEN ITEMS IN PROCESS

Efforts to examine Fulton County ballots

Garland Favorito and David Perdue are pursuing legal actions in an effort to examine Fulton County ballots. See page 117. They are hopeful that the 524,000 ballot irregularities discovered by VoterGA.org (page 107) will convince a court to give them access to high quality imagery of all available Fulton County ballots.

WAS CERTIFICATION OF THE GEORGIA ELECTION PREMATURE?

There are numerous election related uncertainties in Georgia, and especially in Fulton County. As a result, there are hundreds of thousands of questionable ballots that vastly

---

59   Co-prime numbers are pairs of numbers that do not have any common integer factor between them, other than one.

60   "Attention Dominion and ES&S: Sue me please. I volunteer to be sued!" https://www.youtube.com/watch?v=0eNr2qoHKdQ and 642-PA (Declaration of Edward Solomon).

exceed Biden's margin of victory, which was less than 12,000 votes. For that reason, certification of the Georgia election was premature. Here are some specific areas of uncertainty:

- Garland Favorito and his team at VoterGA.org have identified 524,000 questionable ballots and impossible ballots in Fulton County. They hope to present this information in a court of law with the aim of forcing Fulton County to give greater access to election data. The information they already have, if confirmed, would invalidate the Georgia election—without question.

- There is an unfolding ballot harvesting scandal in Georgia, and it may lead to the disqualification of tens of thousands of ballots—all of which probably support one presidential candidate. The allegation, made by True the Vote, is that hundreds of mules harvested between 30,000 and 90,000 ballots in Georgia. A whistleblower said (allegedly) that the ballots were for one party (Democrats). It is believed that the Georgia authorities are investigating the matter.

- In Fulton County, several witnesses, who presumably did not know one another, swore under oath that they saw signs of fake ballots (thin paper, no creases, toner instead of ink marks, and batches that were voted 100 percent for one candidate). Months went by before the Secretary of State's employees did a very limited, nontransparent, and perfunctory review of a few boxes of ballots. A much more comprehensive, independent, and transparent review is needed.

- Georgia had the biggest drop in ballot rejection rates in 2020 (to 1/18th of the 2016 rate). That changed the total vote count by tens of thousands. For Fulton County, that drop was nothing less than incredible: It dropped to 1/128 of what the state average had been four years earlier. There have been allegations made concerning "Ballot Rescue Teams" that cured ballots, using methods that violated the law. *The drop in rejection rates, by itself, justifies a complete (and real) audit of the entire state election.*

- Four months after the election, there were still over 400,000 ballots for which there were no chain of custody records. With regard to Fulton County, thousands of chain of custody records were still missing in October 2021—eleven months after the election. Documents that materialize months after they are due have to be viewed with extreme skepticism. In addition to the missing records, 107,000 chain of custody documents from the 2020 election were found (in January 2022) to be incomplete or otherwise deficient.

- Look Ahead America (LAA) did a detailed analysis of voters who were in the process of moving. It estimated that over 10,000 voted illegally due to residency changes. Another source (Mark Davis) estimated a very similar amount, using a slightly different technique. The LAA estimate of illegal voters for all causes was over 13,000—more than the margin of victory in the election. Those two analyses, by themselves, justify a complete audit of the state election.

- At State Farm Arena in Fulton County, thousands of ballots were processed after partisan observers were misled into leaving the premises. During the hour and one half when they were gone, a huge spike in votes was recorded, with Biden getting about 23,500 votes and Trump getting less than 500.

- The very important "batch tally sheets" for Fulton County were so riddled with errors that a private citizen (Joseph Rossi) was able to identify numerous errors, just using the publicly available information on the internet. Those tally sheets are essential documents that should reconcile to the final vote count for each candidate.

- In auditing, we try to assess the ethics, diligence, and competence of management. We characterize those management characteristics with the moniker, "Tone at the Top." We do that because, when the organization's leadership displays questionable values and competence ("tone"), it makes fraud and irregularities much more likely. The leadership displayed by the Georgia Secretary of State and his Chief Operating Officer is highly suspect for the many reasons already outlined.

These matters should be resolved by means of a comprehensive, independent audit, and a decision to affirm or rescind the certification should be made, based on the results. At a minimum, these areas of examination are needed.

1. A thorough and complete audit should be performed, and should focus on all of Fulton County and parts of other counties. The audit must include verification of signatures, testing of the paper used in the ballots, and verification of the existence of voters, based on door-to-door canvassing of a statistically sound sampling of voter residences. Telephone calls are *not* sufficient.

2. As part of the audit, an analysis of hard drives, data files, and routers should be made by competent cyber experts. Each specific allegation made by VoterGA.org should be investigated and resolved.

3. The ballot harvesting allegations must be thoroughly investigated. This will require law enforcement as well as audit procedures.

4. As part of the audit, chain of custody records must be carefully reviewed for completeness and authenticity. The audit should be focused on ballots listed on chain of custody documents that were produced slowly, or not at all.

5. Two independent studies have shown that about 10,000 people voted, yet may have already moved from their county or even from the state at large. These moving records should be analyzed during the audit, and a sampling of people who may have moved should be contacted.

6. Ballot rejection rates were super low in Georgia and especially in Fulton County. One reason may have to do with ballots subject to adjudication and/or curing. A sampling of such ballots should be selected for testing during the audit process.

7. Independent auditors should test the ballots processed at State Farm Arena during the period when partisan observers were not present.

8. A sampling of batch tally sheets should be examined and tested for accuracy.

When these actions are concluded, it may be possible to affirm the certification of the election. However, this is unlikely.

7

MICHIGAN

[W]hen massive vote fraud was discovered on the island of Corsica—where hundreds of thousands of dead people were found to be voting and even larger-scale vote-buying operations were occurring—France banned absentee voting altogether.

—JOHN R. LOTT, JR.[1]

LOOSE VOTING RULES

Most voters in the United States might be surprised to learn of the much stricter voting requirements in Europe:

> Of the 47 countries in Europe today, 46 of them currently require government-issued photo IDs to vote. . . . When it comes to absentee voting, we Americans, accustomed as we are to very loose rules, are often shocked to learn that 35 of 47 European countries—including France, Italy, the Netherlands, Norway, and Sweden—don't allow absentee voting for citizens living in country.[2]

On the other hand, the U.S. has some of the most lax rules in the world, and for the 2020 election, those voting rules became even looser.

Bloated voter registration list in Michigan

In a controversial move, Michigan's Democrat Secretary of State, Jocelyn Benson, mailed out ballot applications to everyone on the Michigan voter registration list—a total of about 7.7 million people.[3]

---

1   John R. Lott, Jr., "Is ensuring Election Integrity Anti-Democratic?" *Imprimis 50*, no. 10 (October 2021): 2.

2   Ibid. [When Britain requires ID in 2023, 47 of 47 countries will have that requirement.]

3   Adam Brewster, "Michigan sends all voters absentee ballot applications following days of controversy," *CBS News*, May 22, 2020, https://www.cbsnews.com/news/michigan-vote-by-mail-registered-voters-absentee-ballot-applications/.

On its face, Benson's distribution of ballots was of questionable legality because all methods specified in the Michigan Code and the Bureau of Elections "Manual" (Chapter 6) require initiation by the voter. The voter can "...request it in writing [via mail, fax, email, or online] from the clerk." Alternatively, an application for a ballot can be the "...result of an oral request...."

Benson apparently felt that, due to COVID, people could no longer use their cell phones or the internet to acquire applications; and they could no longer write letters. Those methods were now dangerous, so Benson decided to automatically mail ballot applications to everyone. That would prevent acute voter suppression.

A Democrat-leaning appeals court gave its blessing to the instantaneous law change, and I have a feeling that this new "legislation," written by Benson and approved by the Judiciary, is here to stay.

Benson's action was particularly egregious because the state's registration list was bloated and largely out-of-date. Five hundred thousand (500,000) applications came back as "undeliverable," but that wasn't even the problem. At least those applications went to people whom the Post Office knew had moved or died.

The problem was the 4.3 million additional applications mailed to people who were living and breathing Michiganders, but would not use the ballot applications because they had no intention of voting by mail, if at all.[4] You see, the 7.7 million people sent ballot applications were more than twice as numerous as the people who actually wanted to vote absentee.

To a lot of people, the ballot applications were simply junk mail, which ended up in mail boxes, trash cans, on kitchen tables, on sidewalks, or in city dumps. Some applications were probably retained by mail carriers, since the applications could be profitably sold to political operatives.

You might ask, would it be possible for a political operative to use one of the extra ballot applications? Answer: It is not just possible, it's easy. Take a careful look at the current absentee ballot application form used in Michigan (Figure 10, below):

4   Of the 7.7 million ballot applications sent, less than half were requested, and less than half were used.

FIGURE 10 MICHIGAN ABSENT VOTER BALLOT APPLICATION

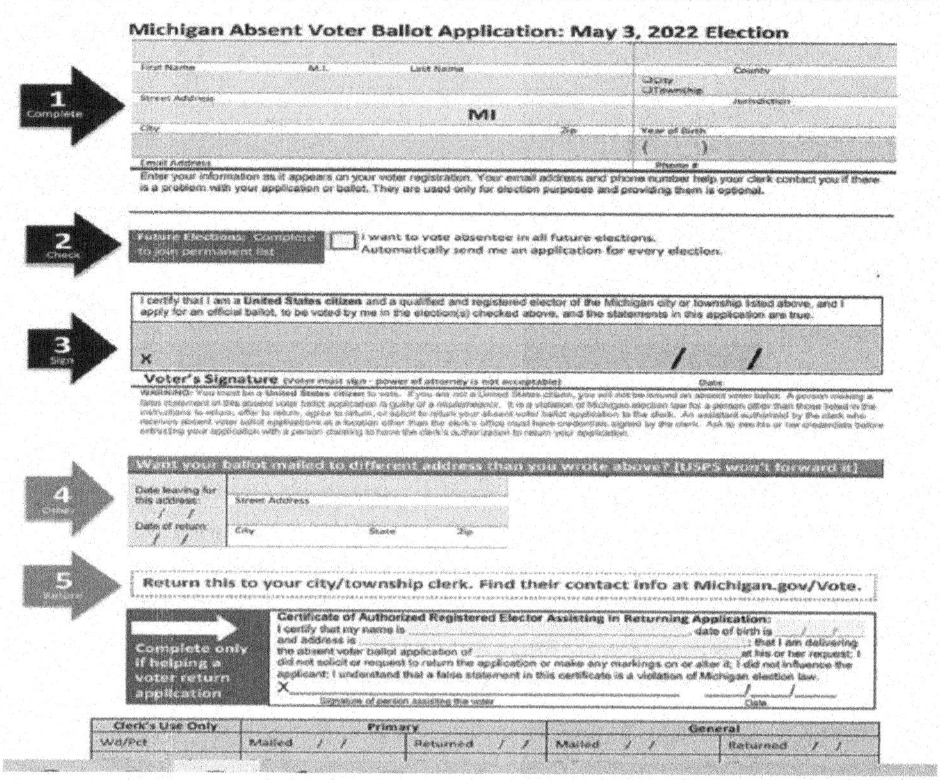

Do you see any requirement for a drivers license number, the maiden name of your mother, the last four digits of your Social Security number, or any other type of ID? No, there is no identification requirement. All you have to do is sign the form and you will be able to vote. And by the way, you can even direct the ballot to another address. (See Item 4 on the application.) That is a wonderful convenience for the busy fraudster on the go.

There is a signature requirement, but it means almost nothing, thanks to another Jocelyn Benson innovation. See below.

Signature checking changed—unlawfully
Compounding the problem of mass-mailed ballot applications was the announcement by Secretary of State, Jocelyn Benson, that all signatures would be *presumptively valid*—even if there were no more than "slight similarities" to registration signatures.[5] This

---

5   M. Dowling, "Michigan state judge rules Secretary of State broke the law on absentee ballots," *Independent Sentinel*, March 16, 2021, https://www.independentsentinel.com/michigan-state-judge-rules-secretary-of-state-broke-the-law-on-absentee-ballots/.

was an awful and unlawful action, and there is no doubt that it affected the final vote tabulation substantially. The announcement was, effectively, an invitation to fraudsters to grab all the extra ballot applications they could find or buy. With the new presumptively valid signature standard, the odds of getting caught would be less than zilch.

Benson had to know she was weakening election rules significantly. Prior to becoming the Secretary of State, she had stated that signatures were the "most secured way of protecting the vote."[6] So, how does *that* work? How are signatures "the most secured way" to protect the vote if Ms. Benson tells election workers to "presume signatures [are] valid"?

Trump strongly opposed Benson's ruling, and he ended up winning in court— *four months after the election was over*. In March, 2021, State Court of Claims Judge Christopher Murray ruled:

> Nowhere in this state's election law has the Legislature indicated that signatures are to be presumed valid, nor did the Legislature require that signatures are to be accepted so long as there are any redeeming qualities in the application or return envelope as compared with the signature on file. Policy determinations like the one at issue—which places the thumb on the scale in favor of a signature's validity—should be made pursuant to properly promulgated rules under the APA or by the Legislature.[7]

Don't think that this fight has ended. After the election, and after the slap down by Judge Murray, it was reported in the Michigan Star that the Secretary of State "is seeking to make permanent a unilateral rule she ordered in 2020 that effectively decreased scrutiny of absentee ballot signatures."[8]

---

6   "Jocelyn Benson Uncertain of Where Jocelyn Benson Stands on Critical Election Integrity Issue," *Michigan Rising Action*, September 9, 2021, https://michiganrisingaction.org/2021/09/09/jocelyn-benson-uncertain-of-where-jocelyn-benson-stands-on-critical-election-integrity-issue/.

7   Beth LeBlanc, "Judge rules Benson's ballot signature verification guidance 'invalid,'" *Detroit News*, March 15, 2021, https://www.detroitnews.com/story/news/politics/2021/03/15/judge-rules-secretary-state-bensons-ballot-signature-verification-guidance-invalid/4699927001/.

8   Cooper Moran, "Michigan Secretary of State Jocelyn Benson Seeks to Decrease Scrutiny of Absentee Ballot Signatures," *Michigan Star*, September 11, 2021, https://themichiganstar.com/2021/09/11/michigan-secretary-of-state-jocelyn-benson-seeks-to-decrease-scrutiny-of-absentee-ballot-signatures/.

> *Benson's goal: Election fraud?*
>
> *According to a group called Rescue Michigan, Secretary of State Jocelyn Benson's new administrative procedures would now mean:*[9]
>
> - *"All signatures are presumed valid."*
>
> - *"Signatures with differences that aren't 'multiple,' 'significant,' AND 'obvious' are valid."*
>
> - *Even with all of those deficiencies, signatures are valid if there is a "redeeming" factor, such as it is shaky or appears rushed.*
>
> - *"Even if every factor imaginable says it's a fake signature, election officials can consider the voter's age or the age of the signature on file to declare it valid."*

If Rescue Michigan is accurate in its portrayal, as characterized by the Michigan Star, then Benson is trying to send a big kiss and roses to people hoping to commit election fraud.

MICHIGAN: EDUCATING WORKERS TO CHEAT?

The Shane Trejo audio

In October 2020, Shane Trejo, reporter with Big League Politics, released a secret audio of an election training session he attended in Detroit. It appears that the audio is authentic, although a very ominous sound track and hyperbolic captions have been added. Here is some of the advice given to the trainees by the woman leading the group:[10]

- She warns that poll challengers will be trying to watch what they are doing. "They's a-coming! I don't know if they're coming to every precinct in the city, but they're coming to many of them in the city [Detroit]."

---

9   Ibid.

10 Patty McMurray, "MI: Radical Dem AG Threatens Reporter With Criminal Prosecution For Publishing Damning Undercover Audio Exposing Crooked Detroit Election Official," *100%FedUp.com*, November 10, 2020, https://100percentfedup.com/mi-radical-dem-ag-threatens-reporter-with-criminal-prosecution-for-publishing-damning-undercover-audio-exposing-crooked-detroit-election-official/.

- She warns the election trainees to keep the poll watchers at least six feet away. If not, they are to call 911. "That's important because they can come behind your table, but if you don't have 6 feet, they can't come back there." According to Trejo, the teacher appears to be mocking the poll watchers and challengers, and the trainees laugh.

- When a trainee says that the observers may not be able to see from six feet away, the teacher responds, "Exactly! Unless they got a really good vision or they got binoculars. [laughter] . . . If they make a scene, get 'em up outa there!"

- Apparently, quite a few people show up and learn that they already voted (supposedly). In those cases, they are required to vote by means of provisional ballots. But the teacher does not seem to like it. She asks, "Where's it going? Not in the tabulator. It's going in an envelope, right? We have how many days? Six! So, what's the department of elections going to do with it? Destroy it!"

At the very least, the recording demonstrates an unserious effort to train election workers in the important work at hand. For his efforts, however, Shane Trejo was rewarded with a very threatening "cease and desist" letter from Michigan Attorney General Dana Nessel.[11] She warned him to delete every copy and every link of the audio recording and his reporting of it from every internet platform.

Nessel's letter justified the cease and desist order by citing a couple of minor reporting errors (nothing to do with the audio recording of the trainer). I read the letter and these were the technical errors cited: (1) Trejo had apparently reported that, before 2020, challenged ballots did not go into the tabulator, and (2) He said that challenged ballots are tabulated and cannot be uncounted later. Obviously, these separate technical issues (whether true or not) did not invalidate the audio.

With her threatening letter, it seems that Nessel inadvertently confirmed the truthfulness of the audio. There was no denial of its authenticity or accuracy. Of course, virtually all media cheerfully complied with the AG's censorship instructions, and for that reason, you most likely never heard this story before.

There is one place the recording can be heard (at least for now)—on this alternative video-sharing platform: https://www.bitchute.com/video/vzjWWJTXpXeO/. (Key audio sections start at 0:16, 0:54, 1:12, and 1:28.)

---

11   Ibid.

Jessy Jacob, Whistleblower
The Trejo audio may be shocking, but it is weak tea compared to the allegations contained in several sworn affidavits. For example:

Jessy Jacob worked for the City of Detroit for about thirty years. In an affidavit filed with the Wayne County Circuit Court, this whistleblower made many startling assertions about the mis-education she received:[12]

- "I worked at the election headquarters in September 2020 along with 70-80 other poll workers. I was instructed by my supervisor to adjust the mailing date of these absentee ballot packages to be dated earlier than they were actually sent. The supervisor was making announcements for all workers to engage in this practice."

- "I directly observed, on a daily basis, City of Detroit election workers and employees coaching and trying to coach voters to vote for Joe Biden and the Democrat party."

- "I was specifically instructed by my supervisor not to ask for a driver's [sic] license or any photo I.D."

- "I was instructed not to validate any ballots and not to look for any deficiencies in the ballots."

- "While I was at the TCF Center, I was instructed not to look at any of the signatures on the absentee ballots, and I was instructed not to compare the signature on the absentee ballot with the signature on file."

- "On November 4, 2020, I was instructed to improperly pre-date the absentee ballots receive date that were not in the QVF [Qualified Voter File] as if they had been received on or before November 3, 2020. I was told to alter the information in the QVF to falsely show that the absentee ballots had been received in time to be valid. I estimate that this was done to *thousands of ballots* [emphasis added]."

12 Cheryl A. Costantino v. City of Detroit, Civil Action 2020cv355443 (Circuit Court for the County of Wayne, 2020), Affidavit of Jessy Jacob filed November 7, 2020, 2–3.

Lisa Gage affidavit: thousands of ballots without review
Based upon the sworn affidavit of one Republican poll challenger, the Wayne School (WCSCEW) did a darn good job of teaching workers how to ignore the law. Lisa Gage was a GOP challenger at the TCF Center in Detroit on November 3 and November 4, 2020. Here is an excerpt from her eight-page affidavit:

> The entire 5-step process [of reviewing ballots and envelopes] was entirely abandoned. There was no scanning of the outside of the envelope to check for registration status, there was no signature, or ballot number verification. . . . There was no postmark verification; there was no ballot review for stray marks; there was no verification of the voter existing in the database; there was no signature comparison or authentication. . . . I estimate that thousands [of] ballots were processed this way.[13]

Later in this section, starting on page 151, you will find excerpts from some of the sworn affidavits of other poll watchers and observers at the Detroit TCF Center. Those affiants were harassed, blocked from observing ballot processing, and sometimes physically removed. While that was going on, hundreds of thousands of ballots were processed. The comments in those affidavits make sense, in view of the disgraceful way election workers were and are (apparently) taught in Detroit.

AT LEAST 125,000 HARVESTED BALLOTS
As noted on page 36, an election integrity organization named True the Vote (TTV) claims it has detected a major ballot harvesting scandal in multiple states, including Michigan. TTV matched cell phone "ping" data, and other data, with video images (where available) to detect ballot harvesting operations. In the movie, *2,000 Mules*, TTV estimates that there were between 125,000 and 225,000 illegally harvested ballots cast in Michigan, depending on the assumptions and definitions used.

DR. SHIVA'S WORRISOME FIND
Concerns about the Michigan 2020 election were raised by pattern specialist and engineer, Shiva Ayyadurai (Dr. Shiva), who was introduced on page 44. This scientist analyzed vote patterns in four Michigan counties: Oakland, Macomb, Kent, and Wayne. His analysis distinguished the straight-ticket voter—an individual who automatically selects all candidates from one political party—from the split-ticket voter (who may vote for a mix of Democrats and Republicans).

---

13   State of Texas v. Commonwealth of Pennsylvania, State of Georgia, State of Michigan, and State of Wisconsin, Motion to Enlarge Word-Count Limit and Reply in Support of Motion for Leave to File Bill of Complaint No. 220155, Original (Supreme Court of the United States, 2021), Affidavit of Lisa Gage filed December 10, 2020, 3.

Dr. Shiva noticed a pattern that seemed to indicate an irregularity: the more Republican the precinct (measured by the percentage of people voting a straight Republican ticket versus straight-ticket voters of both parties), the fewer the individual votes for Trump, relatively to all individual voters.[14] In three counties (Oakland, Macomb, and Kent) the drop-off in Trump's vote percentage was linear and dramatic. His share of the individual, ticket-splitter vote (Trump individual vote divided by total individual vote) dropped relative to straight-ticket Republicans by as much as 20 percent.[15]

When the results are put on a graph they appear ominous. As Trump's share of the straight-ticket vote increases, his share of the individual vote decreases sharply. However, this downward trend line is easily explained: The more Trump supporters use the straight-ticket process, the fewer are available, relative to Democrats, to vote individually.

This same downward slope would be evident for Joe Biden, were we to plot his share of the individual vote against the percentage of all voters who were voting a straight Democrat ticket.

THE EUBANKS CANVASSING EFFORT

In late 2021, a door-to-door canvassing effort was started by Jacky Eubanks, a former candidate to be a Michigan State Representative. Eubanks and her associates were able to reach a random sample of over 1,200 people in Macomb County who, according to information obtained from township, county, and state officials, voted absentee in the November 2020 election.[16,17]

A large percentage of these people, who supposedly voted by absentee ballot (17.6 percent), did not know they had done so. According to Eubanks, sometimes the person who answered the door would say, "I don't know who you're talking about. I've lived here for two years, ten years, twenty years, and they don't know who the person that we're asking for is." In other cases, the person answering the door said they were, indeed, the listed voter, but did not vote in the 2020 election. Some of those people were "upset because they realize they've been defrauded and they sign an affidavit."[18]

---

14   In these Michigan precincts voters have the option to vote separately in each contest or to vote the straight Republican slate of candidates or the straight Democrat slate of candidates.

15   Shiva Ayyadurai, "MIT PhD Analysis of Michigan Votes Reveals Unfortunate Truth of U.S. Voting Systems," *Vashiva. com*, November 10, 2020, https://vashiva.com/dr-shiva-live-mit-phd-analysis-of-michigan-votes-reveals-unfortunate-truth-of-u-s-voting-systems/.

16   Jordan Conradson, "Jacky Eubanks Canvassing Efforts Raise Serious Questions – 'We're Looking At An 18% To 20% Irregularity And Anomaly Rate,'" *Gateway Pundit*, September 29, 2021, https://www.thegatewaypundit.com/2021/09/audit-michigan-jacky-eubanks-canvassing-efforts-raise-serious-questions-looking-18-20-irregularity-anomaly-rate-video/.

17   Christina Bobb, "Interview of Jacky Eubanks," *One America News Network*, November 22, 2021.

18   Ibid.

It is important to understand that Eubanks is not a professional pollster or statistician, and sometimes people misunderstand the questions being asked. However, Ms. Eubanks estimates there could have been 87,000 invalid ballots in Macomb County, assuming the surveyed group of individuals approximately represents the population. If those surveyed people are representative of the state's population, there could have been more than 900,000 invalid ballots in the state. With numbers that large, Eubanks could be off by a factor of five times or more and there still could be enough ballots to disqualify the election results.

During the door-to-door effort, Eubanks collected several sworn affidavits. She had been told by the County Clerk that he would consider doing an audit if she took those affidavits to him. Instead he turned the affidavits over to the state Attorney General (Dana Nessel), and that triggered a real investigation!

Unfortunately, the "real investigation" was not about possible election fraud; rather, it was an investigation of Jacky Eubanks. Dana Nessel, the Michigan Attorney General who threatened Shane Trejo for exposing a corrupt Detroit election worker, threatened Eubanks with legal action related to her canvassing activities. As a result, Eubanks had to hire an attorney, and this is what happened, according to Jacky Eubanks:

> While I am not at liberty to discuss the affair in detail, I can tell you this: We confirmed Nessel's intention was, in fact, to link me to some nebulous crime pertaining to canvassing and collecting affidavits. This was purely political targeting to intimidate myself and other citizen activists from investigating election fraud.[19]

Nessel's intimidation worked. To end the legal threats, Eubanks had to agree to stop canvassing. Mission accomplished! Good job, Attorney General Nessel!

DR. FRANK'S ANALYSIS OF MICHIGAN COUNTIES

As discussed on page 48, Dr. Douglas Frank has produced evidence suggesting that unnatural monitoring and manipulation of voting took place in several states. One of the states is Michigan. By using a six-number "key" (a "6th order polynomial"),[20] voter registration percentages by age, the percentage of voter turnout, and population estimates based on census data, Dr. Frank can predict almost precisely the percentage of voters actually voting at each age level and within each county. That leads him to

---

19   Patrick Colbeck, "Communist Tactics Employed in Michigan," *Let's Fix Stuff.org.* March 16, 2022, https://letsfixstuff. org/2022/03/communist-tactics-employed-in-michigan/.

20   A polynomial is a mathematical expression composed of variables, constants, and exponents that are combined using the mathematical operations such as addition, subtraction, multiplication, and division.

believe that the election results were monitored by and, in some cases, manipulated by computers.

Dr. Frank was asked to predict the vote in nine different Michigan counties, as shown in Table 7. (They were selected for him, without his input.) Notice the near perfect correlations (R) for each. (Average = .997.) Impressively, the correlation for urban Wayne County (Detroit) is similar to the more rural counties. Is that expected?

The predictive ability of Dr. Frank suggests that vote manipulation may have taken place.[21] However, it should be noted that Frank has also produced near-perfect correlations for a few non-swing states. That suggests that high correlations are not necessarily attributable to vote manipulation.

TABLE 7: DR. FRANK'S SUCCESS RATE IN
PREDICTING BALLOTS VOTED IN MICHIGAN

Dr. Douglas Frank
Predicting Ballots with Registration Key

Michigan County	Correlation (R)
Wayne	.999
Oakland	.999
Macomb	1.000
Kent	.999
Livingston	.999
Grand Travers	.996
Barry	.996
Charlevoix	.995
Antrim	.993

PATRICK COLBECK AND THE DIGITAL CONTROLLER THEORY

Most of this book deals with meat and potatoes fraud, where harvesters mail ballots to the election department or place them in drop boxes after the ballots are appropriated from apathetic or confused voters, dead voters, or moved-away voters. A former member of the Michigan State Senate, Patrick Colbeck, has theories that are a bit more

21   Douglas Frank, "Dr Frank's Preliminary Analysis of Michigan's Election Data," June 2, 2021, https://rumble.com/vhy4ml-dr-franks-preliminary-analysis-of-michigans-election-data.html.

sophisticated, more controversial, and worth consideration.

He believes that fraud took place in multiple stages: Preparation, a Main attack, a Back-up attack, and a Defense of the attack. He also believes that digital controllers may have been used to directly modify voter databases. Those digital controllers would have been used as part of the Back-up attack, which is the phase required when last-minute corrections are needed.[22]

Of course, this is just theory. However, Colbeck believes there is some supporting evidence. See Part IV starting on page 253 for more information about Colbeck's theories.

ANTRIM COUNTY AND THE DOMINION MACHINES

To many Trump supporters, Antrim County, Michigan was the smoking gun evidence of Dominion's manipulation of votes. On election night, it appeared that Joe Biden won the county, and this made no sense at all, given the county's normal voting pattern. A day later it became clear that Donald Trump had actually won the county by about 6,000 votes.

Some people, such as Russell Ramsland, Jr., a Harvard MBA with technology experience, believed the error was purposeful, and was caused by the computer system the county bought from Dominion Voting Systems. Ramsland's organization, Allied Security Operations Group (ASOG), analyzed the Antrim errors, and reached this conclusion, as articulated in its report dated December 13, 2020:

> We conclude that the Dominion Voting System (DVS) is intentionally and purposefully designed with inherent errors to create systemic fraud and influence election results. The system intentionally generates an enormously high number of ballot errors.[23]

In the view of ASOG, the high number of errors was an intentional feature of DVS. The plan, supposedly, was to generate a high number of error ballots that could be put into the adjudication process, where county workers could make the final voting decision (in favor of the candidate of their choosing).

I have a problem with the viability of the ASOG theory. It would require help from within election offices (for the adjudication process). But, why would fraudsters rely on collusion from insiders when they merely need to mail harvested ballots to the counties

---

22   Patrick Colbeck, "Election Control System: Did 2020 Election Get an ECO Boost?" *Letsfixstuff.org.*, September 29, 2021, https://letsfixstuff. org/2021/09/election-control-system-did-2020-election-get-an-eco-boost/.

23   Russell James Ramsland, Jr., "Antrim Michigan Forensic Report," *Allied Security Operations Group*, December 13, 2020, 1, https://www.deepcapture.com/2020/12/antrim-county-computer-forensic-report/.

of their choosing (or put them in drop boxes)?

Although other election observers have commented on weaknesses in the Dominion adjudication process, it seems that ASOG presented its theory without much evidence. ASOG also noted that DVS computers are capable of being connected to the internet; however, it has not been shown that Michigan's DVS machines were, in fact, connected to the internet.

To its credit, the ASOG report points out several of the apparent weaknesses of DVS machines. Look Ahead America (LAA), an organization headed by Matt Braynard, analyzed Ramsland's report and reached this conclusion:

> The ASOG Report demonstrated many possibilities where election security could have been compromised, *but failed to prove any actual compromise or intent of compromise from Dominion Voting Systems* [emphasis added].[24]

I concur.

SIDNEY POWELL'S MICHIGAN CASE FAILS

Under extreme pressure and time constraints, Attorney Sidney Powell put together a federal complaint on behalf of Timothy King and various Michigan voters and nominees of the Republican Party to be presidential electors. The defendants were Governor Gretchen Whitmer, Secretary of State Jocelyn Benson, and the Michigan Board of State Canvassers.[25]

The case included dozens of affidavits of individuals who saw questionable activities, were harassed, or were obstructed from performing their duties as poll watchers in Wayne County and the City of Detroit. However, these more traditional types of election complaints were buried under a mountain of more fanciful allegations of deliberate vote manipulation by machines created in a foreign country in order to cheat in the elections of corrupt dictators. Some of the historical references may be true, and many people have serious reservations about the design of Dominion machines. The Powell lawsuit did not, however, provide convincing evidence of specific computer vote changes in the 2020 election.

The main "evidence" of actual wrong doing by Dominion came from Russell Ramsland, Jr., who we just discussed (on page 149) in regard to Antrim County,

---

24   Matt Braynard and Ian Camacho, "The Antrim Report Investigation and Synopsis," *Look Ahead America*, October 20, 2021, 22, https://14oqrc3mu9t3duv5t3o92h75-wpengine.netdna-ssl.com/wp-content/uploads/LAA_AntrimReport_FinalB.pdf.

25   Timothy King v. Gretchen Whitmer, 2:20-cv-13134-LVP-RSW (E.D. Michigan, 2020), 10.

Michigan. According to Powell's civil action, Ramsland "concluded that Dominion alone is responsible for the injection, or fabrication, of 289,866 illegal votes in Michigan, that must be disregarded." However, the Ramsland affidavit does not make a convincing case regarding the number of illegal votes or the cause. In the end, it appears that human error was responsible for the vote problem in Antrim County.[26]

After distracting the court with the weak Dominion allegations, Powell made a strong case for several categories of traditional election misconduct in Wayne County. It is too bad she didn't give more emphasis to these issues, the categories of which are listed below:[27]

1. Republican observers denied access to TCF Center [the Detroit processing facility]

2. Disparate and discriminatory treatment of Republican versus Democratic challengers

3. Republican challenger not permitted to view ballot handling processing or counting

4. Harassment, intimidation, and removal of Republican challengers

5. Republican challenges were not recorded by poll workers

6. Unlawful ballot duplication

7. Democratic election challengers frequently outnumbered Republican poll watchers 2:1 or even 2:0

8. Collaboration between election workers, city/county employees, and Democratic Party challengers and activists

Many troubling affidavits that deserve attention
Here are excerpts from just a fraction of the affidavits from poll watchers (randomly organized). These were attached to Powell's case. As you read these, keep in mind the

---

26   Ibid., 5.

27   Timothy King v. Gretchen Whitmer, 21–27.

comments of Jessy Jacob and Shane Trejo, starting on page 142. They alleged that workers in Detroit were trained to conduct themselves in an unlawful manner and did so with respect to the processing of thousands of ballots.[28]

- [Affiant, Daavettila] "I started talking to someone in a group that was wearing our yellow GOP wristband. They had a packet of instructions with the heading relating to, 'Tactics to Distract GOP Challengers,' which he let me borrow to read. . . . Another man in the group started telling me, 'our main job is to distract and disrupt the GOP challengers,' then a woman in the group grabbed the packet of papers from my hands and said, 'no, no, no, she's a Republican, she doesn't need that, bye, bye.'"

- [Affiant, Daavettila] "I witnessed three white males being thrown out by the police (all on separate occasions), each time it happened, the entire room burst out into cheering and clapping.'"

- [Affiant, Zaplitny] "I experienced intimidation by poll workers wearing BLM face masks and another man of intimidating size with a BLM shirt on, very closely following challengers, including myself, even though there was supposed to be social distancing going on. . . . [I]t was clear that the Precinct Chairperson was directing the voters to the straight ticket Democrat option."

- [Affiant, Antonie] "Persistent hostility from workers. Witnessed duplication [of ballots] with only 1 person, not both parties."

- [Affiant, Kiilunen] "I observed GOP poll challengers being escorted out of the room to the cheers and clapping of all the poll workers."

- [Affiant, Cizmar] "I was present when poll challengers were forcibly removed from the counting room. . . . When these ejections took place, there was a lot of shouting of approval and applause from the poll workers and election supervisors in the room."

---

28   Timothy King v. Gretchen Whitmer, Exhibit 3.

- [Affiant, Steffans] "I was accused by a Democrat volunteer of being part of a 'cult' for my support of Trump. . . . I observed a Republican [sic] contender being prevented from watching during a duplication. He tried to get closer to the table and move around so he could see, but when he did, three people swarmed him to block his view. . . . Democrat volunteers were verbally aggressive with me."

- [Affiant, Papsdorf] "Many of my friends that wanted to help were locked out of the building. . . . Entire room erupting in applause when a GOP kicked out."

- [Affiant, Langer] "[A]rrived at approx. 12:30PM, prohibited entry to the counting floor. Told to wait. Kept door closed. Waited until approx. 10:30PM [10 hours] when returned home."

- [Affiant, Bomer] "At approximately 11:43PM I heard one of the team leads [sic] yell 'this is our house tonight!' At approximately midnight, I heard this same man say racist remarks about black people who support Donald Trump. I believe these remarks were directed at me."

- [Affiant, Pennala] "Throughout the day, I witnessed a pattern of chaos, intimidation, secrecy, and hostility by the poll workers. Poll workers would cheer, jeer and clap when poll challengers were escorted out of the TCF Center."

- [Affiant, Ballew] "There were several instances in which the poll workers used their bodies to prevent me from watching and observing the ballot counting process."

- [Affiant, Gaicobazzi] "The table supervisor, his supervisor, and several other operatives . . . swarmed in and began intimidating me. I was separated from the table at one point by the table supervisor's supervisor and told to stand back. . . . I asked him what his name and job title was and he, along with the rest of the intimidators, refused to give me any information. He made some kind of innuendo about 'playing with' him that made me uncomfortable and he then told me something to the effect that he would either 'kick my ass or kick me out.' In disbelief, I asked him if he was truly threatening me because I was just doing my job. He repeated his mantras multiple times and called the cops over and had me forcibly removed."

- [Affiant, Schneider] "After being called several derogatory names by the entire table (there was a girl videotaping it even though video was not allowed) a man came over to me and told them he was my attorney. Then they started screaming that two Republicans cannot be at the same table, called the police, and the police escorted him out to loud cheers from ALL of the workers."

- [Affiant, Schornak] "At each counting board, the poll workers attempted to block me from observing. I was verbally abused and intimidated by not only the Democratic poll challengers but the ACLU and other organizations."

- [Affiant, Sankey] "I never gained access."

To counter the many affidavits attached to the Powell lawsuit, the defendants (Gretchen Whitmer and Jocelyn Benson) had their own sworn affidavit from Christopher Thomas, a senior advisor to Detroit City Clerk Janice Winfrey.[29] Thomas seemed to respond with authority and sincerity to many of the specific process issues in the complaint and in the affidavits. Those process issues included, for example, the required number of people to observe a certain procedure and the way to complete spoiled ballots. In addition, Thomas attributed some suspicious conduct to the "correction of clerical errors, not some type of fraud."[30] With regard to the delivery of ballots in the early hours of November 4, 2020, the affiant said that "It takes several hours to properly process ballots received on Election Day."

Of course, it may take hours to process ballots, but does it take 7.5 hours to drive them over to the processing center? (More on that is found below.) Also, his response did not cite documentary evidence, such as the chain of custody records that would establish who picked up and delivered the ballots and by when.

The intimidation is ignored

Mr. Thomas completely ignored the many complaints about intimidation, except to imply that the affiants were not following "protocol."[31] His disregard for the claims of intimidation is disgraceful. The affidavits listed in this book are just a fraction of the ones attached to the Powell lawsuit. Until election officials and judges start to take poll watcher intimidation seriously, it will continue unabated. Perhaps some people are fine with that.

---

29   Timothy King v. Gretchen Whitmer, Affidavit Christopher Thomas.

30   Timothy King v. Gretchen Whitmer, Affidavit Christopher Thomas, Item 2.

31   Timothy King v. Gretchen Whitmer, Affidavit Christopher Thomas, Item 6.

In the "Prayer for Relief," Powell asked for (1) decertification of the election, or (2) certification of the election for Donald Trump, or (3) certification after removing ballots processed without adequate observation and without meeting other standards of law.[32] Time was limited, but it might have been better to ask for an immediate, in-depth audit of Wayne County, to see if there were enough questionable ballots to change the election results.

The case was ultimately dismissed by Judge Linda Parker for a number of procedural reasons. However, the judge was clearly not impressed with the merits of the case and indicated that it was likely doomed to failure in any event.

SUSPICIOUS BALLOT SPIKES

As indicated in the section on "Late night ballot dumps," many people noticed suspicious ballot spikes that came late on election night or in the early morning of November 4. These seemed to benefit Biden. In the case of Michigan, there was another factor that made the spikes unusual: By law, all Michigan ballots must be in the hands of county or township clerks by 8:00PM on Election Day. So, why did it take 7.5 hours (all the way until about 3:30AM on November 4) for Detroit ballots to reach the Detroit TCF Center? Is the city that big?

At around 3:30AM on November 4, 2020, reporter Shane Trejo and Pat Colbeck, a former State Senator, witnessed the arrival of a van filled with an estimated 50,000 ballots.[33] Colbeck was concerned by potential chain of custody issues because there was no indication that a Republican and Democrat were present for the transfer. Said Colbeck:

> We don't know if they stopped by a side street in Coney Island and picked up a few more ballots during transfer. We have no way of verifying that information.[34]

A few hours later, even more ballots arrived. Two large ballot dumps were recorded that night (or morning), and are listed below. Presumably, the first one represents the ballots that Trejo and Colbeck saw coming into the garage:

- At 3:50AM (EST) there was an update in Michigan that gave 54,497 votes to

---

32   Timothy King v. Gretchen Whitmer, 72.

33   Cassandra Fairbanks and Jim Hoft, "The TCF Center Election Fraud – Newly Discovered Video Shows Late Night Deliveries of Tens of Thousands of Illegal Ballots 8 Hours After Deadline." *Gateway Pundit*, February 5, https://thetruedefender.com/exclusive-the-tcf-center-election-fraud-latest-video-shows-late-night-deliveries-of-illegal-ballots-8h-after-the-deadline/.

34   Ibid.

Biden and 4,718 votes to Trump.

- At 6:31AM (EST) there was an update in Michigan that gave Joe Biden 141,258 votes while giving only 5,968 votes to Donald Trump.

To be fair, there could be an innocent explanation for the late arrival of these ballots, and Detroit is much more likely to have voted for Biden than Trump. However, the lack of partisan observers, the apparent lack of chain of custody documentation, and the very late arrival of the ballots are cause for unease.

JOCELYN BENSON'S AUDIT REPORT

The Secretary of State issued a report in April 2021, outlining the findings of three types of audits conducted after the 2020 election:[35]

1. Precinct procedural audits

2. Absent voter counting board audits

3. Risk-limiting audits

The first two categories of audit are useful for determining if election employees at the state and county level are carefully following procedures. The third type of audit (risk-limiting) simply determines if ballots add up to the statewide tabulations. In other words, it is just another recounting of ballots.

Audits of this type, however, do little to shed light on the kind of election fraud expected in this particular election. At the risk of being redundant (again), the unique aspect of this election—especially in Michigan—was the automatic mailing of ballot applications to everyone on outdated registration lists. Political operatives could have obtained those lists and figured out who would be unlikely to use his/her ballot. They would have known that certain people had moved or were dead. They also could have determined which people rarely vote. (Such information is available to the public.)

Secretary of State Benson mailed out 7.7 million applications, 4.3 million of which were not used by the named voter. If some of those ballots were submitted fraudulently, it would have been undetectable except by means of the signature match, and that process was emasculated by Secretary Benson's unlawful signature decree.

---

35   Jocelyn Benson, "Audits of the November 3, 2020 General Election," Michigan Department of State, April 21, 2021, 4 ,https://www.michigan.gov/documents/sos/BOE_2020_Post_Election_Audit_Report_04_21_21_723005_7.pdf.

Did Benson Lie?
Benson's audit report states: "Signatures are verified by the clerk's office before envelopes are delivered to the counting board."[36] How does that statement comport with her rule that signatures were to be presumed valid?[37] The presumption-of-validity standard is the real one that Benson put into play. There was no "verification" standard.

THE REPUBLICANS ISSUE A LENGTHY INVESTIGATORY REPORT
In the introduction to his report, Chairperson Edward McBroom, a Republican Michigan State Senator, states, "[T]here is no evidence presented at this time to *prove* either significant acts of fraud or that an organized, wide-scale effort to commit fraudulent activity was perpetrated in order to subvert the will of Michigan voters [emphasis added]."[38] I would generally agree with that statement because we can almost never prove "wide-scale effort to commit fraudulent activity" anywhere or in any activity unless and until a real audit is undertaken. McBroom et al. did not perform an audit.

Specific findings

- The McBroom report "recommends the Michigan Secretary of State discontinue the practice of mailing out unsolicited applications." I concur.[39]

- With regard to Antrim County, the report takes issue with the findings of Ramsland's group, Allied Security Operations Group. The Republicans believe that human error—not Dominion Voting Systems—caused the error.[40] I agree.

- Dr. Frank is criticized in this report—unfairly in some respects. Although I agree that Frank is too definitive in his statements (the correlations are so high there must be fraud), I disagree with the GOP critics in some respects. I don't think they fully understand human nature when they say, "the notable red flags he [Frank] spotted in the data are easily explained."

36   Jocelyn Benson, "Audits of the November 3, 2020 General Election," 11.

37   M. Dowling, "Michigan state judge rules Secretary of State broke the law on absentee ballots."

38   Senator Edward McBroom, "Report on the November 2020 Election in Michigan," Michigan Senate Oversight Committee, June 23, 2021, 6, https://misenategopcdn.s3.us-east-1.amazonaws.com/99/doccuments/20210623/SMPO_2020ElectionReport_2.pdf

39   Senator Edward McBroom, "Report on the November 2020 Election in Michigan," 11.

40   Ibid., 14.

- The Republican report broadly states that the election computers were unhack-able. However, the affidavit of former aerospace engineer Patrick J. Colbeck, who was a poll watcher during the Michigan election, lends credence to the belief that the Michigan election machines were vulnerable and may have been connected via Wi-Fi routers.[41]

- On the issue of ballot harvesting, the report says "no evidence of such was pre-sented." However, subsequent to issuance of the report, evidence of very signifi-cant ballot harvesting was revealed. See page 145.

Bizarre and idiotic findings from the GOP

- Regarding chain of custody issue, the report is surprisingly blasé:
  - » "Frequent demands to decertify . . . are accompanied by high sounding lan-guage regarding the 'chain of custody.' This verbiage evokes images of evi-dence utilized in trials, such as sealed envelopes and locked evidence rooms with sign-out sheets."[42]

- Even worse, the GOP investigators make this naïve statement:
  - » "While concerns about these [chain of custody] systems may be justified, it is incredibly misleading and irresponsible to imply this holds any danger to the official vote counts, the tabulators, or the ballots themselves."[43]

Wow! These Michigan Republicans are clueless regarding the danger posed by an absence of custody documentation. Without chain of custody documentation, we can't be sure if we have all the ballots, or if we have extra ballots. And if we are not sure of the ballot count, we won't be sure of the "official vote counts." I don't understand the McBroom Report's dismissive attitude about this.

- On the issue of poll challenger harassment, the McBroom report is absolutely idiotic. The report refers to the "differing opinions regarding the actual rights and duties of those [poll watchers and challengers]." Then the report describes those "differing opinions"

---

41   Cheryl A. Costantino v. City of Detroit, Civil Action 2020 cv 355443 (Circuit Court for the County of Wayne, 2020), Attached affidavit of Patrick Colbeck, filed November 8, 2020, ¶5 and ¶.

42   Senator Edward McBroom, "Report on the November 2020 Election in Michigan," 30.

43   Ibid.

"Republican challengers were committed to ensuring that challenges were issued and recorded."[44]

Democrats testified that "their specific training regarding the duties and obligations of challengers is to not ever challenge any ballots."[45]

The Democrat view is that challengers should not challenge? That is not a different opinion: It is idiocy![46]

OPEN ITEMS IN PROCESS

Administrative changes to signature verification

As noted, the Michigan Secretary of State, Jocelyn Benson, reduced signature verification standards before the November 2020 election; however, a judge subsequently ruled that the changes were illegal.

Now, Benson is attempting to permanently change the administrative code in such a way that the reduced standards can survive legal challenges. (Also see page 141.) Since signatures are the only form of identification used for mail-in ballots, the proposed Benson changes would be extremely reckless.

An audit of the election is conceivable

An audit is unlikely but possible, even though Michigan is administered by Democrats who are not interested in having an audit. In January, 2022, supporters of former President Trump proposed petition wording that was approved by the Michigan Board of State Canvassers—an organization established by the Michigan Constitution in 1850. According to the Daily News (Iron Mountain, MI):

> Organizers of the . . . audit measure . . . need roughly 340,000 valid voter signatures to send their initiatives to the Republican-led Legislature and, if lawmakers do not adopt them, to the November ballot.[47]

Some Republicans in the legislature are also hostile to the idea of an audit, so the fate of the petition is unclear.[48]

---

44   Ibid., 13.

45   Ibid.

46   Ibid.

47   David Eggert, "Wage, audit ballot drives advance," *Daily News*, January 20, 2022, https://www.ironmountaindailynews.com/news/local-news/2022/01/wage-audit-ballot-drives-advance/.

48   Ibid.

WAS CERTIFICATION OF THE MICHIGAN ELECTION PREMATURE?

The winning margin in Michigan (about 155,000 votes) was a lot larger than that of Arizona or Georgia, so the certification decision is more likely to withstand scrutiny. Nevertheless, the items listed below—especially the first four items—need to be investigated and resolved before the certification should be considered valid. These matters could involve very large numbers of votes that exceed the vote differential between Biden and Trump. Here are some specific areas of uncertainty:

- After the mass-mailing of 7.7 million ballot applications to people who had not requested those applications, Secretary of State Benson effectively and unlawfully eliminated signature matching requirements. Since Michigan does not require identification to be submitted with ballots or ballot applications, Benson's actions gravely undermined the integrity of the election. For this reason alone, there should not have been a certification of the election. A complete and independent audit of the election could remedy this situation, but an audit is very unlikely. It is probable that thousands of defective or fraudulent ballots were approved.

- There are credible allegations of a large-scale ballot harvesting scheme in Michigan and other states. The investigation involves cell phone "ping" technology, videos, and at least one whistleblower describing the operation in detail. The organization conducting the research, "True the Vote," estimates that there were between 125,000 and 225,000 illegal, harvested ballots in Michigan. (See page 145.)

- In Macomb County, Jacky Eubanks surveyed over 1,200 people who voted by means of absentee ballot and found that 17.6 percent said they did not vote that way or did not vote at all. Although Eubanks is not a professional pollster, she claims to have selected individuals randomly from records obtained from township, county, and state records. The error percentage was so high that this survey should not be ignored—especially in view of the True the Vote harvesting allegations. AG Nessel should be expanding the canvassing operation that Eubanks started; instead, it appears that Nessel threatened Eubanks, legally.

- Jessy Jacob, a thirty-year veteran Detroit City employee (a true "whistleblower"), claims that workers were taught to backdate records to circumvent the November 3, 8:00PM deadline. Voters were encouraged to vote for Biden, and workers were told to not look for signature or ballot deficiencies. In addition,

Jacob claims she was instructed to falsify the dates in the Qualified Voter File (to make ballots appear to meet legal deadlines). She said this backdating was done with regard to thousands of ballots. (See page 144.)

- While hundreds of thousands of ballots were processed, there was a huge display of hostility and intimidation at the TCF Center in Detroit. Dozens of poll challengers said that they could not observe results or challenge results. GOP challengers were removed to the cheers of the workers, while GOP replacement challengers were kept waiting outside for hours. This conduct was unethical and illegal, and could have resulted in thousands of improperly-approved ballots in this Democrat stronghold.

- Shane Trejo provided evidence that the hostility displayed by election workers to Republicans was not incidental or accidental. Trejo's audio recording indicates that workers were taught to intimidate poll observers so they could not perform their duties.

- It is not clear that there are chain of custody records on file with regard to the early morning (November 4) ballot "dumps." These records, if they exist, need to be carefully reviewed.

The issues cited above should be resolved by means of a comprehensive professional and independent audit.

AT A MINIMUM, THESE AREAS OF EXAMINATION ARE NEEDED:

1. A thorough and complete audit should be performed, and should focus on all of Wayne County (Detroit) and parts of other counties. The audit must include verification of signatures, testing of the paper used in the ballots, and verification of the existence of voters, based on door-to-door canvassing (not phone calls) of a statistically-sound sampling of voter residences.

2. As part of the audit, an analysis of hard drives, data files, and routers should be made by competent cyber experts.

3. Michigan Attorney General Dana Nessel should stop her threats so that the Jacky Eubanks door-to-door canvassing results can be confirmed or disproven. If necessary, canvassing efforts should be expanded to include Wayne County. Professional pollsters should be used.

4. A test sample of signatures should be reviewed to establish that they are legitimate under the law, as written, rather than the law as corrupted by the Secretary of State. The sampling should include Wayne County.

5. The Qualified Voter File should be examined and tested to ensure that ballot received dates were not backdated to November 3, as claimed by Detroit City employee, Jessy Jacob.

6. All chain of custody documents must be carefully reviewed. That is particularly true for the Wayne County late ballot arrivals.

7. Allegations of ballot harvesting, made by True the Vote, should be investigated by Michigan Attorney General Nessel and U.S. Attorney General Merrick Garland.

8. The woman in the Trejo recording should be investigated and, probably, dismissed. An investigation should be conducted to see if other workers conducted themselves inappropriately. If possible, the ballots and envelopes they handled should be re-examined. People who *teach* cheating will also *do* cheating.

9. If the Secretary of State continues to mail ballot applications to people on obsolete registration lists, and if she succeeds in eliminating or reducing signature verification standards (again), then Michigan law should be changed to impose identification requirements for all voting.

When these actions are concluded, it may be possible to *fairly determine the popular will of the people.*

8

NEVADA

THE "FRAUD TRILOGY" STATE

Trump lost this state by around 33,000 votes, but after the election his lawyers created a detailed list of issues associated with over 130,000 disputed votes. In this section, the Trump claims are evaluated. First, however, we need to review Nevada's brand-new election law.

Just before the 2020 presidential election (in August), Nevada passed emergency legislation to dramatically change voting law. In a party-line vote, Democrats legalized the automatic distribution of ballots to all registered voters (whether requested or not), the unlimited harvesting of ballots, the use of drop boxes, and other policies likely to increase the possibility of fraud. Ostensibly, the changes were made to protect voters from exposure to COVID.

Although the legal changes were temporary in nature, they were made permanent a few months after the election. In my opinion, those changes were an invitation to fraud and will ultimately lead to one-party rule in the state (sort of like California—or Cuba). That said, it is not clear, as I start my analysis, whether the legal changes significantly impacted the 2020 election.

First, Nevada was already tilting to the Democrats. Hillary Clinton won the state in 2016, with a winning margin similar to that of Joe Biden. Also, Nevada has only six electoral votes. For that reason, there was less incentive for nefarious characters to corrupt the election. Finally, the legal changes were enacted so close to the election that fraudsters had limited time to fully take advantages of those laws. If they didn't already, eventually they will.

NEVADA'S NEW ELECTION LAWS: A FRAUD TRILOGY

If bureaucrats in a state want to seize and retain control indefinitely, there are three key mechanisms to use. When employed in combination, they are a most formidable trilogy:

Mail-in ballots for all (not just applications)

Before the election, mail-in ballots were already controversial. In June of 2020, NBC News issued this report:

> A network of deep-pocketed progressive donors is launching a $59 million effort to encourage people of color to vote by mail in November. . . . A nonprofit arm of the donor network Way to Win is working with philanthropic organizations including the Ford Foundation and George Soros's Open Society to raise the money.
>
> [S]ome in the [Republican Party] view broader access as a threat and have voiced worries that mail-in ballots are more susceptible to fraud. That includes President Donald Trump, who tweeted last month that it will lead to "RIGGED ELECTIONS!"[1]

The problem is not with the mailing of ballots, per se: It is with the automatic mailing of ballots to millions of people who are not necessarily interested in voting, who may have already moved to a new location, may be noncitizens, or may be in the city cemetery. If those ballots fall into the wrong hands (and some will, inevitably) they can be used to affect the outcome of an election. Nevada now mails ballots (not just applications) to every registered voter, unless he/she opts out. And it is very easy to register because voter registration is built into the drivers license renewal application—even for noncitizens.

Legalized ballot harvesting

With Nevada's new law, harvesting ballots—no matter how many—is now legal. Barbara Cegavske, the Secretary of State of Nevada, wanted to create a regulation that required ballot harvesters to register with her office. However, Governor, Steve Sisolak, tersely rejected that proposal.[2] That means there will be unidentified people collecting as many ballots as possible, and from anywhere they can get them. The harvesters may include drug addicts, desperate for a "fix," and political zealots, determined to run up the score for their candidate.

If the experience of other states is applicable to Nevada, it is likely that some ballots

---

1   AP, "Mail-in voting gets a $59 million boost from progressive donors," *NBCNews.com*, June 18, 2020, https://www.nbcnews.com/politics/2020-election/mail-voting-gets-59-million-boost-progressive-donors-n1231395.

2   AP, "Nevada Governor Won't Make 'Ballot Harvesters' Register," *USNews.com*, August 25, 2020, https://www.usnews.com/news/best-states/nevada/articles/2020-08-25/nevada-governor-wont-make-ballot-harvesters-register.

will be purchased from people in homeless shelters. Other ballots will be obtained from nursing homes, politically active "civic" organizations, and mail carriers.

Why pay for ballots when you can get them for free?
Jay Greenberg, a journalist with NeonNettle.com News, reported that, in early 2020, thousands of ballots were being mailed to inactive voters in Clark County. He reported:

> The vote-by-mail envelopes are piling up in post office trays, outside apartment complexes, and on community bulletin boards in and around Las Vegas.[3]

Jenny Trobiani, a Clark County postal worker, wondered:

> What's going to happen with these things, they're not secured at all and there are thousands of them just sitting here? This just seems fraudulent to me, something stinks here.[4]

Drop boxes now legal in Nevada
The indiscriminate mailing of ballots ensures the fraudster that he will have plenty of ballots to harvest, but where does he discretely put the many ballots he has acquired? After all, harvesting may now be legal in Nevada, but typical ways of acquiring them (coercion, payoffs, and theft) are not legal. The best and most discrete place is an unguarded drop box, without security cameras, and that is the third part of Nevada's new fraud-conducive trilogy.[5]

WEAK SIGNATURE STANDARDS

> "Based on past experience, at least 90 percent of (ballots mailed to inactive voters) will come back undeliverable," Loreno Portillo, Clark County's assistant registrar of voters, said in a late April affidavit. "There are already pictures and videos of ballots piling up outside of Clark County apartment complexes. *The only safeguard against someone successfully and illegally returning those ballots is signature verification* [emphasis added]."[6]

---

3   Jay Greenberg, "Mail-In Voting Fraud Concerns Emerge as Unclaimed Nevada Primary Ballots Pile Up," *NeonNettle.com* News, May 20, 2020, https://neonnettle.com/news/11324-mail-in-voting-fraud-concerns-emerge-as-unclaimed-nevada-primary-ballots-pile-up.

4   Ibid.

5   The drop box requirements are outlined in Nev. Rev. Stat § 293.8861.

6   Editorial, "Democratic lawsuit seeks to eliminate signature verification on mail ballots," *Las Vegas Review-Journal*, "May 17, 2020, https://www.reviewjournal.com/opinion/editorials/editorial-democratic-lawsuit-seeks-to-eliminate-signature-verification-on-mail-ballots-2030416/.

In the United States, unlike most of the world, we don't require identification when voting, even though almost everyone has a social security number or a driver's license or some kind of government identification card. We put all our faith in a ridiculously subjective standard—the signature. And, some politicians even want that little safeguard eliminated. According to an editorial in the Las Vegas Review-Journal, Democrats sued to get rid of signature verification, just prior to the 2020 primary and presidential elections:

> After Secretary of State Barbara Cegavske announced that June's primary would be conducted primarily by mail, Democrats sued. Among other demands, they wanted . . . ballots mailed to inactive voters and the *elimination of signature verification* [emphasis added].[7]

Frankly, I don't know why anyone would worry about signature standards: Often they are of little consequence. Even if you merely put a scratch or a dash or a dot on a signature line, there is a good chance that the friendly people in the nearby election office will give their blessing to that "signature." If you doubt this, please see Dr. Shiva's test of blank signatures, which he performed as part of the Maricopa County (Ariz.) audit.

Shiva was forbidden from actually reviewing the signatures, but was allowed to look for blanks and scribbles. When he did, he found that the county had accepted, as valid, four times more scribbles than the total number of signatures rejected by the county— out of 1.9 million ballot envelopes! See Dr. Shiva's blank signature test on page 95.

Nevada verifies signatures, but the standard is weak and subjective. First, Republican and Democrat observers are shut out of the process: The matching of signatures is entirely up to employees of the local county clerk. That might sound fair until you realize that, in many areas, the employees reflect the political biases of the neighborhood. For example, in a bright red rural part of the state, the county workers are probably mostly Republican, while the workers in an urban area may be mostly Democrat. For this reason, an employee-only review may not be balanced.[8]

In addition, there may be a bias towards acceptance of the signature as opposed to rejection. In Nevada, the signature must be accepted unless at least two workers find that that it differs from the voter's registration signature in "multiple, significant and obvious respects." It might be difficult to get two workers to agree that a signature's defects are both "significant and obvious."

---

7   Ibid.

8   Nev. Rev. Stat § 293.325 1, 2.

Even if a signature is rejected, it can be cured anytime for several days after the election.[9] What exactly does curing involve? It is probably accomplished with a phone call to the very same cell phone number put onto the ballot envelope by the voter—or by the fraudster.

A signature test is taken, and Nevada gets an F!
Victor Joecks, a columnist for the Las Vegas Review-Journal, created a clever little experiment. He used his own handwriting for the mail-in ballots of nine people. Here is how he did it, in his words:

> I wrote their names in cursive using my normal handwriting. They then copied my version of their name onto their ballot envelope. This two-step process was necessary to ensure no laws were broken.[10]

There was an 89 percent failure rate: Eight of the nine ballots were accepted and voted.

I hope you are convinced that the signature standard—especially in Nevada—does not adequately protect election integrity because it cannot stop the crooked ballot harvester. On the other hand, were we to require real identification, such as the last four digits of a social security number, many ballot harvesters (and some politicians) would be out of business.

People can sign for others
Finally, Nevada law indicates that, if a voter has a disability (undefined in the Code), and "is at least 65 years of age OR is unable to read or write," someone else can sign on his behalf.[11] Hmm! No possible abuse there!

A SUSPICIOUS HIKE IN VOTER TURNOUT AND A DROP IN BALLOT REJECTIONS

The 2020 election was vigorously contested throughout the nation, and that led to a big increase in voter turnout. However, Nevada's increase was extra big, and that could be a sign of weak compliance with election standards and controls. From 2016 to 2020

---

9   Nev. Rev. Stat §293.325 4, 5.

10   Victor Joecks, "Signature verification is a joke. Here's how I beat the system." *Las Vegas Review-Journal*, November 27, 2020, https://www.reviewjournal.com/opinion/opinion-columns/victor-joecks/victor-joecks-signature-verification-is-a-joke-heres-how-i-beat-the-system-2072456/.

11   Nev. Rev. Stat § 293.329.

the nationwide voter turnout increased by 6.7 percent, but in Nevada, the increase was 65.4–57.4 = 8 percent. (See Figure 6 on page 54.) One reason could be the legislative changes (mail-in ballots, harvesting, and drop boxes) that probably increased legitimate and illegitimate voting. Another reason is the 50 percent drop in absentee ballot rejections. Nevada's 2016 rejection rate was 1.6 percent, and it dropped to .8 percent in 2020.[12] A decrease of that magnitude should invite audit scrutiny.

NONCITIZEN VOTING IS A FACT IN NEVADA, AND OTHER STATES

In Nevada, "[a]nyone who goes in to renew their license will automatically have their information forwarded to the Secretary of State and county clerk's office to keep the [voter] rolls up to date" [Nevada DMV.org].[13] Noncitizens and others who can't or won't prove identity get a slightly different license: It is called a "Driver *Authorization* Card." Since non-citizens (and others who are unidentified as residents) are not supposed to vote, you might presume that the application for the Driver Authorization Card doesn't have a "Voter Registration" section. However, you'd be wrong. Noncitizens are also registered on their special card unless they affirmatively indicate that they are not citizens. "What's to stop someone from lying? Nothing and no one."[14]

Don't ask, don't tell

Under federal law (the 1993 Motor Voter Registration Act), all citizens of any state must be automatically registered to vote when they get a license to operate a motor vehicle, unless they affirmatively opt out. Also under federal law, state election departments cannot demand to see citizenship documents. If I were a cynic, I would conclude that the federal government *wants* non-citizens to vote illegally.

As noted by Nevada Secretary of State, Barbara Cegavske:

> [T]here is no federal database that can be accessed for the purpose of evaluating bulk data relative to current immigration status. Furthermore, the U.S. Supreme Court, as well as U.S. Courts of Appeal in the Ninth Circuit and elsewhere, have ruled that election officials cannot lawfully require documentary proof of citizenship as a condition of voter registration.. . .[15]

---

12 "Comparison of rejected absentee/mail-in ballots, 2016-2020," *Ballotpedia*, accessed February 10, 2022, https://ballotpedia.org/Election_results,_2020:_Analysis_of_rejected_ballots.

13 Bridget Clerkin, "Nevada Drivers Will Be Automatically Registered to Vote Now," Department of Motor Vehicles, December 3, 2018, https://www.dmv.org/articles/automatic-voter-registration-at-dmv-a-go-in-nevada.

14 Victor Joecks, "It's easy to vote illegally in Nevada," *Las Vegas Review-Journal*, April 7, 2018, https://www.reviewjournal.com/opinion/opinion-columns/victor-joecks/its-easy-to-vote-illegally-in-nevada/.

15 Barbara K. Cegavske, "Elections Integrity Violation Reports, Office of the Secretary of State, April 21, 2021, https://www.nvsos.gov/sos/home/showpublisheddocument?id=9428.

Ah, but something is amiss! Why should Nevada, or any state, even have a voter registration section on an application for a Driver Authorization Card, which is specifically designed for non-citizens? The Driver Authorization Card is for non-citizens and others who cannot prove identity. The answer is pretty simple: Some people want non-citizens to vote—and thousands do just that.

On page 174 you will find a quantification of the minimum amount of non-citizen voting that took place in Nevada during the 2020 election.

THE BATTLE IN DISTRICT COURT

Shortly after the election, Trump's attorneys, led by Jesse Binnall, filed a lawsuit in Nevada's First Judicial District Court in Carson City. The transcript of the oral arguments shows that Judge James Russell appeared to be attentive and courteous to both parties, but in his subsequent "Order Granting Motion to Dismiss," there were a few statements that do not make sense to me—as an auditor and accountant. My non-legal views seem to coincide with the legal views of the Trump team.

There can be grave doubts about the integrity of an election, even if specific votes cannot be identified, but the Biden lawyers claimed otherwise. Unfortunately, the Judge agreed with them, and his reasoning concerns me. The Judge was not persuaded to

- find "that illegal ballots were cast [simply] because the signature on the ballot envelope did not match the voter's signature [¶89]."

- find that a "signature from Clark County did not appear to match . . . [because the assertion provided] no evidence that it was not the voter's signature [¶87]." [Author's comment: The fact that the signature "did not appear to match" **is** the evidence that it was not the voter's signature.]

- find an illegal vote where a "USPS supervisor instructed her to forward ballot to a deceased person in California [because the assertion provided] no evidence that such ballot was returned as voted [¶108]." [Author's comment: It is illegal to forward a ballot in the mail. *Is there an exception for dead people?*]

- find "that Clark County election workers were pressured to process and count ballots that presented problems and irregularities [¶99]." [Author's comment. The specific allegation was that someone was pressured to count as valid a signature that was merely a picture of a star. I guess His Honor didn't want that embarrassing detail in his ruling.][16]

---

16 Jesse Law v. Judith Whitmer, 20 OC 00163 1B (First Judicial District Court of the State of Nevada in and for Carson City N.D, 2020), Order Granting Motion to Dismiss, ¶ 87.

Thus, the Judge ignored the Nevada laws that specify certain standards for evaluating signatures and that prohibit the forwarding of ballots. It seems that the Judge was seeking absolute proof that a violation of law or policy led directly and ultimately to a specific, identifiable, invalid vote. Apparently, Judge Russell wanted DNA, fingerprints, and three eyewitnesses who could testify that the ballot was mailed, delivered, and run all the way through the Nevada voting system.

The Judge believes the standard requires intent to defraud?[17]
In addition, Judge Russell seemed to dismiss the importance of mistakes, machine errors, or sloppiness. It appears that his focus was on intent and fraud. In paragraph 137 of his order granting dismissal he cited the Nellis Motors v. State case: "In Nevada, a plaintiff must prove a general civil fraud claim, which requires *intent to defraud*, with clear and convincing evidence [emphasis added]." What! If half of Biden's voters couldn't get to the polls because a bridge was rained out, would Judge Russell ignore that? After all there is no "intent to defraud" on the part of Mother Nature.

The judge is unaware of Nevada and federal law?[18]
Judge Russell seemed unaware of the law with regard to providing financial incentives that had been provided to Native American voters. (See "Native Americans selling votes on page 173.) The judge said:

> The record also does not support a finding that any group or individual offered anything of value to voters to *manipulate the voters' choice* for president ¶114 [emphasis added].

Any financial incentive to vote, even if it is not for the purpose of manipulating a voter's choice, is clearly illegal under federal law. It appears that the same standard applies under Nevada NRS 293.700, which states: "It is unlawful . . . to compel, induce or prevail upon any elector to give or refrain from giving his or her vote."[19]

17   Jesse Law v. Judith Whitmer, 20 OC 00163 1B.

18   Ibid.

19   18 U.S. Code § 597 - Expenditures to influence voting; Nevada NRS 293.700 – Bribery of elector.

All other issues[20]

Let's not waste time: Without a single exception, Judge Russell waved off all other matters:

- All of the Trump experts were disregarded and all Biden experts were "persuasive."

- Issues pertaining to double voting, non-resident voting, deceased people voting, untimely ballots, etc. were all dismissed with the phrase: "The record does not support a finding."

- The judge ignored one issue completely because, I suppose, he did not know how to dismiss it. There had been testimony from two county IT workers, who had stepped forward separately as whistleblowers. They reported that the machine tabulation totals changed during the night. In other words, the machines had specific totals when they closed up for the night, and different totals in the morning when they started again. No comment at all from Judge Russell, and no comment from the Appeals Court![21,22]

APPEAL TO THE STATE SUPREME COURT

You don't need to be an attorney to detect the extreme contempt held by the Nevada State Supreme Court with regard to this case. It was docketed on December 7, 2020, competing motions were filed, and the court directed the parties to respond to each other by 2:00PM on the next day—December 8. At 4:30 on that day, the court gave Trump's attorney (Binnall) just two and a half hours to file a supplemental (and final) brief, identifying specific items subject to appeal, "by page and paragraph number, and accompanied by citations to the record in support of their arguments." Incredibly, Binnall and his team got the papers to the court—forty pages in all—with three minutes to spare. That same evening, the Nevada Supreme Court tossed the case.

I have read the brief filed by Binnall, and it is clear and cogent. I am not competent to assess it legally, but I did pick up on a couple of arguments that, to me, as an auditor, are essential in evaluating the credibility of election results. Said Binnall:

---

20   Jesse Law v. Judith Whitmer, 20 OC 00163 1B.

21   Jesse Binnall testimony, "Clip of Senate Hearing on Election Security and Administration," C-Span, December 16, 2020, https://www.c-span.org/video/?c4932084/user-clip-trump-attorney-jesse-binnall.

22   Jesse Law v. Judith Whitmer, 20 OC 00163 1B.

The District Court erred in applying a "clear and convincing evidence" standard

Clear and convincing evidence is not the Contestant's burden of proof for this statutory election contest because the election contest statute is written more in the nature of negligence and malfeasance (preponderance of the evidence) than it is in intentional and fraudulent conduct (clear and convincing evidence).[23]

The argument above, made by Binnall, makes sense: In determining the fair outcome of an election, does it matter if errors were made accidentally, purposely, or maliciously? The only thing that matters is the materiality of the errors. If the errors could affect the outcome, they should and must be addressed—whether they were caused by negligence, accident, or contrivance.

The District Court conflated two alternative elements of election law (NRS 293.410(c))

In basic English, to challenge an election, an appellant has to: (1) find enough votes to close the gap between the two candidates **or** (2) find enough errors to raise reasonable doubt as to the outcome of the election.

The first alternative (find enough votes) is obvious, but consider the second alternative. If election law says that the county election staff must compare a voter's signature against two or more different signatures, but the staff only compares it to one signature, it could "raise reasonable doubt" as to the election outcome. That is true even if no improper votes are specifically identified. Another example: If Democrat and Republican poll watchers have a legal right to observe the processing of ballots but are not allowed to do so, that also could "raise reasonable doubt." It is apparent that Judge Russell and the Nevada Supreme Court rejected that argument.[24]

The Trump team raised several other legal points, but to no avail. In a short, four-page "Order of Affirmation" the Supreme Court rejected the appeal.

Investigation by the Nevada Secretary of State

Shortly after the election there were apparent anomalies that warranted a serious and full-scale audit. Those anomalies were identified during the development of the legal case presented to Judge Russell's District Court. Although an audit never took place, after the election was certified Republican legislators sent the issues and questions (with four boxes of related documents) to the Nevada Secretary of State (SoS), Barbara Cegavske.

---

23   Jesse Law v. Judith Whitmer, Supreme Court of the State of Nevada Case no. 82178, Section V.A. (20 OC 00163 1B First Judicial District Court of the State of Nevada in and for Carson City).

24   Ibid., Section V.B.

The SoS and her associates investigated those matters, and a report was issued on April 21, 2021.[25] Part of Cegavske's effort appears to be sincere and credible, but many issues were not adequately addressed, and remain unsettled to this day. Here is a brief outline of the more significant findings:

NATIVE AMERICANS SELLING VOTES

The Trump legal team had argued that groups linked to the Biden campaign were giving financial incentives to Native Americans, if they voted in the election. The alleged incentives included $25 and $50 Visa gift cards, gasoline cards, beadwork, and some significant raffle prizes. The court disregarded the claim despite obvious photographic evidence, some of which is shown below.

Months after the Court improperly dismissed the claim (see footnote), Barbara Cegavske said she couldn't address the issue, as it was under investigation.[26] I am sure her answer was sincere, but I am equally sure that the federal government (which would probably have jurisdiction) is not doing anything about this—to this day. We have no way to assess the numbers, but the Native American vote is usually significant in Nevada.[27]

It is against federal law to give inducements to directly encourage or discourage voting, even if no particular candidate is involved. However, it is clear that inducements were designed to promote voting for Joe Biden. On Facebook, Native American Janet Davis posted advertisements for "our daily drawing for Early Voting!" she noted that there was "plenty of swag to give away," and made this statement:

> The drawing will be held each day of those that voted that day! [sic] Pretty good chances! So get down the to Tribal Office Chambers to vote [sic]. Or drop off your ballot today.

After noting that the Biden campaign sponsored the "Wild West Burgers," Davis posted a picture of the Biden-Harris campaign bus—similar to one depicted in Figure 11.[28]

---

25 Barbara K. Cegavske, "Elections Integrity Violation Reports.

26 "Improper" because Judge Russell apparently thinks that payments to vote are lawful unless they are "to manipulate the voter's choice for president." In reality, any financial inducement to vote is illegal, even if it is not for a particular candidate. (18 U.S. Code § 597)

27 Barbara K. Cegavske, "Elections Integrity Violation Reports," 3.

28 Janet Davis, "Janet Davis is with OJ Semans and 4 others," *Facebook*, October 20, 2020, https://archive.ph/TmnpQ.

FIGURE 11 RECRUITING THE NATIVE AMERICAN VOTER[29]

3,987 NONCITIZENS VOTING?

As noted on page 168, noncitizens in Nevada are offered a chance to register to vote every time they renew their Driver Authorization Cards (very similar to drivers licenses). Like all other states, Nevada uses the "honor system." On the voter registration form, the applicant answers "yes" or "no" to a citizenship question, but no evidence is required and evidence cannot and will not be obtained.

The Trump's lawyers alleged that 3,987 noncitizens may have voted. The SoS described her actions with regard to this issue. In short, she requested the Department of Motor Vehicles to identify individuals who had "presented an immigration document" during the last five years. The list comprised 110,163 individuals, of which 5,320 were active voters, and 4,057 had voted in the 2020 election.

The 3,987 number calculated by the Trump team and the 4,057 number calculated by Cegavske are probably far too low. Binnall had limited information and the SoS only went back five years, and she only included people who "presented an immigration document." However, non-citizens are not required to present those documents to the DMV.

The real number of non-citizen voters cannot be determined because of the federal prohibition on requesting evidence, as noted on page 168. No official in Nevada, or in any other state in the U.S., can request documents to show citizenship in a federal election.

In the first year of the Biden administration there were an estimated 2 million new illegal immigrants entering the U.S., plus about 1 million more who entered legally

---

29   Cassandra Fairbanks, "PROOF: Democrat Operatives Paid Native Americans to Vote in Nevada With Gift Cards," *Gateway Pundit*, November 29, 2020, https://www.thegatewaypundit.com/2020/11/proof-democrat-operatives-paid-native-americans-vote-nevada-gift-cards/.

and who probably have "green cards." This is on top of the millions (perhaps 20 to 30 million) who were already here illegally. It is unacceptable that the federal government and the State of Nevada cannot, or will not, investigate this problem.[30]

2,479 VOTERS PERMANENTLY GONE?

These are people who filed permanent change-of-address forms with the U.S. Postal Service more than 30 days prior to the election. The SoS acknowledged that most of them (1,892) voted in the 2020 election. Cegavske said it is possible some were still Nevada residents when they voted, despite the permanent change of address, but she claimed there is no cost-effective way to check. That is not an adequate answer.[31]

1,506 DEAD VOTERS?

The Trump people found 1,506 voters who were, allegedly, listed as deceased on the Social Security Administration's Master Death File, and in several other sources. The SoS used the Nevada Office of Vital Statistics, and she claims there were just ten people. However, she has provided no documentation. The SoS should provide a workpaper, listing each of the 1,506 people named by the Trump people and providing the source used by Nevada to confirm the person's status (i.e., dead or alive).[32]

42,284 PEOPLE VOTED TWICE?

The Secretary of State's analysis starts with this statement: "More accurately, this list alleges that 21,142 individuals may have voted twice during the 2020 general election (21,142 x 2 votes each = 42,284 allegations)." I haven't seen the list, but let's assume she is correct: There are only 21,142 people who may have voted twice.

Cegavske then lowered the amount to 18,314 because, according to the Statewide Voter Registration List, 2,828 of the so-called "double voters" had actually voted [only] once in the 2020 election. She didn't offer anything to backup that claim, but again, let's take her word for it.

The status of the remaining double voters (18,314) is very murky. Cegavske implied this when she stated: "Regarding the remainder of the alleged 'double voters' (i.e., the 18,314) there is a significantly *lower chance* that the alleged violation occurred due to the nature of the data comparison [emphasis added]."

"Lower chance" does not sound definitive, especially when determining the winner

---

30   Barbara K. Cegavske, "Elections Integrity Violation Reports," 3.

31   Barbara K. Cegavske, "Elections Integrity Violation Reports," 4.

32   Ibid.," 5.

of a U.S. presidential election. Cegavske needs to be more transparent. She should prepare a workpaper that indicates the analysis that was made for each of the voters who, ostensibly, voted twice.[33]

8,842 VOTERS REGISTERED AT A COMMERCIAL ADDRESS

The Secretary of State acknowledged that it is normally illegal to register to vote from a commercial address unless it is also the residence of the voter. Her staff investigated a sample of 369 specific records (of the 8,842), and of those, only 2.4 percent were questionable. The rest were appropriate locations, such as apartment complexes (37 percent), mobile home parks (20 percent), and hotels with long-term rental options (10 percent). This explanation appears to be reasonable, and the sample size was sufficient to support the analysis. However, she should share a workpaper showing the specific addresses that were checked. The names of voters can be redacted.[34]

8,111 NEVADA VOTERS REGISTERED AT NON-EXISTENT ADDRESSES

Trump's attorneys identified these nonexistent addresses by using the CASS system (Coding Accuracy Support System). According to the SoS, this system only identifies addresses to which the U.S. Post Office makes deliveries. A statistically valid sample of 369 addresses was identified and, using internet search engines, the locations were identified. The SoS claims that 95 percent were "quickly identified as being valid addresses." This resolution may be reasonable but a list of the tested addresses should be provided.[35]

31,643 NEVADANS THAT HAD "ID REQUIRED" FLAGS

These were mail-in voters who were "flagged" by the computer because they registered to vote with questionable identification. Some may be phantoms, so to speak, who do not really exist. In other cases, they may be residents of other states, and were ineligible to vote in Nevada. (A whistleblower alleged that some people were told they could use out-of-state identification.)

On this one, the Secretary of State completely fell down, so to speak. She resorted to the following inappropriate and irrelevant legalistic argument:

33   Ibid.," 6.

34   Ibid.," 7.

35   Ibid.," 9–10.

Much of Contestants' evidence consists of non-deposition evidence in the form of witness declarations. These declarations fall outside the scope of the contest statute, which provides that election contests "shall be tried and submitted so far as may be possible upon depositions and written or oral argument as the court may order."

First, the legal preference for depositions as opposed to sworn declarations has to do with the ability to cross examine witnesses providing evidence in a courtroom proceeding. Because of a lack of time, there was no ability to cross examine during the Trump-Biden legal contest, which ended long ago.

The SoS is not the Nevada Attorney General! She has her own administrative duty to investigate any possible violations of law or administrative standards. She is not limited to deposition evidence (and the court was not really limited either).

The SoS can interview employees, if need be, to see if administrators were telling staff to accept out-of-state drivers licenses and identification cards. In addition, Cegavske can select a sample of Clark County ID-flagged residents, and examine the identifications they provided. Some sort of a statistical evaluation should have been made and publicized.[36]

15,170 NEVADA VOTERS WITH OUT-OF-STATE MAILING ADDRESSES

This is another important issue that was inadequately addressed by Cegavske. She simply speculated that some Nevada-registered voters may live out-of-state "to attend college or to satisfy military orders." She concluded by saying the "request to verify the Nevada residency of more than 15,000 individuals is unreasonable." This was a disingenuous response because nobody was asking the SoS to contact 15,000 people. As she certainly must know, a statistically valid sample would do nicely. When does it become reasonable to verify residency? When there are 25,000 voters with out-of-state addresses; 50,000 thousand?

There probably are college students and military personnel among the 15,170 voters with out-of-state mailing addresses. However, there may also be several residents of California who, knowing their votes are pretty meaningless in that state, seek an opportunity to keep Nevada as blue as possible. This should have been checked, and a report should have been issued.[37]

---

36   Ibid.," 11.

37   Ibid.," 12.

VOTES "APPEARING AND DISAPPEARING IN THE DEAD OF NIGHT"

In the section on the District Court case (starting on page 169) it was noted that Judge Russell and the State Supreme Court each ignored a major issue, without explanation or even comment. Despite the judicial lack of interest, it is a matter of importance that must be raised again. In the words of Trump's lead attorney for Nevada, Jesse Binnall:

> Two Clark County technical employees came forward, completely independent of each other, and explained that they discovered that the number of votes recorded by voting machines, and stored on USB drives, would change between the time the polls would close at night and when they were reopened the next morning. In other words, votes were literally appearing and disappearing in the dead of night.[38]

Binnall explained how the two whistleblowers knew there was a problem:

> What they would do is they would log these disks in and out. Good practice. And the disks had a serial number on them. And numerous times that disk would be logged out with one vote total on it and logged back in the next morning during the early vote period with a different number on it.[39]

Binnall brought in a computer expert to examine the machines, but he was not allowed to get near them:

> We were allowed only a useless, visual inspection of the outside of a USB drive. . . . We were denied a forensic examination.[40]

As noted, Trump's attorney raised the issue with both courts, but neither bothered to comment. For that matter, there was no follow-up (apparently) by the Nevada Secretary of State, the machine vendor, or the people in our country who claim to be journalists. None had interest in this strange, surreal occurrence. I guess machines can do some pretty weird things in Nevada.

---

38   Jesse Binnall, "Clip Of Senate Hearing on Election Security and Administration," *C-Span*, December 16, 2020, https://www.c-span.org/video/?c4932084/user-clip-trump-attorney-jesse-binnall.

39   Ivan Pentchoukov, "Voting Machine USB Drives Had Totals Altered Overnight, Witness in Nevada Election Contest Alleges," *Epoch Times*, December 3, 2020, https://www.theepochtimes.com/voting-machine-usb-drives-had-totals-altered-overnight-witness-in-nevada-election-contest-alleges_3604396.html.

40   Jesse Binnall, "Clip Of Senate Hearing on Election Security and Administration," *C-Span*, December 16, 2020, https://www.c-span.org/video/?c4932084/user-clip-trump-attorney-jesse-binnall.

The impact on votes? Perhaps it was small, but possibly it was huge. If someone risked tinkering with machines in the middle of night, it wasn't for the purpose of altering a handful of votes.

WAS CERTIFICATION OF THE NEVADA ELECTION PREMATURE?

The certification of the Nevada election was premature, given the list of 130,000 questionable votes compiled by the Trump legal team. Unfortunately, the questionable votes and related issues received little consideration in the courtroom. Months later, the Nevada Secretary of State made a more thorough evaluation, and some of the issues were resolved. However, many of the original issues remain unresolved—enough to potentially affect the Nevada election results. Those issues are identified below.

- It is reckless for a state to mail ballot applications to everyone on the registration lists. Nevada did not do that. Instead, it mailed the actual ballots (not just applications) to everyone on the registration lists. And they did not really do it because of COVID. How do we know? Because Nevada enshrined the "emergency legislation" into the Code permanently—after the election. As far as I am concerned, the Nevada state administrators and legislators will be, effectively, conspirators in any abusive ballot harvesting schemes that are uncovered. (And those schemes are a certainty.)

- Nevada obviously has out-of-date voter registration lists, with the names of many people who have moved or died. People have complained to newspapers of piles of ballots strewn near apartment buildings and on pavement. A mail carrier complained, "[T]hey're not secured at all and there are thousands of them just sitting here? This just seems fraudulent to me." This complete breakdown of internal control over ballots disqualifies the results of any close election—and this was a close election.

- Nevada's signature testing law makes it difficult to reject signatures, and the informal test performed by Victor Joecks, a Las Vegas Review-Journal columnist, proves the point. In his test, eight of nine phony signatures were accepted.

- It appears that there were at least 4,000 votes from non-citizens and close to 2,500 who permanently changed address (from Nevada) prior to the election. The number of non-citizen voters could be much larger.

- There has been no evaluation of the 31,643 mail-in voters who registered with questionable identification. They were "ID-flagged" because all or part of their identifications (e.g., names, birthdates, or drivers licenses) did not match the records of the Department of Motor Vehicles. We know that some of them were told to use out-of-state identification, which is unlawful. Thousands of these people could be citizens of neighboring states, or phantoms who do not really exist.

- There has not been a satisfactory resolution of the 42,284 (or 21,142) voters who supposedly voted twice. With regard to 18,314 of those voters, the Secretary of State did not even rule out a violation. She merely said there is a "significantly lower chance" that they voted twice. Speaking as an auditor, that simply is not good enough.

- With regard to 15,170 voters with out-of-state mailing addresses, it appears there was no analysis whatever.

- The Secretary of State must press the federal government on its investigation of financial inducements paid to Native Americans for voting. Even if this cannot be resolved for the 2020 election, it requires resolution for future elections. Also, if the Biden campaign may have participated in providing inducements for voting, it should be investigated.

- There is a dispute concerning the number of dead people who voted. Secretary Cegavske says the number is 10, while the Trump team claimed the number is 1,506. The Secretary of State needs to present a workpaper supporting her number.

- It appears that no one has explained why two Clark County technical employees separately reported that machine totals were changing (somehow) in the middle of night. Those credible reports should have delayed certification until a serious audit was performed.

The issues cited above produce uncertainty with regard to thousands of votes in amounts that exceed Biden's ostensible victory. These matters should be resolved by means of a comprehensive professional and independent audit. A decision to affirm or rescind the certification should be made, based on the results of the audit.

AT A MINIMUM, THESE AREAS OF EXAMINATION ARE NEEDED.

1. As noted on page 164, Nevada's election law was severely weakened by the legalization of mail-in ballots (not just applications) to all people on out-of-date registration lists, by the installation of drop boxes that have no security cameras, and by the legalization of ballot harvesting by unidentified and unregulated people who can be paid for their services—by the piece. Any state with those *ridiculous* election standards needs a serious, independent audit after *every* election.

2. The routine, post-election audits should include verification of signatures, testing of the paper used in the ballots, and verification of the *existence* of voters based on canvassing a sample of voters at their residences. In addition, competent cyber experts should analyze hard drives, data files, and Wi-Fi routers to ensure that no systems or files were hacked or otherwise altered.

3. The voter registration lists are out-of-date, and must be trimmed to include only recent, active voters.

4. A forensic examination of the voting machines should be made in view of the mysterious modification of vote totals in the middle of the night. Fluctuating vote totals may indicate that there was an internet connection between the machines and someone externally. Or, someone may have physically gained access to the machines. Were security cameras used to monitor the machines?

5. Secretary of State Cegavske needs to complete her evaluation. She left many issues unresolved, as noted on previous pages. Those issues involve vote totals that could alter the 2020 election results. Workpapers prepared by the Secretary of State should include these:
    a. What follow-up was performed with regard to the inducements given to Native Americans for voting? Secretary Cegavske said the issue was under investigation. What was the conclusion of that investigation?

b.   There were almost 2,500 people who permanently changed addresses with the Post Office more than thirty days prior to the election. A workpaper should be prepared to show the steps taken to verify the residency of each of the 2,500 people, as of Election Day.

c.   A workpaper is needed for the 31,643 voters who were "flagged" for having inadequate identification. What was the ultimate resolution for each of these voters?

d.   It was alleged that 42,284 people voted twice. Cegavske acknowledges that 18,314 people may have voted twice, although she feels there is a "lower chance" of that. A workpaper should be prepared, and should show the testing performed with regard to each of the 18,314 voters, and the ultimate determination for each. Another workpaper is needed to justify Cegavske's lowering of the total from 42,284 to just 18,314. If it is determined that some people deliberately voted twice, they should be prosecuted, as an example for voters in future elections.

e.   Cegavske said she did not analyze the 15,170 voters with out-of-state mailing addresses. A workpaper must be prepared.

f.   The Secretary of State claims that only ten "dead people" voted, while the Trump team came up with 1,506 dead voters. A reconciliation of these two disparate amounts is needed.

g.   The Secretary of State acknowledged that about 4,000 noncitizens might have voted, but she also said that federal law prevents her from demanding documentation from those (potential) noncitizens. However, Cegavske should demand that the federal government verify the citizenship of the 4,000 people identified. And, if the Biden administration refuses (likely), Nevada should file a legal complaint against the administration. The actual number of noncitizen voters could be vastly higher.

When these actions are concluded, it may be possible to *fairly determine the popular will of the people.*

9

PENNSYLVANIA

Allen: *"Get rid of the pads and the second scanners."*
Savage: *"We can't talk about it anymore."*
Allen: *"Why?"*
Savage: *"It's a felony."*

FRAUD VIGNETTES—CAUGHT ON VIDEO!

If you are certain there was no fraud in the 2020 election, there is a video you need to see. On that video, which was secretly recorded by an election contract worker (Regina Miller), you will see the alleged crimes of two Delaware County election workers: One is James P. Allen, the County Director of Elections, and the other is James Savage, Chief Custodian and Voting Machine Warehouse Supervisor. (See Figure 12.) They are discussing how they need to destroy and/or hide 2020 election information requested under Pennsylvania's "Right-To-Know" (RTK) laws. A link to the video is in the footnotes (assuming it hasn't been censored).[1]

---

1   Wendi Stauch Mahoney, "Stunning Election Fraud Allegedly Found in Delaware County, Pa," *Uncoverdc.com*, November 19, 2021, https://uncoverdc.com/2021/11/19/stunning-election-fraud-allegedly-found-in-delaware-county-pa/.

FIGURE 12 TWO MEN CAUGHT CHEATING IN DELAWARE COUNTY? (FROM WHISTLEBLOWER VIDEO RELEASED BY MARGOT CLEVELAND OF *THE FEDERALIST*).

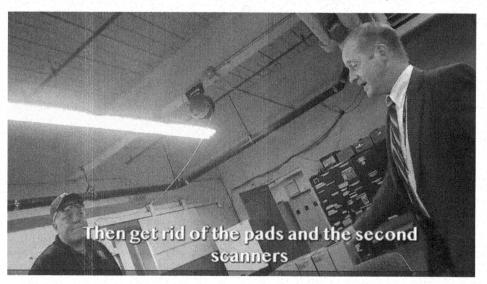

There is an additional video featuring two other men who are doing similar and equally destructive acts. The stars of that film are Thomas Gallagher, an attorney for Delaware County, and James Ziegelhoffer, who held the title, "Judge of Election" (sort of the head of poll workers). Based on their recorded actions and words, it is apparent that they are doing things they don't want you, or anyone else, to see.

In a third recording, even more damning evidence is revealed. In that one, a worker admits:

> There were six precincts in one location and all of the machines were, all of the scanners were, programmed to accept any ballot of those six precincts.[2]

Other secretly-recorded videos reveal missing chain of custody documentation for provisional ballots and for V drives (removable drives containing county election results).[3]

---

2   Margot Cleveland, "Systemic Voting Issues in Pennsylvania County Even More Extensive than Previously Known," *Federalist*, February 15, 2022, https://thefederalist.com/2022/02/15/exclusive-systemic-voting-issues-in-pennsylvania-county-even-more-extensive-than-previously-known/.

3   Margot Cleveland, Whistleblower Videos Show Systemic Issues With Pennsylvania Elections," *Federalist*, February 7, 2022, https://thefederalist.com/2022/02/07/exclusive-whistleblower-videos-show-systemic-issues-with-pennsylvania-elections/.

It's smoking gun video evidence that has been available for a long time, but I bet many or most Americans have no idea it is out there. Do you remember about the tree in the forest that falls but makes no sound—because no one is there to hear it? Well, it is a similar situation. A major scandal has little impact when there are no honest reporters to report it.

The Delaware County workers in the videos, and many other Delaware County employees, are now defendants in a civil case that was filed on November 18, 2021 by Ruth Moton and myriad others. In addition to the rising film stars, defendants include the former Pennsylvania Secretary of State, Kathy Boockvar, and at least a dozen other government employees.

The introduction to the case states:

> Defendants intentionally and fraudulently conspired to destroy, delete, secrete, and hide November 3, 2020, election law violations in Delaware County, which the Defendants also conspired to commit and did commit while carrying out the November 3, 2020, election.[4]

Midway through the complaint, the broader objectives of the illegal actions are stated succinctly. The actions were taken:

> to prevent the discovery of the fraudulent results of the November 3, 2020 election, and the violation of various state and federal election laws.[5]

District Attorney announces investigation

In November 2021, Delaware County District Attorney Jack Stollsteimer announced an investigation into the videos, which appear to show blatant destruction of election records and equipment. In May 2022, Stollsteimer closed the case without taking further action. The plaintiffs in the civil case filed a 21-page response to the District Attorney, alleging that he had conducted a "sham investigation." Based upon the videos, that appears likely.

In any event, it is not the purpose of this book to dwell on any specific example of illegality or fraud. I don't know how much trouble these video stars are in, and I don't know what impact their alleged illegal acts had on the vote totals. I have heard, however, that the overwhelmingly Democrat County of Delaware was the very last county

---

4   Ruth Moton v. Former Secretary of State Kathy Boockvar, Case 2021 (Court of Common Pleas for Delaware County), Complaint, Introduction.

5   Ruth Moton v. Former Secretary of State Kathy Boockvar, ¶118.

in Pennsylvania to report its vote totals. Before it reported those results, Trump was winning the state.

This scandal is interesting for a couple of other reasons. First, it is amusing that one of the video characters, James Savage, had just filed a lawsuit against Donald J. Trump, alleging that Trump made malicious and defamatory statements and insinuations about him. I don't imagine his video performance will help his case against Trump![6]

The other point of interest is a little skirmish that took place in the summer of 2021 between former Attorney General William Barr and former U.S. Attorney in Philadelphia, William McSwain. The former U.S. Attorney in Philadelphia wrote a friendly letter to Donald Trump, seeking his endorsement in the Pennsylvania governor's race. (McSwain was a gubernatorial candidate.) In his letter, McSwain mentioned that he had wanted to investigate some possible Pennsylvania fraud, but had been blocked by Barr. I wonder if the fraud in Delaware County is what he had in mind, or was it Jesse Morgan's missing trailer? (See page 188.)

McSwain's letter enraged the former president, and it angered William Barr. The former Attorney General (AG) wasted no time getting an interview with Politico, in which he declared that McSwain's letter "is written to make it seem like I gave him [McSwain] a directive. I never told him not to investigate anything."[7]

It is hard to say which man is telling the truth. The general impression I have is that neither man is completely trustworthy.

The two key elements for massive voter fraud

Many attorneys, even those who are prosecutors, lack the experience required to detect and assess certain types of white-collar crime, and this may be true of William Barr. In an interview with Jonathan Karl in the summer of 2021, Barr said: "Any issue posed by a computer error or malicious software intrusion . . . would have shown up in recounts of the paper ballots produced at the time of voting."[8] That statement is quite naïve, and I hope you understand, before finishing this book, that it is very easy to cheat in an election without detection—even where there are paper ballots in addition to computer records.

6 Alex Rose, "Delco election official sues former president Donald Trump, supporters for defamation," *Delaware County Daily Times*, November 4, 2021, https://www.delcotimes.com/2021/11/04/delco-election-official-sues-trump-supporters-for-defamation/.

7 Josh Gerstein, "Barr shoots down former prosecutor's election-fraud claims," *Politico*, July 13, 2021, https://www.politico.com/news/2021/07/13/barr-election-fraud-claims-499519.

8 John Bowden, "William Barr thought Trump's election fraud claims were 'bull***'," new book reveals," *Yahoo News*, June 27, 2021, https://news.yahoo.com/william-barr-thought-trump-election-193414404.html.

There are only two ingredients needed to produce massive and nearly undetectable election fraud. We did not have those ingredients a few years ago, but we have them now. For almost undetectable fraud you just need:

1. Some sort of real-time voter turnout surveillance system. The surveillance is essential. Without it, a fraudster could end up putting more ballots in a precinct than the number of registered voters. That would give the scheme away. The surveillance can be done high-tech, via internet hacking. It also can be done as it was in Wisconsin. There, an election official printed voter turnout reports every night and sent them to a political operative—an ex-Obama man to be specific. That story is on page 222.

2. The second required element is lots and lots of harvested ballots. A harvested ballot is the real deal. It is a genuine ballot, and it is undetectable if the election officials don't carefully check signatures (as was the case in Pennsylvania, Michigan, Arizona, Georgia, and other states), and if the drop boxes are unmonitored (which was also the case in most states).

If you'd like to hear the thoughts of a real and highly experienced vote harvester (in an anonymous interview with the *New York Post*) please go to page 33. One of his interesting comments has to do with mail carriers. Some of them cooperate with harvesters, and some of them work directly in harvesting "work crews." On the other hand, some postal workers are whistleblowers. They try to sound the alarm when there is corruption at the Post Office. Here is the story of a postal whistleblower.

THE RICHARD HOPKINS—PROJECT VERITAS SAGA

I am not scaring you. But I am scaring you.

—RUSSELL STRASSER, USPS OFFICE OF IG

Shortly after the election, a Pennsylvania mail carrier named Richard Hopkins claimed "he had heard [Erie Postmaster Robert] Weisenbach and another supervisor discussing the back-dating of mail-in ballots that arrived after Election Day." Presumably, the purpose of the illegal act was to make the ballots appear qualified for the election.[9]

---

9   Ed Palattella, "Free speech or libel? Erie postmaster, Project Veritas face off in court over election claims," *Goerie News*, January 27, 2022, https://www.goerie.com/story/news/2022/01/28/free-speech-case-erie-postmaster-project-veritas-james-okeefe-richard-hopkins/6632611001/.

Hopkins's claims were made to and reported by Project Veritas (PV), the conservative undercover reporters. Weisenbach and other Post Office bigwigs denied the claims, and Hopkins was suspended without pay for placing "the reputation of the U.S. Postal Service in harm's way [not something easy to do]."[10] When asked why Weisenbach wanted the ballots backdated, Hopkins said, "He's actually a Trump hater."[11]

The mailman was grilled for four hours by federal agents (without an attorney, according to PV), after which time investigators claimed Hopkins recanted his allegations. Hopkins immediately and emphatically denied recanting his allegations in a video on YouTube.[12]

Hopkins was also intimidated (allegedly) by Russell Strasser, an employee of the Postal Service Inspector General's office. The conversation was recorded by Project Veritas, and can be heard on NTD News Today, at the link in the footnote.[13]

In April of 2021, Hopkins resigned from his employment, and the Erie Postmaster filed suit against Project Veritas and Hopkins for defamation, a claim that was strongly denied by PV and Hopkins. As of July 2022, the case was still winding its way through the courts.

JESSE MORGAN'S DISAPPEARING TRACTOR TRAILER
The next day it just got weirder.

—JESSE MORGAN, TRUCK DRIVER AND USPS CONTRACTOR

Here is another Post Office story: an interesting one that involves a lot of ballots. It's the story of Jesse Morgan, a man who drove tractor trailer rigs for the U.S. Postal Service. He claims that he took hundreds of thousands of completed ballots from New York State to Pennsylvania, was given strange instructions by Postal authorities, and then his truck disappeared—with the ballots.

Morgan told his story at an Arlington, Virginia, press conference, hosted by The Amistad Project of the Thomas More Society (edited for brevity):[14]

---

10   Kevin Flowers, "Postal Service investigators: No evidence of mail ballot fraud in Erie," *Erie Times-News*, March 18, 2021, https://www.goerie.com/story/news/local/2021/03/18/richard-hopkins-erie-mail-ballot-probe-postal-service-finds-no-fraud-investigation/4746818001/.

11   Ed Palattella, "Free speech or libel? Erie postmaster, Project Veritas face off in court over election claims."

12   Staff, "USPS Pennsylvania Whistleblower: 'I Did Not Recant,'" *NTD News Today*, November 12, 2020, https://www.ntd.com/usps-pennsylvania-whistleblower-i-did-not-recant_527272.html.

13   Ibid.

14   Staff, "What Happened to Jesse Morgan's Trailer," *Baltimore Post-Examiner*, December 3, 2020, https://baltimorepostexaminer.com/what-happened-to-jesse-morgan-trailer/2020/12/03.

- "I drive a tractor trailer (subcontractor) for U.S. Postal Service."

- "On October 21st, when I arrived for my usual route in Bethpage, New York, the expediter [said] 'Hey, you've got ballots today.' 'Someone really wants their ballot to count.'"

[Morgan saw twenty-four large trays of ballots (called "Gaylords"), containing as many as 288,000 completed ballots, in his estimation.]

- "At Bethpage, I was first loaded with two tall Gaylords that had mixed mail pieces bound for Lancaster. . . . The remainder of the truck was loaded with completed ballots bound for Harrisburg. I then drove to Harrisburg with the ballots."

- "I wasn't allowed to off-load."

- "After waiting six hours, I went inside to figure out what's going on. I was told to wait for the transportation supervisor."

- "Sixteen months I've been doing this, I haven't ever talked to the transportation supervisor for United States Postal Service."

- "The supervisor told me to drive to Lancaster without being unloaded in Harrisburg. This made no sense to me." [Author's note: Perhaps it made no sense because the Harrisburg load was put in the truck after the Lancaster load. Would it be blocking the Lancaster load?]

- "I wanted my ticket. A ticket is always provided to a driver. . .That proves you are there."

- "I wanted my late slip, too, because I wanted to be paid for sitting in that yard for six hours."

- "The transportation supervisor refused to give me a ticket and told me to leave. I then demanded he give me a late slip. . . . He refused to give me that too."

- "He was kind of rude and wouldn't explain anything to me. He just told me to go Lancaster."

- "I then drove to Lancaster, unhooked my trailer in its normal place and then drove my truck to where I always park it in a nearby a lot."

The trailer and ballots disappear

- "The next day it just got weirder. I went to hook up to my trailer and my trailer was gone. Not there no more."

- "What happened on October 21 was a series of unusual events that cannot be coincidence. I know I saw ballots with the return addresses filled out—thousands of them—thousands loaded onto my trailer in New York and headed for Pennsylvania."

- "But as things became weirder, I got to thinking and wondered why I was driving completed ballots from New York to Pennsylvania. I didn't know why, so I decided to speak up. And that's what I'm doing today."

Mainstream media fact-checked this story by warning readers about the Amistad Project. It's a *conservative* organization, you know, and it is headed by Phill Kline, who used to investigate abortion clinics. Next, the fact-checkers noted that it is normal for some Pennsylvania residents, such as students, to vote from out-of-state. (That is true, of course, but is it normal to have their mail transported in a trailer that disappears?) Finally, the fact checkers pointed out that every ballot in Pennsylvania is matched to a voter, so it would be impossible to have thousands of illegal ballots in the system. Now that is the point I really wish to address.

Is this the reason Pennsylvania's ballots exceed the number of voters?
You see, this missing truck story meshes perfectly with another unexplained phenomenon. A little later in this section you will see that, shortly after the election, *Pennsylvania could not identify a voter for each ballot cast.* When the election was certified there were 202,000 more ballots than voters in the Commonwealth. For that reason, the election certification may have been illegal under Pennsylvania law.

Presently, the 202,000 number has been whittled down somewhat, but the excess of ballots over voters is still a huge number, and it still exceeds Biden's winning margin. See page 197 for additional explanation.

But, back to our story. In a September 2021 interview, Phill Kline said that he found Jesse Morgan to be credible, based on his own preliminary investigation. Kline still doesn't know what happened to the trailer and ballots, and he continues to investigate.[15]

Where is the case today?

A Pennsylvania attorney, Tom King, claims he has been involved in the case, and has tried to get information released:

> I was involved in that case and we worked directly with the US Attorney Bill McSwain who is now a candidate for governor. . . . We got the truck driver over to the FBI offices in DC and to date we have met nothing but resistance from the postal authorities to release the report done by the postal police and the FBI. We're close to getting it but that's still unresolved as I speak to you today [in April 2022].[16]

Attorney King says he is still in touch with Jesse Morgan, who reports that the Postal authorities and the FBI have yet to even interview certain people about this incident. Have patience, Jesse: It's only been two years.

As for transparency, it may take a while to find out what happened. I made a FOIA request of the U.S. Postal Service, but my request was denied because releasing this information "could expose witnesses, victims, subjects, and law enforcement personnel to harassment and intimidation."

Perhaps Rod Serling knows where we might find the missing trailer . . . and ballots.

275,000 ILLEGALLY HARVESTED BALLOTS

As noted, an organization with the name, True the Vote (TTV) matched cell phone "ping" data with video images (where available) to detect and map-out ballot harvesting operations. In the movie, *2,000 Mules*, TTV estimated that 1,150 "mules" visited forty-five drop boxes and delivered between 210,000 and 275,000 illegally harvested ballots in the Commonwealth. This appears to be a credible allegation, but so far there is no indication of investigation by the Pennsylvania Attorney General, Josh Shapiro, or by the U.S. Attorney General, Merrick Garland. Of course, 275,000 (or 210,000) disqualified ballots would invalidate the certification of the election.

TTV and this multistate harvesting scheme are discussed in more detail on page 36.

---

15   Jim Hoft, "A conversation with Amistad Project Director Phill Kline: The investigation of the mysterious USPS Truckloads of ballots continues," *Gateway Pundit*, September 14, 2021, https://www.thegatewaypundit.com/2021/09/conversation-amistad-project-director-phill-kline-investigation-mysterious-usps-truckloads-ballots-continues/.

16   Joe Hoft, "US Postal Service Refuses to Release Investigative Report on Whistleblower Truck Driver Who Hauled 288,000 Suspicious Ballots Across State Lines Before 2020 Election," *Gateway Pundit*, April 1, 2022, https://www.thegatewaypundit.com/2022/04/breaking-exclusive-us-postal-service-withholding-investigative-report-whistleblower-truck-driver-hauled-288000-suspicious-ballots-across-state-lines-2020-election/.

THE PRE-ELECTION "ACT 77" LEGAL BATTLE

It might be fair to say that Donald Trump already lost the Pennsylvania election before voting began. If so, he lost it in the chambers of the Pennsylvania Congress, in the offices of the Board of Elections, and in various Commonwealth courtrooms. Here are some of the more significant legislative, administrative, and judicial hurdles faced by Trump.

In 2019, the Pennsylvania legislature passed Act 77, which made significant changes to election procedures, commencing with the presidential primary election in April 2020. No longer would voters need a good reason to vote by mail, although they would still need to apply. Ballot harvesting became legal, within tight limits. If a voter had a long-term disability, he or she could request to be put onto a permanent absentee voting list (periodic applications would no longer be required.)

Straight party voting was eliminated. A voter could still vote for candidates of one party, but he/she could not do it all at once with one button. Ballot counting would no longer be done at the separate polling places. Instead, ballots would be counted centrally, at the location of the county board of elections.[17]

Act 77 would turn out to be a disaster for Republicans but, to a large extent, it was a disaster of their own making. In the book, Rigged, Mollie Hemingway summaries the GOP problem:

> The Republican Party was not in any way prepared for what hit it. The Republicans in the legislature were thrilled to get rid of straight party voting that they thought helped Democrats, and they didn't put much thought into growing integrity problems associated with mail-in-voting. GOP chairman Val DiGiorgio resigned in disgrace months prior to the passing of the [Act 77] legislation in a sexting scandal. Election integrity was clearly not his focus at the time.[18]

Democrats sue one of their own

Although the Democratic Party liked many elements of Act 77, it did not like all of them, so the party went to court to file a petition for review. Technically, it was a Democrat versus Democrat case because the review was filed against the Secretary of Elections, Kathy Boockvar, a Democrat.[19] However, Petitioner and Respondent were actually on

---

17   "Act 77 Changes to the Election Code," Pennsylvania Department of State, 2019, accessed December 15, 2021, https://berksweb.com/wtf/Act%2077%20-%20Election%20Reform%20Bill%20summary.pdf.

18   Mollie Hemingway, *Rigged* (Washington DC: Regnery, 2021), 254.

19   Pennsylvania Democratic Party v. Kathy Boockvar, 133 MM 2020 (Supreme Court of Pennsylvania Middle District), September 8, 2020.

the same side. Indeed, Boockvar helped the cause by requesting the Supreme Court of Pennsylvania to exert "extraordinary jurisdiction" over the claims of the Party.[20]

By this time, the presidential election was a mere three months away, and it was unusual for a judicial review so close to an election. However, the Democrat-leaning Pennsylvania Supreme Court took the case and issued a split decision ruling, mostly favorable to the Democratic Party. It allowed the unlimited use of drop boxes, and it extended by three days the deadline for the receipt of ballots (and even for the filing of ballots as long as there was no evidence of post-election filing). Also, the court ratified the favored position of Democrats that limited the number of poll watchers.

The case was not completely a win for the Democrats. The high court did not agree that it was okay for voters to send in ballots without envelopes (so-called naked ballots), and it did not agree that election officials could lawfully complete ballots and contact information for voters.[21]

THE GREEN PARTY GETS THE BOOT

Just like in Wisconsin, the high court removed the Green Party from the ballot, citing a technical deficiency in the Party's filing. This was a helpful ruling in the eyes of Democrats, who felt that the Green Party had taken nearly 50,000 votes from Hillary Clinton in 2016. The two Republicans on the high court agreed that the Green Party had filing defects, but they felt those could be remedied retroactively.[22]

ZUCKERBERG'S DROP BOXES

In October 2020, a group called the Pennsylvania Voters Alliance, along with fourteen individual voters, filed a civil rights action in the Middle District of Pennsylvania to enjoin the City of Philadelphia and Centre County and Delaware County from receiving $10 million from The Center for Technology and Civic Life (Zuckerberg's CTCL organization) to install no fewer than 800 drop boxes in (primarily) Democrat-leaning areas of Philadelphia. The court dismissed the case for lack of standing.[23] That was another blow to the Trump re-election effort.

---

20   "State Court Docket Watch: Pennsylvania Democratic Party v. Boockvar," *Federalist Society*, November 5, 2020, https://fedsoc.org/commentary/publications/PADemvBoockvar2020#_ftn5.

21   Pennsylvania Democratic Party v. Kathy Boockvar, 62–63.

22   Sam Gringlas, "Pennsylvania Supreme Court Extends Vote By Mail Deadline, Allows Drop Boxes," *National Public Radio*, September 17, 2020, https://www.npr.org/2020/09/17/914160122/pennsylvania-supreme-court-extends-vote-by-mail-deadline-allows-drop-boxes.

23   Pennsylvania Voters Alliance v. Centre County, et al., 4:20-cv-01761 (United States District Court for the Middles District of Pennsylvania), Memorandum Opinion.

A regulation that is not enforced

The Capital Research Organization has studied the Center for Tech and Civic Life (CTCL) and its spending patterns in various states. This was not easy because CTCL "refuses to reveal where its hundreds of millions went in the last election." According to Scott Walter, President of Capital Research Organization, CTCL's spending in Pennsylvania heavily favored Democrats in the last election, just as it did in every other state. In testimony before a Pennsylvania House Committee, Walter stated: "Trump counties received an average of $0.59 per capita, while Biden counties averaged $2.93 per capita—over five times more funding per capita."[24]

As explained on page 64, this disparate political treatment appears to violate the regulations pertaining to CTCL's tax exempt status under IRC 501(c)(3) but, with Democratic administrations in both Pennsylvania and Washington, DC, it is unlikely that CTCL will face legal consequences.

A SHAMEFUL RULING REGARDING SIGNATURES

I said this is an objective book, but that does not mean I will let myself become stupid. At midnight on an early Sunday in October, Secretary of State Kathy Boockvar asked the Commonwealth's high court to back her up in a dispute with candidate Donald Trump. Boockvar felt that all mail-in ballots should be accepted and counted, even if the signatures on them did not match the registration signatures. Naturally, Trump objected.

Incredibly, the high court agreed with Boockvar. Although ballot transmittal documentation has to be signed, there is no signature *matching* requirement. Indeed, the high court ruled that signature matching could not be used to reject a ballot. (I must admit, however, that the signatures do make pretty decorations on the ballot envelopes.)[25]

Possibly you think that the wise justices on the Pennsylvania high court made this ruling because signatures are not really needed—because Pennsylvania requires the mail-in ballot to be accompanied by other forms of identification. No, that is not so. When a voter returns his/her ballot there is no required identification other than the signature—which was not used for the 2020 election!

---

24 Scott Walter, "Should Pennsylvania's Elections be Privatized," *Capital Research Organization*, April 15, 2021, https://capitalresearch.org/article/should-pennsylvanias-elections-be-privatized/.

25 Angela Couloumbis, "Counties cannot reject mail ballots because of mismatched signatures, Pa. Supreme Court rules," *Philadelphia Inquirer*, October 23, 2020, https://www.inquirer.com/politics/election/spl/pa-mail-ballot-signature-match-supreme-court-ruling-20201023.html.

PENNSYLVANIA COURTS LET PHILLY KEEP TRUMP OBSERVERS FAR AWAY

When counting began on November 3, Republican watchers and challengers in Philadelphia were kept at least fifteen to eighteen feet away, and they complained that it was impossible to observe the processing of ballots. One such observer, attorney Jeremy Mercer, said he was "not able to discern whether, if there is a secrecy envelope, whether the secrecy envelope has any markings on it. . .[or] what, if anything, is being pulled out."

For some observers it was even worse. "They will not allow us within 30 to 100 feet to supervise the ballots being counted," said poll watcher Brian McCafferty, who said he is a registered Democrat.[26]

Trump's team went to court, but a Philadelphia judge ruled that the distances were reasonable. Trump's people then went to a Commonwealth court, where Judge Christine Fizzano Cannon ruled that observers should be allowed within six feet of the tables.[27] But they were already two days into counting, and the Philadelphia Sheriff simply refused to enforce the judge's ruling.[28]

Democrats joined the City of Philadelphia in its quest to have the Pennsylvania Supreme Court overrule Judge Fizzano Cannon, which it did in a 5 to 2 (Democrat to Republican) ruling. Thereafter, Republicans in Philadelphia had to stay fifteen to eighteen feet away, and their ability to effectively view the process of ballot processing was eliminated.[29]

This was an absurd Supreme Court ruling. Aside from the fact that meaningful observation is impossible from fifteen to eighteen feet away, there is the issue of disparate treatment of Pennsylvania citizens. Effectively, the court ruled that, in the Democratic stronghold of Philadelphia there would be no observation of ballot processing, while in other parts of Pennsylvania (mostly Republican parts) there would be close observation of ballot processing.

26   Cristina Laila, "'I can't believe what I'm seeing – This is a coup,'" *Gateway Pundit*, November 5, 2020, https://www.thegatewaypundit.com/2020/11/cant-believe-seeing-coup-registered-democrat-poll-watcher-details-corruption-philly-vote-counting-center-video/.

27   Mosk, Siegel and Hosenball, "Pennsylvania judge permits campaign observers up-close view of ballot count after Trump complaint," *ABC News Radio*, November 5, 2020, http://abcnewsradioonline.com/politics-news/pennsylvania-judge-permits-campaign-observers-up-close-view.html.

28   Ivan Pentchoukov, "Philadelphia Sheriff Not Enforcing Court Order on Poll Observers, Trump Campaign Says," *Epoch Times*, November 5, 2020, https://www.theepochtimes.com/philadelphia-sheriff-not-enforcing-court-order-on-poll-observers-trump-campaign-says_3567159.html.

29   Alexandra Jones and Jack Rodgers, "Pennsylvania High Court Rules Against Trump in Poll Watchers Case," *Courthouse News Service*, November 17, 2020, https://www.courthousenews.com/pennsylvania-high-court-rules-against-trump-in-poll-watchers-case/.

WHAT HAPPENS WHEN JUDGES IGNORE THE LAW?

In Pennsylvania, the Democrat-controlled City of Philadelphia, its Democrat Sheriff, and the five Democrat Justices on the Commonwealth Supreme Court made decisions that seem partisan and very hard to justify, or even to understand. Those decisions significantly degraded election internal control.

There is confusion regarding the role of judges, justices, and the legal system generally, in relation to the unique process for electing U.S. presidents. Under one theory (the "independent state legislature" doctrine), the U.S. Constitution gives state legislatures plenary authority to certify the election, and those legislatures can even ignore state court decisions that seem to undermine election law.

This is an untested area of the law and the Constitution; however, there may soon be clarity. On the last day of the Supreme Court's 2021-2022 term, it announced that it would hear a case from North Carolina that concerns the manner in which states set the rules for federal elections. It is possible that the Court will use that case to consider the merits of the independent state legislature doctrine. Arguments are expected in the fall of 2022, with a ruling in the summer of 2023.

NO RELIEF IN FEDERAL COURTS

The Trump team found no judicial relief in Pennsylvania courts so they went to federal district court. They had multiple claims that included disparate treatment of voters (depending upon where they lived) and lack of administrative transparency. They claimed that 680,000 absentee ballots in two counties were processed without giving Republican observers meaningful opportunity to watch the process. (As noted, they had to stay fifteen to eighteen feet away.) Trump's people also complained that, in Democrat counties, mail-in ballots were pre-canvassed, and voters were given opportunities to fix deficient ballots (in violation of law). No such opportunity was given to voters in Republican counties. The legal case failed both in district court and upon appeal to the third circuit court (lack of standing).[30]

TRUMP FINALLY WINS IN COMMONWEALTH
COURT, AND THEN HE LOSES AGAIN

Subsequently, U.S. Representative Mike Kelly, and a few other Republican candidates who participated in the 2020 election, went to Commonwealth court, where they argued a case of great importance to the Trump team. The Kelly ensemble asserted that the law passed a year earlier, known as Act 77, was unconstitutional because the

---

30   Donald J. Trump for President, Inc. v. Kathy Boockvar, 4:20-cv-02078-MWB (United States District Court for Middle District of Pennsylvania, 2020), Verified Complaint for Declaratory and Injunctive Relief.

absentee provision (legalizing mail-in ballots) was not approved in accordance with the Pennsylvania constitution. The provisions of the Act, which was signed into law, are discussed on page 192.

On November 28, Commonwealth Judge Patricia McCullough issued an order preventing the Commonwealth from certifying the election until the Trump's case could be heard. She ruled that Act 77 was likely unconstitutional, and the Trump team would probably prevail in their challenge to it.[31] However, the Pennsylvania Supreme Court threw out the Kelly case, unanimously ruling that the challenge to Act 77 was filed too late (laches).[32] At first glance, the ruling seems reasonable: Kelly and the other Republicans should have filed their complaint a year earlier, when the law was passed. However, it is not that simple, as noted by Senator Ted Cruz:

> [T]he plaintiffs point out that the Pennsylvania Supreme Court has also held that plaintiffs don't have standing to challenge an election law until after the election, meaning that the court effectively put them in a Catch-22: Before the election they lacked standing; after the election, they've delayed too long. The result of the court's gamesmanship is that a facially unconstitutional election law can never be judicially challenged.[33]

202,377 MORE BALLOTS THAN VOTERS MADE THE CERTIFICATION ILLEGAL

On November 24, 2020, the Pennsylvania Secretary of the Commonwealth, Kathy Boockvar, certified Pennsylvania's election. On its face, the certification was illegal under commonwealth law because the Secretary had not investigated a very large excess of ballots cast over the number of participating voters. At that point in time there were 202,377 more ballots cast than the number of people who actually voted, according to SURE (the statewide listing of registered voters who actually voted).[34] In fact, this was one of several reasons some Republican legislators wanted Vice President Mike Pence

---

31 "Judge rules pro-Trump case established a 'likelihood to succeed on the merits' in Pennsylvania," *BPR Business & Politics*, November 28, 2020, https://www.bizpacreview.com/2020/11/28/judge-rules-trumps-case-established-a-likelihood-to-succeed-on-the-merits-in-pennsylvania-1000222/.

32 Staff, "Pa. Supreme Court throws out lawsuit seeking to invalidate mail-in ballots and overturn Biden's win," *WITF*, November 28, 2020, https://www.witf.org/2020/11/28/pa-supreme-court-throws-out-lawsuit-seeking-to-invalidate-mail-in-ballots-and-overturn-bidens-win/.

33 "Mike Kelly, US Congressman, et al., v. Commonwealth of Pennsylvania, et al.," The Center to Protect Voters and their Voices of the ACU, No. 620 MD 2020, https://elections.rootshq.net/case/kelly-v-pennsylvania/.

34 Pennsylvania State Representative Russ Diamond, "Numbers Don't Add Up, Certification of Presidential Results Premature and In Error," repdiamond.com, December 28, 2020, http://www.repdiamond.com/News/18754/Latest-News/PA-Lawmakers-Numbers-Don.

to delay counting the electoral votes on January 6, 2021. They knew that there was a 202,377 discrepancy, and they wanted time to resolve it.

On December 28, 2020 (well-before the January 6th debacle), Pennsylvania Representative Frank Ryan issued a statement titled: "Numbers Don't Add Up, Certification of Presidential Results Premature and in Error."

The lengthy statement reflected the views of Ryan and at least sixteen other Pennsylvania legislators. Here are a couple of excerpts:

> We were already concerned with the actions of the Supreme Court of Pennsylvania, the Executive branch, and election official in certain counties contravening and undermining the Pennsylvania Election Code by eliminating signature verification, postmarks, and due dates while allowing the proliferation of drop boxes with questionable security measures and the unauthorized curing of ballots, as well as the questionable treatment of poll watchers. . . .
>
> However, we are now seeing discrepancies on the retail level . . . . These findings call into question the accuracy of the SURE system. . . .
>
> *These numbers just don't add up, and the alleged certification of Pennsylvania's presidential election results was absolutely premature, unconfirmed, and in error* [emphasis added].[35]

A reading of Pennsylvania Code (25 PA. Stat. §3154) suggests that the Republicans had the law on their side:

> If. . . it shall appear that the total vote returned for any candidate or candidates . . . exceeds the total number of persons . . .who voted in said district. . .such excess shall be deemed a discrepancy and palpable error, and shall be investigated by the return board, and *no votes shall be recorded* from such district until such investigation shall be had . . ..[emphasis added].

In other words, if there is an unidentified excess of ballots cast over persons who voted, and it is of significant magnitude, you can't legally certify without an investigation. That is just common sense, right?

The counter-argument, which was made by Boockvar's spokesperson, Wanda Murren, was simply ridiculous. After insulting the GOP representatives for their "uninformed, lay analysis," Murren conceded, in a statement made *after* the certification:

---

35   Pennsylvania State Representative Russ Diamond, "Numbers Don't Add Up, Certification of Presidential Results Premature and In Error"

At this time there are still a few counties that have not completed uploading their vote histories to the SURE system. These counties, which included Philadelphia, Allegheny, Butler, and Cambria, would account for a significant number of voters.[36]

When Murren said the tardy counties "would account for a significant number of voters," she was being modest. Those counties have well over 2 million voters! How is it possible to certify an election when millions of vote histories have not yet been uploaded into the SURE system? And, what about the investigation required by Pa. Stat. §3154? . . . Details, details!

Well, the slow-poke counties have now submitted their voter information into the SURE system, and there no longer is a discrepancy of 202,377 votes, but it appears that the number of excess ballots still exceeds Biden's winning margin of 81,000 votes.

The Verity Vote analysis

Verity Vote (described on page 100) prepared a detailed analysis of the quantity of excess ballots over voters, and calculated the number to be 121,240, as of February 1, 2021. I reviewed the Verity Vote methodology, as outlined in its report, and discussed those results with Verity personnel. The logic seems to be sound.

To calculate the voter deficit, Verity converted the officially-reported total votes into total ballots by adjusting for write-in votes and over/under votes. Using information received via Right-to-Know requests, Verity determined that the SURE system's record of voters had increased after the election due to the receipt of 71,893 late ballots. Those late ballots increased the number of voters who voted (according to SURE) but not the number of ballots counted. Therefore, to determine the actual voter deficit it is necessary to adjust for the 71,893 amount.

There is one more complication. After Verity calculated the 121,240 voter deficit amount, the Secretary of the Commonwealth upwardly revised her estimate of the number of voters. That revision lowered the Verity calculation of the voter deficit to about 90,000—a result that remains larger than Biden's winning margin and large enough to call into question the legitimacy of the Pennsylvania certification.

In conclusion, it appears that the Pennsylvania certification was and is of questionable legality. In my judgment there is no auditor on earth who would certify these election results unless and until:

---

36   Daniel Payne, "Amid claims of unexplained ballots, Pennsylvania officials unsure how many voted in 2020," *Just the News*, December 30, 2020, https://justthenews.com/politics-policy/elections/nearly-two-months-after-election-pennsylvania-still-uncertain-how-many.

- The ballot versus voter discrepancy is investigated and explained

- There is an explanation for the tardy submissions to SURE made by the four identified counties.

- There is an explanation for all post-election adjustments made to voter totals and ballot totals.

(When documents are submitted months after they are due, it strongly suggests the possibility of error or corruption.)

POOR PROFESSOR MILLER

Dr. Steven Miller, a professor of mathematics at Williams College, probably knows what it feels like to be a professor in a Beijing university: Toe the line or get sent to a re-education camp. Miller was approached by Matt Braynard, a man who has much experience in surveys and canvassing, but not too much in statistics. Braynard had conducted a fairly large survey of Republican voters in Pennsylvania, and he asked Dr. Miller to analyze the results and reach some statistical conclusions. Miller did an analysis and issued a report. He estimated that there were between 89,397 and 98,801 ballots that may have been requested by someone other than the registered Republican or requested and returned by a Republican but not counted. That was an amount greater than Biden's winning vote margin.

All hell broke loose. Outraged teachers and students from academia, including his own college, expressed their disgust with Miller for doing something that could be used by the Trump team in its legal fight with the Biden forces. I imagine that Miller slept with one eye open for weeks.

Samuel Wolf, writing for The Williams Record, the student-run paper for Williams College, described the critical views of Miller's colleague, Richard DeVeaux, a statistics professor at Williams College:

DeVeaux described Miller's document as "completely without merit" and "both irresponsible and unethical."[37]

---

37   Samuel Wolf, "Professor Steven Miller issues legal statement suggesting PA ballot irregularities; conclusions repudiated by statisticians, political scientists," *The Williams Record*, November 25, 2020, https://williamsrecord.com/434506/news/professor-of-mathematics-steven-miller-issues-legal-statement-suggesting-ballot-irregularities-in-pa-conclusions-repudiated-by-statisticians-and-political-scientists/.

Miller was also "strongly criticized" by George Marcus, a political science professor at Williams College, and by Charles Stewart III, an MIT professor of political science. It is notable that Miller's statistics were not really the target of their ire:

> All three professionals found Miller's calculations themselves routine and uncontroversial, but took serious issue with Miller's assumption that the data that he analyzed was accurate and representative. They pointed to the fact that the survey's response rates were low, that the survey only reached out to registered Republicans and that voters often tell pollsters untrue statements on their voting history.[38]

I agree with the critics, but only to an extent. First, the sample size was plenty big enough—much larger than the many samples I have seen served up by college professors—especially ones in the area of political science.

Gambling in Casa Blanca

Miller's analysis would have been strengthened if Democrat respondents were in Braynard's survey results, but there are many published statistical studies that lack such controls. For example, how often have you read the results of a survey of women, where men were not asked comparable questions, as a control? It is always better to add as many control variables as possible, but let's not pretend Miller's work is unique in this regard.

The critics also said that people often tell pollsters untruthful things about their voting records, and I definitely agree with that. For this reason, I don't see the Miller analysis as strong evidence of fraud—just possible evidence. But again, I must comment about these high-minded professors who just discovered gambling in the Casablanca casino. There are probably hundreds of political polls and surveys conducted each year, and it is likely that some people lie or exaggerate in each one of them.

I suspect that, had Miller produced the very same findings in support of Biden, within days there would have been around—say, fifty-one political scientists and statisticians writing an Op-Ed in the *Washington Post*—supporting the high-quality work of Miller.

According to the Williams Record, "Miller did not recant," and he subsequently had additional conversations with Braynard that made him more confident in Braynard's methods. Miller did, however, apologize for a "lack of clarity and due diligence." I guess that apology might be enough to keep him out of the academic gulags!

---

38 Ibid.

SETH KESHEL'S VERY INTERESTING ANALYSES

Seth Keshel is a tall, articulate, and no-nonsense former U.S. military intelligence officer. He is also a statistical analyst who noticed some interesting election trends. Those trends don't prove anything conclusively, but they add to the risk that the election results might be wrong. His results should be considered when we assess the need for a comprehensive audit.

FIGURE 13: INCREASE IN NEW REGISTRATIONS FROM 2016 TO 2020

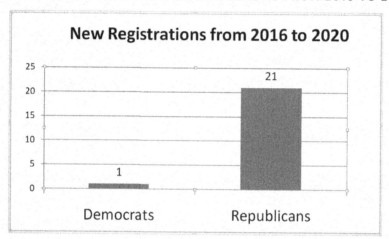

Figure 13 is a representation of the findings of Seth Keshel regarding the growth of new voter registrations in Pennsylvania Democrats and Republicans. Normally, a growth in the relative registration rate is predictive of a victory in the ensuing election. However, the normal trend did not hold up in 2020. Between 2016 and 2020, new voter registrations for Republicans increased much more than did Democrat registrations. In fact, there were more new GOP registrations by a factor of 21 to 1, according to Keshel. (Actually, the true ratio is closer to 23 to 1 according to the Pennsylvania Secretary of the Commonwealth.[39]) Nevertheless, Trump lost in Pennsylvania. Again, this is merely something to consider when we assess the validity of the election certification.[40]

---

39   Veronica W. Degraffenreid, "The Administration of Voter Registration in Pennsylvania," Secretary of the Commonwealth, June 2021, https://www.dos.pa.gov/VotingElections/OtherServicesEvents/VotingElectionStatistics/Documents/Annual%20Reports%20on%20Voter%20Registration/2020-Annual-Voter-Registration-Report.pdf.

40   Doug Wade, "Interview of Seth Keshel," *PureSocialTV*, January 1, 2021, https://www.youtube.com/watch?v=xXMW9VNMPT4.

"THREE EVERYDAY MOMS" SPRING INTO ACTION

After the election, it seemed that "something wasn't right" to three young Pennsylvania women, so they decided to do something about it. The three women, Toni Shuppe, Karen Taylor, and Jamie Sheffield, formed a group called Audit the Vote PA (ATVPA), with the goal of gaining support for a full forensic audit of the Pennsylvania 2020 presidential election. Among other activities, they launched a petition in support of the audit, and they began canvassing residents in several counties, to see if their survey responses jibed with the official Pennsylvania voting records. They didn't.

So far they have released complete results for a couple of counties: York and Lancaster. For those two counties, in combination, they knocked on almost 900 doors and were able to survey 462 respondents. The responses showed a 16.2 percent "phantom vote rate," with a margin of error of 3.34 percent (95 percent confidence). In other words, the estimated number of people who officially voted, *but did not know they voted*, was somewhere between 12.8 and 19.6 percent. This suggests the possibility of harvested mail-in ballots being stuffed into drop boxes or mail boxes.[41,42]

On March 28, 2022, the group released additional survey data for eight more counties. The total number of respondents for the eight additional counties was over 2,500. The lowest phantom voter percentage for any of the counties was 12 percent.

ATVPA is not a professional polling outfit; the respondents were not necessarily selected randomly, and we can assume that some respondents may have misunderstood the questions. Nevertheless, these percentages are of great concern when we consider that a phantom vote of just 3 percent could possibly change the outcome of the election.

Update
On May 5, 2022, Carter Walker, a journalist for Lancaster online, reported results from an analysis he'd performed of ATVPA's canvassing operation in Lancaster County. He had these general findings:[43]

- ATVPA sometimes relied on responses from people answering the door instead of the voters themselves. For example, a wife might answer for the husband, or vice versa.

---

41   "See the Data," *Audit the Vote PA*, accessed February 2, 2022, https://www.auditthevotepa.com/.

42   Toni Shuppe, "Canvassing Results," *Audit the Vote PA*, February 1, 2022, https://rumble.com/vtrrgt-canvassing-results-what-does-the-data-mean.html.

43   Carter Walker, "Audit the Vote gave us its canvassing data to check the results. It was riddled with errors," *Lancasteronline*, May 5, 2022, https://lancasteronline.com/news/politics/audit-the-vote-gave-us-its-canvassing-data-to-check-the-results-it-was-riddled/article_8f0a6c2a-cd6e-11ec-9f73-b3e07fd7b64b.html.

- ATVPA portrayed some answers as definitive, when the respondent was not entirely confident of his/her recollection.

- In most cases the canvasser did not bother to document whether the respondent lived in the home during the 2020 election.

- The sample selection was not representative of the county.

In addition, Walker visited eleven households where ATVPA identified specific anomalies of various types (concerning missing votes, phantom votes, or phantom registrations). From his article, it appears that four of the eleven "anomalies" were either classified in error or were questionable.

These appear to be legitimate criticisms, and provide helpful context to the ATVPA results.

THE ANALYSIS OF DR. DOUGLAS FRANK

As mentioned on page 248, and with regard to Arizona and Michigan, Dr. Douglas Frank uses a 6th order polynomial "key" to precisely predict the voter turnout, by age, for most or all counties in several states. After he did this for Pennsylvania counties, Dr. Frank reached this conclusion:

> The same algorithms are operating in Pennsylvania as in other states. . . . A machine algorithm is being used to harvest ballots at the precinct level, artificially control the number and proportion of ballots at the county level, and achieve a target outcome at the state level.[44]

These results seem to reinforce the findings of Audit the Vote PA, which found a huge number of people who voted, but did not know they had voted. However, I am not entirely convinced by Frank's interpretation of these results because he has also predicted accurately for a few non-swing states. He needs to explain why people would bother to manipulate election results in places where elections are not normally close. I tried to contact Dr. Frank to query him on this issue, but was unable to reach him. More information can be found on page 249.

---

44   Dr. Douglas Frank, "Pennsylvania Election Analysis," *ElectionFraud20.org.*, accessed on February 27, 2022, https://electionfraud20.org/dr-frank-reports/pennsylvania/.

OPEN ITEMS IN PROCESS

The trailer filled with ballots

We still don't know what happened to Jesse Morgan's trailer and the hundreds of thousands of ballots within it. It appears that the Biden administration is withholding the results of its investigation. See page 188.

Audit of the election is underway?

In September 2021, the Republican-controlled Pennsylvania Senate subpoenaed many election records held by the Secretary of the Commonwealth. In addition, the Senate retained a firm, Envoy Sage, LLC, to perform an audit of the 2020 election results. Pennsylvania's Attorney General, Josh Shapiro sued to block the Senate subpoena, claiming it had no legislative purpose and violated privacy laws by requesting sensitive voter information, such as drivers licenses and partial Social Security numbers.

In early January 2022, a Commonwealth court ruled that there was a valid legislative purpose for the Senate's subpoena, and the audit could proceed.[45] A few days later, the PA Supreme Court intervened to stay the lower court's ruling, until it reaches a final decision. In all likelihood, the audit is dead: another defeat for election transparency.

WAS THE CERTIFICATION OF THE PENNSYLVANIA ELECTION PREMATURE?

There are numerous election-related uncertainties in Pennsylvania. For that reason, certification of the Pennsylvania election was premature. Here are some specific areas of uncertainty, starting with legal decisions that increased the likelihood of fraudulent ballots and ballot processing errors.

- The Commonwealth Supreme Court allowed 800, unmanned "drop boxes" to be placed in the areas near Philadelphia, as required by the private financiers of the boxes—Mark Zuckerberg and spouse Priscilla Chan (via their organization, CTCL). If that seems OK to you, imagine the likely reaction were the Koch brothers to fund the placement of hundreds of drop boxes solely in areas that traditionally vote for Republicans. The Zuckerberg boxes do not necessarily invalidate the ballots within them, but they raise questions of election fairness and internal control over the ballots.

---

45 Anton Carillo, "Pennsylvania Senate's Investigation Of 2020 Election Results Moves Forward Despite Opposition Following Court Decision," *Christianity Daily*, January 13, 2022, https://www.christianitydaily.com/articles/14591/20220113/pennsylvania-senates-investigation-of-2020-election-results-moves-forward-despite-opposition-following-court-decision.htm.

- The Commonwealth Supreme Court agreed with the Democratic Party's request to limit the number of poll observers. Poll observers are an essential element of the election internal control system.

- Incredibly, the Commonwealth Supreme Court decided that the law requires the voter to sign the ballot envelope; however, election officials are prohibited from rejecting ballots that cannot be matched to registration records. Signatures are the only form of identification in Pennsylvania, so when this crazy ruling was announced it became an engraved invitation to fraudsters.

- After the election, Republicans complained that, in Philadelphia, they were prevented from getting close enough to observe the processing of ballots. A lower court agreed, and said they should be allowed to get as close as six feet from the processing tables. The Commonwealth Supreme Court stepped in to state that the observers can be kept fifteen to eighteen feet away, thus eliminating meaningful oversight of more than 600,000 ballots. Without that oversight, we should expect a much higher rate of ballot processing errors—unintentional and deliberate.

As noted on page 196, a state legislature's authority with regard to certification of a U.S. presidential election is unclear. Under one theory (accepted by a minority of scholars), legislative authority supersedes that of state administrators and state courts, especially when court decisions undermine the specific election laws created by the legislature.[46] If that legal theory is applicable, the Pennsylvania legislature's certification decision should be considered inappropriate on the basis of the legal decisions that undermined election laws. In addition, there are these factors that cast doubt on the certification decision:

- It appears that the Pennsylvania Secretary of the Commonwealth cannot or will not reconcile the total of voters to the total of ballots cast. The potential discrepancy is large enough (90,700) to invalidate the certification.

- To this very day, U.S. postal authorities refuse to disclose information about Jesse Morgan's trailer and the hundreds of thousands of ballots inside it. Transparency is required. This may be a Biden administration cover-up, and it may relate to the 90,700 excess ballots, mentioned in the first bullet point.

---

46   I don't believe that the U.S. Supreme Court has decided this issue.

- Volunteer canvassing efforts show a very large "phantom" vote (at least 12–17 percent). These amateur canvassing efforts may be flawed, but they should not be ignored. Rather, they should be expanded, and professional canvassers should be employed to obtain a clearer understanding of the problem.

- There are credible allegations of a large-scale ballot harvesting scheme in Pennsylvania and other states. The investigation involves cell phone "ping" technology, videos, and at least one whistleblower describing the operation in detail. The organization conducting the research, "True the Vote," estimates that there were about 275,000 illegal, harvested ballots in Pennsylvania. This claim needs to be thoroughly investigated, but probably won't be.

- There is an unresolved scandal, unraveling in Delaware County. We don't know if it impacted the overall vote totals but we do know that it allegedly involved the unlawful destruction of 2020 election data.

As noted, the Commonwealth Senate hired independent auditors who are supposed to review the 2020 election results, if they are not blocked from doing so by the Pennsylvania administration and by a very political Commonwealth Supreme Court. Let's hope that an audit is completed in a thorough and fair manner, without additional obstruction. The audit should address all of the issues listed above so that the election certification can be confirmed, or rescinded, based on complete and impartial information.

When these actions are concluded, it may be possible to *fairly determine the popular will of the people.*

10

WISCONSIN

"All machines in Green Bay were ESS machines and were connected to a secret, hidden Wi-Fi access point at the Grand Hyatt hotel."

—OFFICE OF SPECIAL COUNCIL, MARCH 1, 2022

BLOCKBUSTER REPORT FROM OFFICE OF SPECIAL COUNCIL

On March 1, 2022, the Office of Special Council (OSC), which was established in 2021 by the Wisconsin State Assembly, released a 136-page interim report on its investigation into several election related issues. It was not a complete and final report because, according to the OSC, State Administrators were angry and uncooperative. Special Council Mike Gableman noted:

> WEC and the State Attorney General have refused to cooperate with the Legislature's investigation and actively obstructed it. . . .
>
> [V]oting machine companies have refused to comply with the OSC's legislative subpoenas, and have provided no data.
>
> Despite this cover-up, or perhaps because of it, the OSC can still reach certain conclusions about the integrity of election administration in the state of Wisconsin, and we can still make baseline recommendations.[1]

Here is one of the OSC findings:

Outside operative has secret access to ballots, machines, and Wi-Fi
One municipality under investigation admitted to having its election machines connected to the internet on election night, and:

---

1   Office of Special Council, "Second Interim Investigative Report," Wisconsin State Assembly, March 1, 2022, 5,14,6, https://legis.wisconsin.gov/assembly/22/brandtjen/media/1552/osc-second-interim-report.pdf.

[A]ll machines in Green Bay were ESS machines and were connected to a secret, hidden Wi-Fi access point at the Grand Hyatt hotel, which was the location used by the City of Green Bay on the day of the 2020 Presidential election. The OSC discovered the Wi-Fi, machines, and ballots were controlled by a single individual who was not a government employee but an agent of a special interest group operating in Wisconsin.[2]

Please consider the gravity of having one person, representing a special interest group, secretly in control of the ballots, the Wi-Fi, and the election machines, via a secret access point at a nearby hotel. This is a major finding, and here is another one:

On Election Day, Spitzer-Rubenstein [a Democrat political operative from New York] had access to ballots and determined which ones would be counted or not counted. . . . Forty-seven boxes of ballots were expected to be delivered and apparently, according to Spitzer-Rubenstein's email, some of them were late but he decided that despite some of them being late, they were to be counted anyway because no one "challenged them."[3]

To my non-legal eyes, it appears that Spitzer-Rubenstein knowingly broke the law by processing ballots that he knew were late.

It is not clear that the special access given to Democrat operatives resulted in a huge change in votes (it might have), but in any event, this was corruption, pure and simple.

Nursing home scandal much bigger than we realized

The OSC also investigated reports of nursing home patients who were pressured into voting in the 2020 election. To guard against that kind of pressure, Wisconsin normally sends "special voting deputies" into nursing homes to assist elderly residents who may be cognitively impaired, to help them fill out and cast absentee ballots, and to ensure that they are not coerced or influenced in exercising their voting rights. Claiming concern over COVID, the Wisconsin Elections Commission (WEC) decided to suspend the special voting deputies program and to allow nursing home workers to assist the residents.

After the change made by WEC, family members of some nursing home residents complained that their elderly relatives were being pressured to vote, even when those relatives suffered from dementia or other cognitive issues. When this came to the attention of the Sheriff of Racine County, Christopher Schmaling, he referred criminal

---

2   Ibid., 14.

3   Ibid., 70.

charges against five or the six WEC commissioners.[4] He was widely criticized for that action, but now he has been vindicated.

TABLE 8: OSC REPORT ON NURSING HOME VOTER "TURNOUT"

County	# of nursing homes vetted	# of registered voters	# of voters November 2020	Percentage of registered voters who voted
Milwaukee	30	1084	1084	100%
Racine	12	348	348	100%
Dane	24	723	723	100%
Kenosha	9	866	841	97%
Brown	16	280	265	95%
Totals	91	3301	3261	

Imagine: 66 nursing homes had 100% voter turnout!
Special Counsel Gableman's team investigated the nursing home allegations brought forth by the Sheriff and discovered serious potential election fraud in addition to the immoral and unethical treatment of nursing home patients.

Ninety-one (91) homes were investigated, and it was determined that all of the nursing homes had voting rates of between 95 and 100 percent. The voter "turnout" was 100 percent in 66 of the 91 nursing homes. Healthy people don't vote at rates approaching 95 to 100 percent, so we can safely assume election fraud was in play. See Table 8.[5]

Who are some of these amazing senior citizens? One of them is 104-year-old Maryl Barrett, who has had serious memory problems for up to twenty years and is "not capable of making decisions" . . . or even "remaining awake for more than a few minutes [according to her guardians]." I was going to put her photo here, but decided it was wrong to picture someone who is obviously incapacitated and incapable of giving permission for a photo, or for that matter, a vote.

There are many other cases of nursing home abuse, documented by the OSC and the Thomas More Society, which also investigated the matter. The people who abused

---

4   Henry Redman, "Racine Co. Sheriff alleges elections commission broke the law," *Wisconsin Examiner*, October 29, 2021, https://wisconsinexaminer.com/2021/10/29/racine-co-sheriff-alleges-elections-commission-broke-the-law/.

5   Office of Special Council, "Second Interim Investigative Report," March 1, 2022, Chapter 7.

these patients in order to satisfy their own political goals should be legally prosecuted (but probably won't be unless there is a change in Wisconsin management).

IMPORTANT NOTE: The OSC investigated just ninety-one nursing homes in five of Wisconsin's seventy-two counties. However, according to "SeniorHomes.com," a website for seniors looking for nursing homes, there are 581 nursing homes in Wisconsin, statewide.

Ninety-one nursing homes happen to behave in the same way?
More food for thought: The OSC found ninety-one separate nursing homes, presumably owned by different entities, and each one had an unusually high turnout rate. What does that tell you? It suggests to me a possible criminal conspiracy to commit election fraud. It would be irrational to assume that ninety-one facilities spontaneously and separately started pushing 100 percent of their residents to vote. More likely, one person or a small group of people was manipulating the absentee ballot process at nursing homes across the state.

Now, someone might say, this is no big deal; it only involves about 3,000 people—not enough to overturn the state election. But it is a very big deal because there are 581 homes in the state. Also, the people who would abuse elderly nursing home residents in order to accomplish their political ambitions would probably commit fraud in other aspects of the election process.

Other findings of the OSC:

- "The cities of Milwaukee, Madison, Racine, Kenosha, and Green Bay [engaged] private companies [i.e., Zuckerberg's CTCL and CEIR] in election administration in unprecedented ways, including tolerating unauthorized users and unauthorized uses of WisVote private voter data."

- "WEC [failed] to record non-citizens in the WisVote voter database, thereby permitting non-citizens to vote, even though Wisconsin law requires citizenship to vote [as does federal law]."

- "Wisconsin election officials and WEC" violated "Federal and Wisconsin Equal Protection Clauses by failing to treat all voters the same in the same election."

- "The OSC learned that one machine company representative stated that the voting machines were "wiped" during updates, meaning they did not retain federally required voter data."

Perhaps the most important thing to remember is this: Despite these very significant findings, which should be of importance to all Wisconsin citizens, there has been a wall of obstruction from the Wisconsin Attorney General, Josh Kaul, and from other election administrators, including those in the very liberal cities. They have resisted every subpoena, and have refused to respond to Open Records requests from private watchdog groups. They believe, I guess, that you can get away with anything when the media are on your side, and when the clock is ticking away.[6] Unfortunately, they are probably right. In August of 2022, Robin Vos (R), Speaker of the Assembly, closed the Office of Special Council, leaving pending lawsuits in limbo.

THE REPORT OF THE WISCONSIN INSTITUTE FOR LAW & LIBERTY
Democracy dies in darkness. (It also dies when a newspaper lies!)

Starting on page 265, there is a section in this book that is devoted to the "debunkers"—those self-appointed defenders of democracy who crusade against misinformation and conspiracy theories. One such crusader, the *Washington Post* (WAPO), warrants special notice here because of its concise debunking of the claims of fraud in Wisconsin's 2020 election.

Journalism students take note! Here is how the big boys debunk election lies. WAPO reduced a 127-page investigative report issued by the Wisconsin Institute for Law & Liberty (W.I.L.L.) to a few carefully-selected and fragmented quotations—about a paragraph. Context need not apply.

After stating that the W.I.L.L. investigation "found no support for theories that the election was stolen," the Post added:

> In particular, a 10-month review by the conservative Wisconsin Institute for Law & Liberty released last week found there was "no evidence of widespread voter fraud." It concluded that "in all likelihood, more eligible voters cast ballots for Joe Biden than Donald Trump." And it debunked specific myths spread by Trump and his allies.[7]

That is how WAPO framed 127 pages of (supposedly) nasty election conspiracy theories. Very concise—and totally false! Let's prove this WAPO lie by reviewing several sections of the W.I.L.L. report.

---

6   Henry Redman, "Legal Battle Over Gableman Subpoenas Drags On," *Urban Milwaukee*, March 18, 2022, https://urbanmilwaukee.com/2022/03/18/legal-battle-over-gableman-subpoenas-drags-on/.

7   Rosalind Helderman and Josh Dawsey, "A real conflagration: Wisconsin emerges as front line in war over the 2020 vote," *Washington Post*, December 16, 2021, https://www.msn.com/en-us/news/politics/a-real-conflagration-wisconsin-emerges-as-front-line-in-war-over-the-2020-vote/ar-AART2Ib.

WISCONSIN

At the very beginning of the report, where it smacks you right in the face, there is this bold type statement:

It is almost certain that in Wisconsin's 2020 election the number of votes that did not comply with existing legal requirements exceeded Joe Biden's margin of victory.[8]

That statement alone, if correct, means that some sort of independent audit should have been performed before Wisconsin certified its election. However, we are just starting our review. As you read this, keep in mind that Trump lost Wisconsin by just 20,600 votes. (The bold type and underlining is presented as it appears in the report.)

- "[The] widespread adoption of absentee ballot drop boxes, not provided for under Wisconsin law, was correlated with an increase of 20,000 votes for Joe Biden. ..."[9]

- "We found that 23,361 Wisconsin voters in 2020 cast ballots despite failing their DMV identity check this year, meaning their name, address, and/or birthdate doesn't match what is on file with the Department of Motor Vehicles (DMV) . . . . Democratic-leaning counties were disproportionately represented among DMV checks [more on this, below]."[10]

- "We found that 31,664 Wisconsin voters were in the National Change of Address Database. Among the subset where a new address was known, 7,151 moved to an address in a different state."[11]

- "State law provides no legal authority for local election officials to fix, or 'cure,' defects, mistakes, or missing information on absentee ballots. But the Wisconsin Elections Commission (WEC) said they could—resulting in some municipalities curing ballots while others did not. . . . W.I.L.L. estimates that if absentee ballot rejection rates were similar to the rates in 2016, the final election margin would have narrowed by 6,000 votes."[12]

---

8   Will Flanders, Kyle Koenen, Rick Esenberg, Noah Diekemper & Miranda Spindt, A Review of the 2020 Election," *Wisconsin Institute for Law and Liberty* (December 2021), https://will-law.org/wp-content/uploads/2021/11/2021Electio nReviewStudy.pdf.

9   Ibid., 11,34.

10   Ibid., 12.

11   Ibid.

12   Ibid., 14.

213

- **"Private funding disproportionately benefited Democrats. A statistical analysis finds significant increases in turnout for Democrats, approximately 8,000 votes statewide, as a result of [Zuckerberg-supplied] CTCL grants** [emphasis as written]."[13]

- "Our poll [of sample of 2,000 absentee ballot requesters] found a surprisingly high percentage of respondents who say they did not request absentee ballots. A higher percentage of Republicans than Democrats claim they did not request an absentee ballot than of Democrats [sic] [emphasis as written]." [Author's note: The percentage was 8.3 percent for Democrats and 16.6 percent for Republicans—a statistically significant difference that could indicate (potentially) thousands of fraudulent votes. Were those the "harvested" ballots identified by True the Vote? See page 223.[14]

- **"More than 265,000 Wisconsin voters adopted the 'indefinitely confined' status, meaning they received an absentee ballot and were exempt from the statewide photo ID requirements.** The number of indefinitely confined voters increased from 66,611 in 2016 to 265,979 in 2020. . . . Many of these votes were cast illegally [emphasis as written]."[15] [Author's note: Without a doubt, many people abused the "indefinitely confined" classification to evade ID requirements.]

- "Drop boxes were largely unmonitored. Out of 24 communities that reported having drop boxes, only 10 reported using chain of custody logs to track absentee ballot pickups." [Author's note: If the drop boxes without chain of custody logs had ballot quantities aggregating to more than the election margin of 20,600, that should have prevented certification of the election.][16]

In addition to these damning findings, the report touches on other controversies—all of which hurt Trump. For example, there were at least 17,721 ballots collected by Madison City volunteers at a Biden-advertised campaign called "Democracy in the

---

13   Ibid., 14–15.

14   Ibid., 16.

15   Ibid., 11,13.

16   Ibid., 35.

Park."[17] These ballots were collected improperly and illegally, although the Wisconsin Supreme Court ultimately declined to decide the case, based on a supposed lack of timely filing.[18]

An issue of concern for many Trump supporters was an apparent spike of votes in the middle of the night on November 4, 2020. That spike moved Biden from a vote deficit of 109,000 to a lead of 11,000. W.I.L.L. could not find any evidence that this influx of votes, primarily from Madison, was fraudulent. However, the report chided the Milwaukee Election Commissioner and a Democratic Party activist for an "ill-advised and unprofessional e-mail exchange" in which they joked (they claimed) about "delivering just the margin needed at 3a.m."[19]

The W.I.L.L. report also took aim at the super low ballot rejection rates for the 2020 election, as contrasted with previous elections. These rates are shown in Figure 14 from the W.I.L.L. report:

FIGURE 14: REJECTION RATE TRENDS IN WISCONSIN

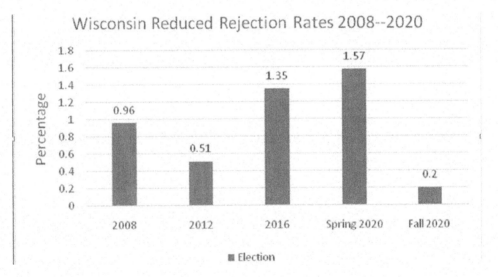

According to the report, if 2016 rejection rates were in place, instead of the lower 2020 rates, the election would have been about 6,000 votes closer.[20]

---

17   It is estimated that there were thousands more ballots collected at Democracy in the Park events, but they were co-mingled with other ballots, making them impossible to quantify.

18   Ibid., 54.

19   Ibid., 62.

20   Ibid., 44,45.

Some of these issues are addressed in more detail on subsequent pages, but right now let's get back to that conspiracy-crushing crusader, the *Washington Post*. I said the *Post* lied, but that is not exactly true, and I apologize.

The *Post* merely engaged in a little trickery. WAPO wrote something that is supposed to make you think that W.I.L.L.'s report supported the Biden victory, and "debunked" the claims of Trump.

Let's look again at the words of the *Post*—more carefully. It said the W.I.L.L. report found "no evidence of widespread *voter fraud* [emphasis added]." The two key words are "voter" and "fraud." First, there is a difference between voter fraud and election fraud, and the authors of the W.I.L.L. report make it very clear that they are not accusing *voters* of anything.

And when it comes to election fraud, the authors do not exonerate Wisconsin officials: They simply side-step the legal determination. The report cites many instances of deliberate law breaking by election officials (instances which meet the definition of "Election Fraud" per Wisconsin statute 12.13), but the authors of the report explicitly say that they are not utilizing the Wisconsin legal definition: They state: "Note that the statutory definition of 'election fraud' is far broader than [our] definition."

So, the *Washington Post* was technically correct because the W.I.L.L. report chose to not use the legal definition of election fraud (although they found plenty of it), and the report did not accuse voters (as opposed to election officials) of misconduct. The W.I.L.L. report simply outlined a litany of illegal acts that very likely changed the election victor from Trump to Biden.

Washington Post, please accept my apologies. Some of us need a bit more time to grasp the meaning of words that journalists use so deftly.

More on the 23,361 voters who can't be matched to DMV!
I want to impress upon you the seriousness of this particular finding, which was first presented on page 213. As noted, W.I.L.L.'s investigation found that 23,361 voters had provided registration information that could not be tied to Department of Motor Vehicle records, yet those 23,361 people voted in the November 2020 election.

In Table 9, a breakout of the types of mismatched information is provided. For example, 15,260 had names that did not match, 4,885 had mismatched drivers license numbers, and 1,815 had no matching information at all. The information in the table came from the Wisconsin Institute for Life and Liberty (W.I.L.L.). The organization said it requested the underlying records (e.g., drivers licenses and birth information) from the Wisconsin Elections Commission (WEC), but the request was denied.

TABLE 9: VOTERS WITH IDENTITIES THAT DON'T TIE TO DMV

Reason	Count
Name and DOB doesn't match	274
Name does not match	15,260
DOB doesn't match	1,061
No record of license #	4,885
Invalid data	66
No matches at all	1,815
Total	23,361

Of course, there will be innocent explanations for some of these mismatches. However, when we start with more than 23 thousand questionable voters, many are likely to be invalid.

WISCONSIN POLITICOS DENY BALLOT ACCESS TO THE GREEN PARTY

In a blow to the Green Party, and a blow to the Trump campaign, the Wisconsin Elections Commission (WEC) denied ballot access to the Green Party presidential candidates, and the Wisconsin Supreme Court upheld that denial. It was a decision for which WEC and the Wisconsin Supreme Court should feel great shame.

In a dissenting opinion, Wisconsin Justice Annette Kingsland Ziegler opined:

> [T]he Court issues a perfunctory order in perhaps one of the most important cases in a judicial lifetime. . . . It is ultimate voter suppression when a candidate who presumptively belongs on the ballot is denied ballot access.[21]

In the view of Ziegler and two other dissenting justices, WEC acted unlawfully in ruling against the Green Party, and the Supreme Court's ruling upheld that unlawful activity. In her separate dissenting opinion, Chief Justice Patience Drake Roggensack stated:

---

21   Howie Hawkins and Angela Walker v. Wisconsin Elections Commission, 2020AP1488-OA, 2020 WI 75 (Supreme Court of Wisconsin), September 14, 2020, ¶30 (Justice Ziegler).

Howie Hawkins and Angela Walker, Green Party candidates for President and Vice President, followed all the requirements of Wisconsin law necessary for ballot access, yet the Commission denied them and the people of Wisconsin the right to have Hawkins' and Walker's names on the ballot for the November 3, 2020 general election.[22]

Here is the background of this shameful case. According to Chief Justice Roggensack, "On August 4, 2020, the Green Party candidates filed nomination papers containing 3,966 signatures with the Commission [Wisconsin Election Commission, or "WEC"]. At least 2,000 signatures but not more than 4,000 signatures must be filed to gain ballot access."[23]

Just imagine: A person moves and, somehow, her address changes!
A few days later, a retired attorney, Allen Arntsen, filed a complaint with the WEC, challenging the validity of 2,046 of the signatures of the Green Party vice presidential candidate, Angela Walker. Mr. Arntsen stated that he had no personal knowledge of a problem with the signatures; rather, his allegation was based upon "information and belief."[24] In other words, it was his belief based upon things he had heard or was told.

The specific issue, a red herring, was that Angela Walker used two different home addresses for the documents. She did that for a simple and valid reason: She had moved during the time signatures were being requested, and when she moved her address changed. (I don't know any other way that works.)

The attorney for the Green Party, Andrea Merida, was told she could argue the matter before the WEC on August 20, 2020, and she appeared as directed. But in the words of dissenting Chief Justice, Patience Roggensack:

> Ann Jacobs, who served as chair of the [WEC] Commission, prevented the presenta-
> tion of evidence about the dates of Walker's move. The Commission then voted 6-0
> to sustain Arntsen's challenge to 57 signatures and rejected it for 48 signatures.[25]

In other words, Ann Jacobs behaved in a disgraceful and political manner. What about the rest of the disputed signatures? Regarding those signatures, the Commission deadlocked 3-3, implicitly along party lines. (Democrat appointees voted to disallow the signatures and Republican appointees voted to allow them.)

---

22   Howie Hawkins and Angela Walker v. Wisconsin Elections Commission, ¶14 (Chief Justice Roggensack).

23   Howie Hawkins and Angela Walker v. Wisconsin Elections Commission, ¶17 (Chief Justice Roggensack).

24   Ibid., ¶18.

25   Howie Hawkins and Angela Walker v. Wisconsin Elections Commission, ¶21 (Chief Justice Roggensack).

According to the three dissenting Supreme Court Justices, the Green Party had 3,909 presumptively valid signatures—far more than the required 2,000. The Justices said the reason is rooted in Wisconsin law:

> Since Crane v. Wiley, 14 Wis. 658 (1861), we have held that allegations based *upon information and belief* in a complaint make a verification insufficient for material facts. However, the Commission's votes showed it did not honor the presumption of the nomination papers' facts as Wis. Admin. Code section EL 2.05 (4) requires [emphasis added].[26]

To make a long story short, after the deadlocked vote, and after Jacobs denied the Green Party a chance to make its case, the WEC Administrator simply denied ballot access to the Green Party candidates. Hawkins and Walker sued, but by the time the case got up to the Wisconsin Supreme Court, a 4-3 majority on the court said there was no time to "provide meaningful relief."[27]

Claiming that they wanted to prevent "confusion and disarray," the Democrats on the Wisconsin Supreme Court kept Howie Hawkins and Angela Walker off the ballot—even though they had done nothing wrong, and had every right to be on the ballot. People who follow this particular court may recognize a pattern in its rulings.

Many people think the Green Party was collateral damage in the Democrats' fight to hurt Donald Trump. Democrats were openly bitter after the 2016 election, and felt Hillary Clinton had been defeated in Wisconsin due to the votes absorbed by Green Party candidates.

Had the Green Party been on the ballot, Trump would have (probably) won the state. Keeping the Green Party off the ballot required corruption by two entities: the Wisconsin Elections Commission (WEC) and the Wisconsin Supreme Court.

DO YOU THINK THERE MIGHT BE CHEATING IN MADISON?

In an effort to spot possible irregularities, the Wisconsin Institute for Law & Liberty (W.I.L.L.) did a statistical analysis of the top ten voter turnout changes for Republican wards and Democrat wards. The results are shown in Table 10, and are graphed in Figure 15.[28]

---

26   Ibid.,¶20.

27   Howie Hawkins and Angela Walker v. Wisconsin Elections Commission, ¶10.

28   Will Flanders, Kyle Koenen, Rick Esenberg, Noah Diekemper & Miranda Spindt, "A Review of the 2020 Election," *Wisconsin Institute for Law and Liberty* (December 2021):78, https://will-law.org/wp-content/uploads/2021/11/2021ElectionReviewStudy.pdf.

TABLE 10: INCREASES IN VOTER TURNOUT FROM 2016 TO 2020

— WHAT??

Democrat ward	% increase from 2016 to 2020	Republican ward	% increase from 2016 to 2020
Madison 124	1285.7	Milwaukee 170	354.6
Sun Prairie 24	393.8	Milwaukee 110	266.7
Oshkosh 33	308.3	Milwaukee 149	240.0
Appleton 2	287.5	Milwaukee 121	230.0
Fox Crossing 3	149.4	Milwaukee 162	225.0
Fox Crossing 6	149.3	Sun Prairie 24	213.6
Fox Crossing 5	149.0	Milwaukee 156	194.1
Madison 107	139.2	Oshkosh 33	191.3
Wright Crossing 4	117.7	Milwaukee 155	172.7
Kenosha 75	113.7	Milwaukee 151	155.0

FIGURE 15: PERCENTAGE INCREASE IN VOTER TURNOUT 2016 TO 2020

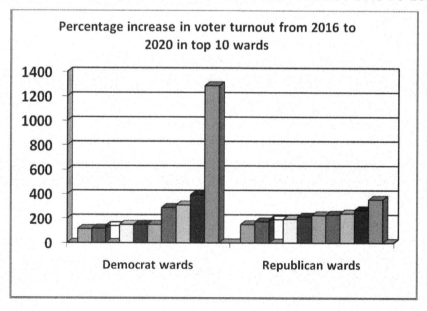

Madison Ward 124 increases voter turnout by 1,285 percent!

Look at that tall column to the right side of the Democrat wards—the one that nearly goes to the top of the chart. That is Madison Ward 124, and in some amazing way the voter turnout increased in that ward by 1,285 percent. In other words, it grew by nearly 13 times. That is a very unnatural increase, and it could explain why Madison refused to give ballot certificate access to the Legislative Audit Bureau. (See "Question to Consider" on page 3.)

There are a several things that might explain the sharp increase in Madison's voter turnout. It could be due to lots of voter enthusiasm. Or, it might be due to the 200 drop boxes that were placed in Madison for special voting days called "Democracy in the Park." That issue is described on page 228.

It could indicate something more sinister, like the situation in Pima County, Arizona, where 35,000 votes were allegedly added to Biden's tally (page 71). Or, the super high turnout rate might relate to the claims of Ethan Pease, regarding alleged corruption within the U.S. Postal Service. You will find that story on page 225.

Finally, the increase could be attributable to the work of Zuckerberg's organization, CTCL, and the ballot harvesting that may have resulted from CTCL activities. That is our next topic.

ZUCKERBERG TAKES OVER THE ELECTION

To increase voter participation in Wisconsin, almost $9 million was spent by Mark Zuckerberg and his wife, Priscilla Chan. Their organization, Center for Tech and Civic Life (CTCL), spent most of the funds in five Democrat strongholds that were key to Biden's success in the election: Madison, Milwaukee, Racine, Kenosha, and Green Bay. The money was spent with strings attached, according to Wisconsin Representative Janel Brandtjen:

> In Green Bay we had an individual from New York [former Obama staffer, Michael Spitzer-Rubenstein] who had the ability to pick the poll workers, pick the curing ballot process, had an ID that said he was an employee of the City of Green Bay, had access to the room with the counting equipment, and had all of the internet codes, including one for sensitive machines.[29]

---

29   Benjamin Yount, "Rep. Brandtjen: Gov.'s 'Zuckerbucks' veto puts Wisconsin elections 'up for bid,'" *The Center Square*, July 1, 2021, https://www.thecentersquare.com/wisconsin/rep-brandtjen-gov-s-zuckerbucks-veto-puts-wisconsin-elections-up-for-bid/article_62e503f0-daab-11eb-9809-870d2f45c198.html.

A former Wisconsin elections clerk, Sandy Juno said: "If this is how elections are going to go, we won't have election integrity."[30] In an interview with Just the News, Juno said that CTCL was redoing forms and documents used for the election.[31] Although they had no right to do that, it appears they were given privileges because of the money they contributed. In the end, power was taken from county clerks (who are supposed to have authority) and was given to CTCL and local mayors (who are not supposed to have power).

Stunning emails reveal likely ballot harvesting

At hearings sponsored by the Wisconsin Assembly, Representative Brandtjen revealed emails between Michael Spitzer-Rubenstein (the Obama guy from New York) and Claire Woodall-Vogg, the Executive Director of the Milwaukee Election Commission. These emails, which were obtained using Open Record requests, reveal that Spitzer-Rubenstein requested, and received, unnatural access to WisVote, which is a state-owned database containing "[e]ach municipality's election data, e.g., voter registration, ballot access, ballot tracking, polling place, etc."[32]

Before the election, Spitzer-Rubenstein asked Woodall-Vogg if:

> WisVote has an API [application programming interface] or anything similar so that it can connect with other software apps? That would be the holy grail (but I'm not expecting that to be easy).

To her credit, Woodall-Vogg did not give him the requested API, but she did promise to access the database each night and send him a report (which she did). Later, Spitzer-Rubenstein told Woodall-Vogg that the nightly reports were no longer needed because, "through partners, we should be able to access the voter file and pull the data from WisVote."[33] My guess is that some Wisconsin election worker was getting the

---

30   Anton Carillo, "Former Wisconsin Elections Clerk Says Facebook-Funded Activists Took Control Of 2020 Race In State," *Christianity Daily*, June 24, 2021, https://www.christianitydaily.com/articles/12361/20210624/former-wisconsin-elections-clerk-says-facebook-funded-activists-took-control-of-2020-race-in-state.htm.

31   Daniel Payne, "'No business doing that': Wis. official says Zuckerberg-funded group seized control of 2020 election," *Just the News*, June 22, 2021, https://justthenews.com/politics-policy/elections/sandy-juno-wisconsin-election-clerk-2020-election.

32   Wendy Strauch Mahoney, "Wisconsin Hearing Emails Show Democrat Operatives Coordinating With City Election Officials," *UncoverDC.com*, December 10, 2021, https://uncoverdc.com/2021/12/10/wisconsin-hearing-emails-show-democrat-operatives-coordinating-with-city-election-officials/.

33   Ibid.

information to him. (Or, perhaps, Spitzer-Rubenstein had a direct Wi-Fi hookup, like the one described on page 208.)

According to Representative Brandtjen, the voter information given to Spitzer-Rubenstein, coupled with other information he was provided, would make it easy to harvest ballots, if he were so inclined. On a micro-level, he could determine exactly when ballots would be put in the residential mail boxes, which ballots were returned, and which were not.[34]

Of course, harvesting has not been proven yet—but see the following:

14,000 TO 83,000 ILLEGALLY HARVESTED BALLOTS

True the Vote's multistate cell-phone ping ballot-harvesting probe determined that 138 individuals (sometimes called mules) made 3,588 harvesting trips in the Milwaukee County area—largely in the dead of night. True the Vote (TTV) is the group that uses cell phone pings and drop box videos to track illegal ballot harvesters. (Background information for this group is found on page 36.) In the movie, *2,000 Mules*, TTV estimated that a total of 14,000 to as many as 83,000 ballots were illegally cast, depending on the assumptions made.

TTV's cyber expert, Gregg Phillips, describes the harvesting as "an organized crime against Americans." Harvesters got the ballots (somehow), and gave them to "nongovernmental organizations" (NGOs). After the ballots were received (and perhaps altered) by the NGOs, they were given to mules for nighttime distribution to various drop boxes. TTV claims that it knows the identity of many of the participants (NGOs and mules), but it is not disclosing that information at this time.[35]

> *Question: If these were ballots from legal voters, why did the nongovernmental organizations feel the need to hand them off to mules for nighttime delivery to various drop boxes? Why didn't the NGO simply take them to the post office in the light of day?*

Another question: How did the NGO harvesters get the ballots in the first place? As noted, Democrats had unnatural (and possibly illegal) access to the Wisconsin database of voters (*WisVote*), and that information could have been used to track the delivery of ballots to registered voters. Once located, the voters could be persuaded, cajoled, or

---

34 Ibid.

35 Steven Kovac, "Election Watchdog Finds 137,500 Ballots Unlawfully Trafficked in Wisconsin," *Epoch Times*, March 30, 2022, https://www.theepochtimes.com/voting-integrity-group-uncovers-over-137000-ballots-that-were-trafficked-in-wisconsin_4369214.html.

bribed (free concert, free restaurant coupon, etc.) to give away their ballots. Perhaps the ballots were simply swiped out of mailboxes. The WisVote access was explained on page 222.

"Zuck Bucks" bribery lawsuits
On March 23, 2022, the Thomas More Society filed a complaint with the Wisconsin Elections Commission (WEC), alleging that election bribery was committed by the acting and former mayors of Milwaukee and the City Clerk. This complaint follows other complaints filed against officials in Racine, Green Bay, Kenosha, and Madison.[36]

The allegation is that the city officials violated Wisconsin law by accepting a "bribe" (funding of millions of dollars) from Zuckerberg's CTCL nonprofit organization, in exchange for the city's encouragement of people to vote in certain neighborhoods. It is a violation of Wisconsin law (and Federal law) to offer and/or receive private funds as an inducement to encourage voting:

> *Wisconsin§12.11- Election bribery*
> *(1m) Any person who does any of the following violates this chapter:*
> *(a) Offers, gives, lends or promises to give or lend, or endeavors to procure, anything of value, or any office or employment . . . in order to induce any elector [voter] to :*
> *1. Go to or refrain from going to the polls.*

The theory of the case is that CTCL's funding for the city, which was ostensibly for COVID relief, was actually used to encourage voting in certain city neighborhoods by the placement of drop boxes and by other means. Therefore, the funding was effectively a bribe.

I don't know if the case is legally sound but, in my opinion, WEC is perfectly capable of ignoring the statutes to achieve the political aims of its members.

THE POST OFFICE ALLEGATION—NOT PROVEN BUT NOT DEBUNKED
The Wisconsin Elections Commission (WEC) and the United States Postal Service Office of Inspector General both concluded that the following allegation has been debunked—but it wasn't. The allegation is presented first, followed by the so-called debunkings.

---

36 Staff Writer, "Election Complaint Charges Milwaukee with Election Bribery for Taking 'Zuck Bucks' to 'Get out the Vote,'" *Thomas More Society*, March 23, 2022, https://thomasmoresociety.org/election-complaint-charges-milwaukee-with-election-bribery-for-taking-zuck-bucks-to-get-out-the-vote/.

The allegation

Ethan Pease started working for United Mailing Services (UMS) on August 26, 2020 as a Madison route driver, picking up mail and delivering it to UMS, a company that sorts and then delivers bulk mail to the United States Postal Service (USPS).

Pease's basic allegation, as summarized by the Epoch Times, is:

[H]e was told by two postal workers on two separate occasions that the USPS in Wisconsin was gathering over 100,000 ballots on the morning of Nov. 4 to be back-dated so that they would be counted even if they arrived after the statutory deadline.[37]

In a December 1, 2020 press conference, Pease stated that, on the day before the election, he noticed there was only one absentee ballot in the UMS "ballots only" box. That is the box from which he would normally get mail—specifically ballots—to take to the USPS.

The next day, Election Day, there were no ballots in the special box.

On November 4, a senior USPS employee (named Monty?) told Pease that the Wisconsin/Illinois chapter of the USPS sent a communication indicating that 100,000 ballots were missing. Monty asked Pease if he had forgotten any ballots at UMS. He also said that someone was sent to UMS to look for ballots and found seven or eight. Pease felt this was not true because he was certain there were no ballots at all at UMS.

On November 5, a different postal worker (Rachel) told Pease that USPS employees were ordered to backdate ballots that were received too late to be included in election results. Pease asked the employee if he (Pease) was going to get in trouble because of the alleged missing 100,000 ballots, mentioned by the first USPS employee. She answered, "No you wouldn't as long as they were postmarked for the third."

Pease said he heard the same two postal workers making jokes about throwing away the absentee ballots for Trump. Pease also stated that he did not vote for Trump or Biden.[38]

You can view Ethan Pease stating his case on a video at the link in the footnotes. He is extremely credible, and it seems unlikely to me, given his demeanor and the specificity of his claims, that he made up his story. However, it is definitely possible that

---

37   Isabel van Brugan, "Wisconsin USPS Subcontractor Alleges Backdating of Tens of Thousands of Mail-In Ballots," *Epoch Times*, December 2, 2020, https://www.theepochtimes.com/wisconsin-usps-subcontractor-alleges-backdating-of-tens-of-thousands-of-mail-in-ballots_3601580.html.

38   Hannah Bleau, "Watch: Ex-USPS Subcontractor Says Colleagues 'Ordered to Backdate Ballots,'" *Breitbart.com*, December 2, 2020, https://www.breitbart.com/politics/2020/12/02/ex-usps-subcontractor-says-colleagues-ordered-to-backdate-ballots/.

the employees he talked to (Monty and Rachel) were misinformed or were deliberately deceiving Pease.

The "debunking" of Ethan by the Wisconsin Elections Commission (WEC)

- WEC pointed out that UMS provides services to the Post Office, but is not officially a subcontractor [Author: irrelevant].

- Someone [unidentified] at UMS said that "nobody came to their facility to look for absentee ballots." [Author: Someone else may have seen the person who looked for ballots, or perhaps Monty made up the claim about seven or eight ballots.]

- WEC wondered why people would backdate ballots when, under the law, "if a clerk receives a ballot after that deadline, or in the days after the election, it cannot be counted." [Author: If a parcel is postmarked on the fourth, it is pretty difficult to pretend it arrived on the third. Someone in the Post Office could have been colluding with one of the county clerks to support the pretense that ballots were both postmarked on time and received on time. Remember, we are talking about Madison County—the one with a precinct having a 1,285 percent increase in voter turnout, and the very same county that violated state laws in multiple ways with its "Democracy in the Park" campaign.][39]

Onward to the next debunking!

The "debunking" of Ethan by the Post Office Inspector General
The Post Office Inspector General's report is heavily redacted, but in the part that can be read, these arguments are presented:

- "All of the parties cited by Pease denied that they did anything wrong or considered backdating forms." [Author: Of course, such denials would be expected.]

- "No information has been developed that USPS or the Madison Post Office employees mishandled any voter ballots on November 3, 2020." [Author: We don't know if investigatory efforts were even made.]

---

39 "Did clerks receive backdated absentee ballots to be counted after the deadline of 8:00 p.m. on Election Day? Wisconsin Elections Commission, accessed March 29, 2022, https://elections.wi.gov/node/7292.

- "There is no evidence of USPS employees collecting late ballots after November 3, 2020 or being dispatched to 'collect forgotten ballots.'" [Author: except, of course, for the testimony of Ethan Pease].

- There was a "miscommunication between individuals." [Author: That sounds a bit like an admission.]

- "Pease interpreted [name redacted]'s conversation as misconduct by the USPS." [Author: Hmm! The IG seems to concede that someone said something that could be construed as "misconduct by the USPS." The IG needs to tell us more about that conversation.]

- Pease's information is "not based on any direct observations" [true].[40]

I don't think the arguments of WEC or the IG come close to debunking the claims of Ethan Pease. For fun, I am going to summarize my overall conclusion by using one of those cool, fact-checking meters. Here is my "ruling" regarding Ethan Pease's allegations:

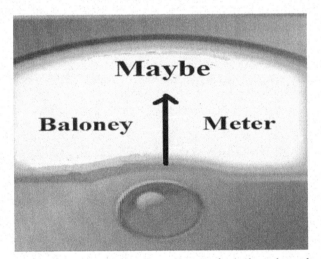

I have "ruled" it to be a "maybe" because no people (other than the ones he accused) have contradicted Pease's core statements, he has not recanted, and no one has shown that Pease had a motive to lie about this subject. Given the 1,285 percent turnout increase in Madison Ward 124, this allegation has some credibility.

---

40 "Case Summary Report # 21INV 00707," United States Postal Service Office of Inspector General, November 9, 2020 to December 9, 2020, https://elections.wi.gov/sites/elections/files/2021-02/USPS-IG%20Report.pdf.

TRUMP LAWSUIT: "DEMOCRACY IN THE PARK:" ILLEGAL AND UNFAIR

I'm Joe Biden, candidate for president, and I approve this message.[41]

Those were the ending words of a Biden campaign radio ad, promoting a get-out-the-vote effort in the Democrat stronghold of Madison, Wisconsin.

FIGURE 16: DEMOCRACY IN THE PARK—MADISON: BALLOT DROP OFF LOCATIONS

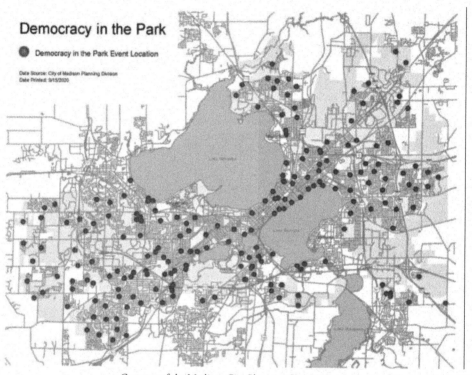

Courtesy of the Madison City Planning Commission

"Democracy in the Park" was actually two days of events (on September 26 and October 3, 2020) taking place in 206 parks in the City of Madison. Volunteer poll workers ("election inspectors") were available at each of the 206 parks to assist would-be voters, to complete and correct ballot applications if needed, and even to provide witness services (required in Wisconsin). Later, the special City-appointed election inspectors took the ballots back to the election headquarters. Some might call that harvesting.

---

41   M.D. Kittle, "Is Biden Sponsoring Madison City Voter Event?" *Townhall*, September 25, 2020, https://townhall.com/columnists/mdkittle/2020/09/25/is-biden-sponsoring-madison-city-voter-event-n2576920.

Over 17,000 ballots were collected at the parks by the special volunteers, recruited by the city. According to James Troupis, Trump's lead attorney for Wisconsin, tens of thousands of additional ballots were collected at the 206 parks, but those ballots could not be identified because they were co-mingled with ballots collected in the normal way.[42]

A little context is required. Wisconsin has some of the strictest election laws in the country, and it does not allow advance voting. A vote prior to Election Day comes under the strict rules for absentee voting. Here are some of those rules, in the words of Patience Drake Roggensack, Chief Justice of the Wisconsin Supreme Court.

- "Wisconsin Stat. §6.87(2) provides that absentee ballots must be accompanied by a certificate . . . and directs that certificates must be in 'substantially' the same form as the model."[43]

- "[T]he plain language of §6.87(2) requires that it is the witness who must affix his or her signature and write in his or her name and address. Section 6.87(2) does not mention an election official taking any action."[44]

- Wisconsin Stat. 6.87(6d) provides that "[i]f a certificate is missing the address of a witness, the ballot may not be counted."[45]

- The requirement that such ballots not be counted is found in Wis. Stat. §6.84(2), which provides that the provisions in §6.87(6d) are "mandatory."[46]

- "[T]he envelope [containing the ballot] shall be mailed by the elector, or delivered in person, to the municipal clerk issuing the ballot or ballots."[47]

The Trump campaign had four different election complaints that it took to the Wisconsin Supreme Court, in one filing. One of the complaints pertained to the

42   James Troupis, "Clip of Senate Hearing on Election Security and Administration," *C-Span*, December 16, 2020, @4:07, https://www.c-span.org/video/?c4932085/user-clip-trump-campaign-attorney-james-troupis-testimony.

43   Donald J. Trump v. Joseph Biden, 2020AP2038 2020 WI 91 (Supreme Court of Wisconsin), December 14, 2020, ¶75 (Justice Roggensack dissent).

44   Ibid.

45   Ibid., ¶77.

46   Ibid., ¶78.

47   Ibid., ¶98.

"Democracy in the Park" activities. The Trump team said that those activities violated many of the mandatory provisions of state law. The broken provisions, as related to "Democracy in the Park," were:

- Election workers are not supposed to be the witnesses for the ballot certificates.

- Election workers are not supposed to complete or correct information on the forms.

- Voters are required to mail their own ballots or deliver them in person. If a volunteer election worker gathers up a bunch of ballots at a park and delivers then, she is, essentially, harvesting.

THE THREE OTHER COMPLAINTS IN TRUMP'S LAWSUIT

The other complaints embodied in Trump's case before the Wisconsin Supreme Court pertained to:

- Ballots from "indefinitely confined" voters. These voters did not produce the normally required identification, and the Trump people said there was evidence that thousands were not truly indefinitely confined.

- An alleged lack of a "written application," which is required for in-person voting.

- Ballots that were (unlawfully) witnessed by municipal officials.

In each case, Trump argued these ballots were illegal and should not be counted. His case addressed the issues only with regard to two counties: Dane and Milwaukee. That may have been a tactical mistake.

WISCONSIN SUPREMES SPLIT 4/3

. . .You want us to overturn this election so your king can stay in power.

—JUSTICE JILL KAROFSKY

In oral hearings, several justices questioned whether they could disqualify ballots in only the two Democrat-leaning counties of Dane and Madison. Justice Jill Karofsky said Trump's case "smacks of racism."[48] Watching her in action, she reminded me a lot of Congresswoman Maxine Waters, especially when she referred to Trump as "Your King," and complained that the case was un-American. Her demeanor from the bench left no doubt as to her views or the degree of her impartiality.

On December 14, 2020, all of the complaints were dismissed by the court on the basis of laches. In other words, the court said the Trump campaign should have brought the case sooner. It was another 4–3 Wisconsin Supreme Court "process" decision, and not without controversy. Indeed, the three justices in the minority each wrote separate, blistering dissents, the likes of which I have never seen:

Justice Rebecca Grassl Bradley:

- "How astonishing that four justices of the Wisconsin Supreme Court must be reminded that it is THE LAW that constitutes 'the rulebook' for any election— not WEC guidance—and election officials are bound to follow the law, if we are to be governed by the rule of law, and not of men. [emphasis as written]."[49]

- "Surely the majority understands the absurdity of suggesting that the President [Trump] should have filed a lawsuit in 2016 or anytime thereafter. Why would he? He was not 'an aggrieved party'—he won."[50]

Justice Annette Kingland Ziegler:

- "LACHES DOES NOT AND SHOULD NOT BAR THIS CASE [emphasis as written]."

- "Once again, the majority imposes its definition of laches, which is tailored to its judicial preferences rather than based on well-established legal principles."[51]

- "The respondents cannot demonstrate that laches bars a single one of these claims, and, even if they could, the court could still and should exercise its discretion to hear these issues."[52]

48 Scott Bauer, "Wisconsin Supreme Court tosses Trump," *AP News*, December 14, 2020, https://apnews.com/article/wisonsin-supreme-court-trump-lawsuit-e6b3aa222b4141c0844d541c4b041964.

49 Donald J. Trump v. Joseph Biden, 2020AP2038 2020 WI 91 (Supreme Court of Wisconsin) ¶147.

50 Ibid., ¶146.

51 Ibid., ¶113.

52 Ibid., ¶114.

Chief Justice Patience Drake Roggensack:

- "Once again, four justices on this court cannot be bothered with addressing what the statutes require to assure that absentee ballots are lawfully cast."[53]

- "The Milwaukee County Board of Canvassers and the Dane County Board of Canvassers based their decisions on erroneous advice when they concluded that changes clerks made to defective witness addresses were permissible."[54]

Because the ruling was based on "process" (laches), these matters may present themselves again in 2022, 2024, or beyond.

119,283 "ACTIVE VOTERS" REGISTERED FOR MORE THAN 100 YEARS?
Stunning testimony was given by software and database engineer, Jeff O'Donnell, before a Wisconsin Campaigns & Election Committee hearing on December 8, 2021. Here are the highlights of his analysis of the Wisconsin voter database:

- According to WEC records, 119,283 citizens, classified as "active voters," have been registered for more than 100 years.

- If you add inactive voters with the active voters, there are more than 500,000 Wisconsin citizens who have been registered for more than 100 years.

If we assume these people could not register until they were eighteen years old, that means there are over one half million people in the state who are at least 118 years. It must be the benefits of all that cheese!

Actually, it isn't. Although O'Donnell's work is, apparently, completely accurate, it probably is not an indicator of fraud. Instead, it shows extreme sloppiness on the part of the Wisconsin Elections Commission (WEC). Here is what happened: In 2002, the "Help America Vote Act" made statewide voter registration mandatory for all states with more than 500,000 citizens. However, some municipalities had not been tracking registration dates and birth dates. As a "placeholder," so to speak, Wisconsin stuck in January 1, 1900 for the unknown birthdates and January 1, 1918 for the unknown registration dates.

---

53   Ibid., ¶62.

54   Ibid., ¶63.

Why do I criticize WEC for extreme sloppiness? I do so because it is not possible to verify voter information if you don't have accurate information on file, and have not had it for nearly twenty years. The records should have been updated long ago.

Mr. O'Donnell also noted some other red flags that may still be of concern:

- Forty-two thousand (42,000) people who voted in the November 2020 election, dropped off the voter rolls by August 2021. Maybe they ate too much cheese!

- Nine thousand seven hundred (9,700) active voters registered prior to 2016, but did not vote until November 2020. And 1,500 active voters registered prior to 2011 but did not vote until November 2020.

- The database engineer also reported that 31,872 voters who registered during the six months leading to the 2020 election were listed as "inactive" shortly after the election.[55]

These statistics may indicate that ballots were obtained and voted in the name of inactive but registered voters. It is hoped that WEC will check these data points to ensure that no laws were broken or errors were made.

SEVERAL LEGAL ISSUES SHOULD BE RESOLVED BEFORE FUTURE ELECTIONS

For future elections, several legal issues need to be resolved because auditors and other investigators have to make their evaluations in the context of applicable rules, regulations, and laws. There is the issue of private organizations, like CTCL, and their relationship to those who manage elections. Specifically, is it legal for private organizations to obtain voter information and special access in exchange for their financial contributions?

In addition, there are the four legal issues that comprised Trump's legal claims before the Wisconsin Supreme Court. These are still unresolved:

- Was the "Democracy in the Park" operation legal?

- Who is an "indefinitely confined" voter?

---

55 Jeremy Porter, "Wisconsin Election Hearing Finds Over 100,000 Voters Have Been Registered For Over 100 Years," *Red Voice Media*, December 9, 2021, (includes video), https://www.redvoicemedia.com/2021/12/wisconsin-election-hearing-finds-over-100000-voters-have-been-registered-for-over-100-years-video/.

- Can ballots be legally witnessed by election officials?

- What constitutes a "written application" for in-person voting?

Unfortunately, the Wisconsin Supreme Court did not render a decision based on the merits of the case. Instead, its controversial ruling was based on process: specifically, laches (basically, not filing as soon as you could have and should have). If the case had been tried on the substance of the claims, two things might now be known:

- Would Trump have won the state if WEC had faithfully applied the statutes?

- Will courts force the WEC to adhere to statutes in future elections?

Until those issues are settled, auditors will not know how to analyze and tabulate votes in future elections. For example, should the auditor count the vote from ballots collected at semi-partisan events like "Democracy at the Park"? Or, should those votes be disregarded as illegal? Should the auditor obtain verification that "indefinitely confined" people have been, in fact, confined due to some physical condition? If ballot applications are incomplete, should the related votes be counted? Can government clerks complete applications for voters?

You see, real audits are more than counting. They do involve counting, but only after delving into the nature of people, transactions, events, and the law.

OPEN ITEMS IN PROCESS

Jeff O'Donnell work is unresolved
Jeff O'Donnell raised several questions pertaining to changes to active voter lists and registration records. Many of the concerns have been resolved, but some remain open. See page 232.

Supreme Court limits drop boxes but questions remain
On Friday, July 8, 2022, the Wisconsin Supreme Court issued a ruling that sharply limits the use of drop boxes. The Court stated that absentee ballots can be returned to a clerk's office or to a designated alternative site, but not to an unmanned box. Voting rights activists are already claiming that harvesting of ballots remains legal if sent to the clerk's office by United States mail. More legal battles are likely. [56]

---

56   Scott Bauer, "Wisconsin Supreme Court disallows absentee ballot drop boxes," *Associated Press News*, July 8, 2022, https:// apnews.com/article/2022-midterm-elections-biden-donald-trump-wisconsin-supreme-court-05166e3f3ef970b5cde8ac1 5cd30e18b.

Election laws undecided by the courts

Several legal issues are unresolved because courts issued rulings based on process, rather than merit. See page 233 for a summary of the issues.

WAS CERTIFICATION OF THE WISCONSIN ELECTION PREMATURE?

The certification of the Wisconsin election results was premature because there are unresolved issues that involve a total vote number that is far greater than the margin of victory in this state's 2020 election.

- There is the serious anomaly in Madison Ward 124. That is where the vote *increased by about 1,285 percent*. That increase is particularly troubling in view of the allegations of Ethan Pease regarding possible USPS misconduct. Those allegations were not proven, nor were they debunked (despite claims to the contrary). An audit of the county should be performed. Questioning a few Post Office workers is not nearly enough.

- The Special Counsel (Mike Gableman) for the Wisconsin State Assembly recommended that the Assembly consider rescinding its certification of the presidential election, based on his preliminary findings concerning nursing home irregularities, lawbreaking, and voting and machine irregularities. See page 208.

- As noted, the Office of Special Counsel (OSC) faced a wall of obstruction from the Wisconsin Attorney General, Josh Kaul, and from other election administrators, including those in the very liberal cities. They resisted every subpoena, and have refused to respond to Open Records requests from private watchdog groups. Now that the OSC has been terminated, many of those subpoenas and open record requests are now in limbo.

- In December 2021, W.I.L.L. reported that 23,361 voters cast votes *despite failing their DMV check*, meaning that their identity, or some aspect of it, does not match the information on file at the DMV. The Wisconsin Elections Commission would not provide W.I.L.L. with underlying information sources.

- According to W.I.L.L., 31,664 voters were in the national change of address database. Many of those voters had apparently moved out of state prior to Election Day.

- Ballot rejection rates dropped dramatically from the 2016 election to the 2020 election. The 2016 rate (1.35 percent) is 6.75 times greater than the 2020 rate (.2). This suggests a need to verify that ballot envelopes were properly completed and signatures were properly verified.

- As noted on page 214, there is a type of Wisconsin voter who has special status, and is exempt from the normal identification requirements: the "Indefinitely Confined Voter." The number of such voters in Wisconsin jumped from 66,600 in 2016 to 266,000 in 2020. That increase means that *nearly 200,000 individuals evaded (properly or improperly) the normal voting ID rules.* The testing of signatures, by competent and independent experts, is required to determine that voters were not misusing the Indefinitely Confined Voter category.

- Ballot harvesting is more than possible. On a real-time basis, Democrat operatives had unnatural access to WisVote—the Wisconsin database of voters. (See page 222.) The information acquired from WisVote may have been used in an elaborate "ballot harvesting" scheme. According to True the Vote, at least 14,000 ballots (and as many as 83,000 ballots) were obtained by mules from nongovernmental organizations. Those ballots were distributed among several drop boxes in the Milwaukee County area.

- The ballot harvesting cited above would have been easy, since most drop boxes in Wisconsin were unmonitored and lacking basic documentation. W.I.L.L. said that only ten of twenty-four communities using drop boxes bothered to keep chain of custody logs. This fact, alone, may have precluded a fair certification of the election.

- In a survey of 2,000 people who supposedly requested ballots, 8.3% of Democrats and 16.6% of Republicans said they did not request ballots. This could indicate wide-spread fraud.

AT A MINIMUM, THESE AREAS OF EXAMINATION ARE NEEDED.

1. Professional pollsters or auditors should perform door-to-door canvassing of registered voters in high turn-out districts, including Madison wards. Respondents should be asked whether they voted, and by what means they voted.

2. The Office of Special Council, which was working on behalf of the Wisconsin Assembly, is now disbanded. However, the Assembly must seek compliance with all subpoenas that had been issued by the Special Council. The withholding of information requested during an audit is a serious "red flag" that may indicate law breaking.

3. The Wisconsin Institute for Law and Liberty (W.I.L.L.) reported that 23,361 voters cast votes despite having information that did not match DMV records. It appears that another 31,664 voters may have permanently moved out of state prior to the election. That would invalidate their votes. Resolution of these issues is required. At the very minimum, statistically significant samples should be evaluated by independent auditors (not the Wisconsin Elections Commission).

4. Because the ballot rejection rate fell dramatically (to about one seventh of the 2016 rate), a sample of the signatures on ballot envelopes should be evaluated by a qualified panel of forensic document examiners.

5. It is likely that some of the so-called "Indefinitely Confined Voters" claimed that status to evade identification requirements. Therefore, a sample of such voters should be checked via door-to-door canvassing and signature review.

6. It appears that some members of the Wisconsin Elections Commission may have behaved unethically. Legislative reform of WEC is required.

7. As noted, W.I.L.L. surveyed 2000 people who supposedly requested ballots, but said they had not requested them. This survey needs to be expanded with professional document examiners and auditors.

When these actions are concluded, it may be possible to affirm the certification of the election.

PART IV

THE GRAND THEORIES OF MIKE LINDELL, DR. DOUGLAS FRANK, AND STATE SENATOR PATRICK COLBECK

11

A LITTLE HISTORY OF LINDELL AND FRANK

In many parts of this book there is discussion of mail-in ballots and how they may be intercepted and used to stuff ballot drop boxes. In addition, there is frequent mention of the primary means to detect such fraud: through canvassing a statistically meaningful sample of voters at their homes. This section adds another, more complicated element: how computers may have been used to facilitate the fraud. We analyze the theories of election fraud that have been expounded by Mike Lindell, Dr. Douglas Frank, and Patrick Colbeck. Their arguments are not proven, but there is some supporting evidence. In particular, please refer to the cyber analysis performed in Mesa County, Colorado by Jeff O'Donnell and Walter C. Daugherity. They found evidence of vote manipulation and apparent cover-up by Dominion machines. That analysis is discussed on page 261.

MYSTERIOUS MARY

On January 9, 2021 Mike Lindell was given access to computer script that, supposedly, showed Chinese hacking of the United States 2020 presidential election. Lindell got the information from Mary Fanning, according to a statement she made on a January 2021 broadcast on a Brannon Howse show called, "The Situation Room."[1] This mysterious woman "has no internet footprint, displays no photographs or history, and is only a voice over the telephone in numerous radio broadcasts and video productions

---

[1] Brannon Howse, "Situation Room," *WVW Broadcast Network*, January 18, 2021, https://www.worldviewweekend.com/situation-room/audio/brannon-howse-january-18-2021.

over the last several years."[2] She says the lack of photos is needed for purposes of security. Some claim that she was a CIA agent before being "drummed out" of the agency.[3] Fanning considers herself to be a national security journalist, and she posts articles at TheAmericanReport.com.

DEVIOUS DENNIS?

In 2017, Fanning wrote a series of articles concerning the claims of Dennis Montgomery, a controversial software designer and former defense contractor. Montgomery alleged that the government had a supercomputer, called "The Hammer," which was used to illegally spy on American citizens. Some of Fanning's articles allegedly include descriptions of, and graphs and charts from, Hammer's output. The government denies there is such a supercomputer, and several sources say that Montgomery is dishonest and unreliable.[4]

Years later, in early January 2021, Fanning contacted Mike Lindell via his Website associate, Brannon Howse. Fanning told Lindell that she had computer evidence showing that the 2020 election was stolen. The information she presented to Lindell looked a whole lot like the things that were produced by the Hammer, and the guy who gave it to Fanning was, once again, Dennis Montgomery.[5]

Lindell already believed that Donald Trump was cheated in the election, so he was pleased to give Fanning's information to the president. In January 2021, he presented the evidence to President Trump in the Oval Office.[6]

Although Trump's legal team was wary of Lindell and his newly acquired information, the pillow CEO promoted the alleged evidence with gusto on his own television/internet programs such as "Absolute Proof."

ENTER DR. FRANK

Dr. Frank was introduced to Mike Lindell by a mutual acquaintance, Kathy Barnette, who had unsuccessful run for a U.S. House seat. At that time, Frank had already analyzed election results from several states, and Lindell had released his documentary, "Absolute Proof." Sixteen of Lindell's attorneys and four technical people (presumably

2   Sharon Rondeau, "Is Mary Fanning a Real Operative?" *The Post and Email*, July 27, 2021, https://www.thepostemail.com/2021/07/27/is-mary-fanning-a-real-operative/.

3   Ibid.

4   Ibid.

5   Brannon Howse, "Situation Room," *WVW Broadcast Network*, January 18, 2021.

6   Ibid.

cyber and statistical experts) arranged a Zoom call grilling of Douglas Frank. They were so impressed with Frank's findings that they wanted him to participate in Lindell's second documentary, "Absolute Interference," which was being produced in Tennessee. Could he get there right away?

The next Monday, Frank arrived in Memphis, where he met General Mike Flynn in a heavily guarded steel-walled room with shuttered doors and no windows. Dr. Frank estimates that there were twenty people—about half had guns and the other half had cameras. (He did not say what the guns were for.) Frank spent much of that day working on his own projects.

Dr. Frank and Mike Lindell were supposed to meet early the next morning to discuss Frank's findings, but Lindell was late. "I'm so sorry," he said, as he rolled in around 10:05. The cameras were ready to roll, so Lindell said, "Just start." "Start what?" asked Frank. "Whatever you have," replied Lindell.

With the cameras recording, Lindell heard, for the first time, Frank describe the election "keys" (6th order polynomial algorithms) he had discovered. These could be used to predict election results with remarkable precision for every age group within every county in a state. Frank had already developed keys for all of the counties in five states. (Eventually he would do the same for many other states.) According to the scientist, his work proved beyond any doubt that election fraud took place.

After just five minutes, an animated Lindell jumped up, with arms waving. "Stop everything! Reset the cameras. I want to do a full hour documentary just on Dr. Frank's work." That hour-long production would become "Scientific Proof," another documentary on Lindell's website. Both men realized that their findings meshed well, and reinforced each other.[7]

---

7   Pete Santilli, "Video interview of Dr. Douglas Frank," *The Pete Santilli Show*, November 12, 2021, https://rumble.com/vp4i7h-dr.-frank-epic-interview-with-pete-santilli-november-12-2021.html, @5:10.

12

THE CLAIMS OF MIKE LINDELL

I went out and bought a $70 pillow in 1977. Who does that as a teenager?

—MIKE LINDELL

My Pillow CEO, Mike Lindell, states that he was given vast amounts ("thousands of pages") of computer script, showing these specific parameters of a massive hack starting on November 1, 2020 and lasting several days:

- Date

- IP Source (the Internet Protocol of the originating system)

- Source owner (e.g., China Mobile Communications)

- ID of source (exact computer)

- IP target (the Internet Protocol of the target system)

- State target (e.g., Wisconsin)

- Target entry point (e.g., Clark County)

- ID of target (specific computer)

- Method of intrusion (using credentials, breaking firewall, or both)

- Successful? (yes or no)

- Change of votes (e.g., "Trump down 3000")

In Lindell's video, "Absolute Proof," several lines of script are displayed, and the voice of Mary Fanning is heard describing each parameter. Fanning states that 66 percent of the intrusions originated from China or China-related sources. Votes were altered when they exited the offices of state secretaries of state.[1]

FIGURE 17: PARTIAL SCREENSHOT FROM LINDELL'S "ABSOLUTE PROOF"

IP TARGET	STATE TARGET	TARGET ENTRY POINT / OWNER	ID TARGET	METHOD INTRUSION	SUCCESS	LOG TRACE	VOTES CHANGED
66.129.42.43	MICHIGAN	EMMET COUNTY	04:cf:6f:5c:8b:aa	*	Y	Y	TRUMP: 3477
159.233.2.2	ARIZONA	PIMA COUNTY ELECTION	10:2e:49:35:68:fa	CREDENTIALS		Y	TRUMP: DOWN 33066
74.174.32.228	GEORGIA	GWINNETT COUNTY ELECTION	ea:87:b2:68:81:53	*	Y	Y	TRUMP: DOWN 10433
207.38.72.55	GEORGIA	EFFINGHAM COUNTY ELECTION	84:60:04:6f:50:f1	FIREWALL	Y		TRUMP: DOWN 1116
67.192.61.135	MICHIGAN	HOUGHTON COUNTY	5b:f9:5b:9d:a5:fa	FIREWALL	Y	Y	TRUMP: DOWN 1143
216.245.224.78	MICHIGAN	ANTRIM COUNTY	d8:c7:22:d5:34:ce	BOTH		Y	TRUMP: DOWN 1201
104.16.0.195	GEORGIA	COBB COUNTY ELECTION	37:a2:23:d8:ef:d1	FIREWALL	Y	Y	TRUMP: DOWN 13044
66.96.149.31	GEORGIA	CALHOUN COUNTY ELECTION	08:f0:bd:cd:08:f0	BOTH			TRUMP: DOWN 13244
34.192.0.65	MICHIGAN	OAKLAND COUNTY	26:3d:af:6b:03:1e	CREDENTIALS	Y	Y	TRUMP: DOWN 13449
172.217.18.19	WISCONSIN	ADAMS COUNTY	6b:bf:df:e8:59:65	FIREWALL		N	TRUMP: DOWN 17044
50.62.172.113	GEORGIA	ROCKDALE COUNTY ELECTION	28:8a:59:5c:d9:b9	FIREWALL	Y	Y	TRUMP: DOWN 17175
205.213.0.76	WISCONSIN	WINNEBAGO COUNTY	02:8e:82:65:6d:16	BOTH	Y	N	TRUMP: DOWN 17833
99.83.180.235	NEVADA	CLARK COUNTY	91:26:91:5d:e2:79	BOTH	Y	Y	TRUMP: DOWN 18044
205.213.0.202	WISCONSIN	WAUKESHA COUNTY	ce:79:f4:18:12:10	CREDENTIALS	Y		TRUMP: DOWN 18404
13.82.40.73	GEORGIA	FULTON COUNTY ELECTION	6a:f3:a0:59:44:71	CREDENTIALS	Y	N	TRUMP: DOWN 18409
23.185.0.1	GEORGIA	DEKALB COUNTY ELECTION	49:d8:c9:d1:67:09	*	N	N	TRUMP: DOWN 18445
104.16.0.1	GEORGIA	COBB COUNTY ELECTION	d0:98:3a:88:e6:c4	CREDENTIALS		Y	TRUMP: DOWN 18904
2.16.186.47	WISCONSIN	RACINE COUNTY	07:59:bb:8c:3b:11	BOTH	Y		TRUMP: DOWN 19011
13.64.0.146	PENNSYLVANIA	DELAWARE COUNTY	1c:d3:b4:d3:8c:cd	CREDENTIALS	Y		TRUMP: DOWN 19359
208.90.188.132	PENNSYLVANIA	MONTGOMERY COUNTY	63:0f:47:a0:9d:5a	BOTH			TRUMP: DOWN 22033
204.194.248.251	WISCONSIN	MILWAUKEE COUNTY	4f:3e:00:26:83:a9	*	Y	N	TRUMP: DOWN 22215
13.64.0.219	GEORGIA	FULTON COUNTY ELECTION	f1:01:f9:71:99:d4	CREDENTIALS	Y	Y	TRUMP: DOWN 22519
75.98.160.227	MICHIGAN	MACKINAC COUNTY	bf:2a:69:8d:8c:8d	FIREWALL	Y	N	TRUMP: DOWN 22765
68.185.163.98	WISCONSIN	CLARK COUNTY	52:39:48:5f:4c:35	FIREWALL	Y	N	TRUMP: DOWN 23909

An implicit part of the scheme was that cyber intrusions could be concealed by manipulating votes in election machines, such as those made by Dominion Voting Systems, and through the use of paper ballots, which would be harvested and used as "backfill."

According to other audio recordings made by Fanning, the computer and software used to capture this cyber information was developed by the U.S. government as part of its war against terror. She claims that John Brennan (Director of CIA until 2017) and James Clapper (Director of National Intelligence until 2017) eventually began using the supercomputer for domestic spying and election hacking.[2]

In 2015 a whistleblower allegedly brought the existence of the supercomputer, and its misuse, to the attention of then FBI Director, James Comey. Fanning believes Comey "knew, in fact, that our election machines were open for hacking."[3]

---

1   Mike Lindell, "Absolute Proof Documentary," *Lindell-TV*, April 18, 2021, https://frankspeech.com/tv/video/absolute-proof-exposing-election-fraud-and-theft-america-enemies-foreign-and-domestic.

2   Dr. Meri Crouley, "Video of interview of Mary Fanning," *The Hammer Archives of TheAmericanReport.org.*, September 22, 2021.

3   Mike Lindell, "Video interview of Mary Fanning on Absolute Proof Documentary," *Lindell-TV*, April 18, 2021, @1:45:47, https://frankspeech.com/tv/video/absolute-proof-exposing-election-fraud-and-theft-america-enemies-foreign-and-domestic.

SUPPORTING ARGUMENTS

- It appears to be factual that Dennis Montgomery once had government cybersecurity contracts, and had helped develop government programs.

- In a sworn affidavit, an experienced expert in cyber security, Dr. Navid Keshavarz-Nia, attested to the existence of a supercomputer and software developed by the U.S. Intelligence Community (known as the "Hammer and Scorecard"). According to Keshavarz-Nia, the secret of this computer and software was released by Wiki Leaks and confirmed by Lt. Gen. Thomas McInerney and Dennis Montgomery. It was developed to conduct man-in-the-middle attacks against foreign voting systems.[4] For more information on Keshavarz-Nia, see "The Smartest Man in the Room" on page 58.

- Lindell hired people to check some of the IP addresses for the target computers, and he reports that the IP addresses that were checked appear to be genuine.[5] That much of Lindell's theory could be true: The IP addresses are real, and foreign governments were monitoring the election. Lindell goes further, however, and asserts (or at least implies) that foreign powers were directly changing election results in most states in the union. That broad assertion is not supported.

- After analyzing a copy of the hard drive from a Dominion machine (in March 2022), Jeffrey O'Donnell and Walter C. Daugherity determined that votes were manipulated in one of two ways: by hacking or by an internal, pre-set algorithm in the machine. The cyber experts could not rule out hacking because access logs had been erased. (See page 261.)

ARGUMENTS AGAINST LINDELL

- Has anyone seen Mary Fanning? What is her background and what are her credentials? We can't assign credibility to a phantom.

---

4   A man-in-the-middle attack involves three entities: There are two computers communicating with each other, and a hacker in between them, intercepting communications without their knowledge.

5   Mike Lindell, "Absolute Interference," *Lindell-TV*, May 3, 2021, @1:35, https://frankspeech.com/video/absolute-interference-sequel-absolute-proof-new-evidence-foreign-and-domestic-enemies-used.

- Dennis Montgomery has a very controversial past. After 9-11, he sold terrorist tracking software to the U.S. Defense Department and foreign governments. It was supposed to alert them to terrorist threats. He claimed that there were "embedded coded messages for future terrorist attacks in Al Jazeera's broadcasts."[6] The government concluded that the software was worthless, and some speculated that the government was conned by Montgomery.

- At his multi-day and well-hyped cyber symposium in August 2021, Lindell guaranteed that the world would see the computer "PCAPs" (Packet Captures) associated with the purported election hacking and alteration of vote totals. (A PCAP is an application programming interface that captures live network packet data.) However, Lindell did not produce the PCAPs. [In a video interview on November 12, 2021, Dr. Douglas Frank claimed that Lindell could not produce the PCAPs because law enforcement was at the symposium, and he believed he would have been arrested on the spot for a breach of national security.][7]

- The star of Lindell's cyber symposium, Dennis Montgomery, did not show up. At the very last minute it was claimed that he had suffered a stroke.

- Lindell's allegation that a supercomputer changed votes thousands of times in all fifty states lacks credibility. Why would vote alterations be made in fifty states? It would involve needless effort and risk of detection. Why not concentrate on the swing states?

- Last, but not least, some election officials around the country saw their own computer IP addresses displayed during the Lindell Symposium. In a fact check published by the Wisconsin Elections Commission (WEC) on its own website, the WEC noted that "some of the alleged Wisconsin IPs are actually in other states." It also stated that their computer vote totals appear to be correct and could be reconciled to paper ballots on file. As a counterargument, Lindell has challenged authorities everywhere and anywhere to prove him wrong by providing access to routers.

---

6   Adam Klasfeld, "Risen cleared on labeling CIA contractor a 'con artist,'" *Courthouse News Service*, July 18, 2016, https://web.archive.org/web/20160719125830/http://www.courthousenews.com/2016/07/18/risen-cleared-on-labeling-cia-contractor-a-con-artist.htm.

7   Pete Santilli, "Video interview of Dr. Douglas Frank," November 12, 2021.

13

THE CLAIMS OF DR. DOUGLAS FRANK

For me to get 1.00 and I'm a physicist. . . that ain't natural, buddy

—DR. DOUGLAS G. FRANK

As noted, Dr. Frank began analyzing the 2020 election in an effort to help Kathy Barnette, after she lost her 2020 race for the U.S. 4th congressional house seat in Pennsylvania. Before long, Frank noticed some patterns that seemed unnatural, so he extended his analysis to the voting patterns in other states. His source data were U.S. census figures (population by age in each county), voter registration data (available from state election offices), and overall voter turnout numbers.[1]

Dr. Frank discovered that, once he determined a pattern in a few counties (actual votes for each age level), he could develop a mathematical "key" that could be used to predict the voting pattern accurately for all other counties in the state.[2,3] Specifically, he could estimate the number of voters in each age group.

The "key" used by Dr. Frank is a "6th order polynomial," and it predicts so accurately that, for a given county, estimated voter turnout correlates almost perfectly with actual turnout.[4] In each case the correlation factor (R) is very close to 1.0, which is perfection. Frank believes that the extreme accuracy of those results indicates fraud,

---

1 Mike Lindell, "Video interview of Dr. Douglas Frank in the Scientific Proof Documentary," *Lindell-TV*, August 9, 2021, https://frankspeech.com/video/scientific-proof-internationally-renowned-physicist-absolutely-proves-2020-election-was.

2 Some states have a lot of counties. For example, Pennsylvania has 67, Wisconsin has 72, Michigan has 83, and Georgia has 159.

3 Frank refers to these keys as "6th order polynomials." They are sometimes referred to as "6th degree polynomials."

4 A polynomial is a mathematical expression composed of variables, constants, and exponents that are combined using the mathematical operations such as addition, subtraction, multiplication, and division.

committed using computers to monitor and change the voting results.[5] You can see Dr. Frank's graphs for several of his counties at his website: https://electionfraud20. org/dr-frank-reports/.

FRANK'S ANALYSIS REVEALS TWO UNNATURAL VOTING PATTERNS

Why don't economic and ethnic factors affect the "key"?
To me, there are two aspects of Frank's predictions that could indicate possible election irregularities: There are ethnic and economic variations between the populations of different counties within a state. Some counties are poorer and some are whiter, some counties are urban and some are rural, etc. Yet, Dr. Frank is able to predict the voter turnout by age level in all counties in a state, using the very same "key."

For example, Table 11 shows Dr. Frank's results for seven (7) Pennsylvania counties. The first one is the very urban county of Philadelphia, while the others are found in less populated parts of the Commonwealth. I picked those other counties arbitrarily, yet all of them (urban or rural) have the same super-high correlation rates. Perhaps race and economics have no impact on turnout levels of different age groups, but it seems odd.[6]

TABLE 11: COMPARISON OF URBAN PHILADELPHIA COUNTY WITH OTHER COUNTIES

County	Dr. Frank's Correlation Factor
Philadelphia	.998
Crawford	.998
Beaver	.999
Bedford	.998
Blair	1.000
Berks	1.000
Bradford	.999

---

5   Mike Lindell, "Video interview of Dr. Douglas Frank in the *Scientific Proof* Documentary," August 9, 2021.

6   Douglas Frank, "Pennsylvania Election Analysis by Dr. Douglas Frank," accessed March 6, 2022, https://electionfraud20. org/dr-frank-reports/pennsylvania/.

Why does the "key" change at the state border?

Frank's findings seem unnatural in another respect. Although his 6th order polynomial key will work for every county within a state, that same key won't work well in other states. In other words, the key that works in all eighty-eight counties in Ohio will not perform well in any of the sixty-seven counties in Pennsylvania. However, Dr. Frank is able to produce a different key (a different 6th order polynomial) that will work with precision for all Pennsylvania counties.

Dr. Frank analyzed several states, and the same pattern held. (i.e., each state has its own unique key that predicts voting in all counties but only within that state.) I can think of only one explanation for the changes at the border: state and local issues and candidates. For example, if State A has a referendum on the ballot for smoking marijuana, and State B does not, we would expect State A to have a higher percentage of young voters.

If you'd like to see a visual comparison of five different keys (for Penn., Ohio, Fla., Mich., and Ariz.), please go to the Arizona page of Dr. Frank's site at https://electionfraud20.org/dr-frank-reports/arizona/. Click on the "Video Presentation: Fifteen Arizona Counties." The image is displayed at 25:50.

Frank believes that these patterns do not occur naturally: Someone has to adjust the votes. However, he is certain that no human or group of humans would have the computational power to make such adjustments in real time. It would take massive computer power before, during, and after the election. That is why he is receptive to Mike Lindell's theory, as espoused in "Absolute Proof."[7]

Unlike Lindell, Frank does not presently believe that manipulation of votes took place in all or most states, although he believes that many states were monitored. Dr. Frank believes that computers were used to change votes only where victory in the state election was in jeopardy. In those situations, electronic vote changes were followed by the insertion of harvested ballots to ensure that the paper counts matched the electronic tabulations. The insertion of harvested ballots was easy: They could be mailed to election centers or placed into drop boxes.

It is just a theory, but given the unwillingness of most counties to allow inspection of computers and routers, we cannot rule it out.[8]

---

7   Ibid.

8   Brannon Howse interviews Dr. Douglas Frank, "Introduction to the key," Defending the Republic.org. June 30, 2021, https://rumble.com/vj98g1-introduction-to-the-key-dr.-frank.html.

SUPPORTING ARGUMENTS

- Frank has produced numerous graphs of counties, and the high correlations (R) appear to be consistent.[9]

- There have been some volunteer canvassing efforts that support his findings.[10]

- It is odd that the polynomial formulae seem to change at the boundary of each state (although the variations might be attributable to differences in state and local candidates).

- It is odd that the same formula can be used for urban counties as well as rural counties. Due to variations in economic levels and ethnicity, we might expect different voting patterns.

ARGUMENTS AGAINST DR. FRANK

- To my knowledge, the specific formulae being used (i.e., the 6th order polynomials) have not been not revealed.

- Dr. Frank uses voter roll data ending on October 31, 2020 rather than on November 3, 2020. It is an important distinction in the case of states that allow voter registration up to the day of the election.

- Frank has analyzed a few states where presidential elections are not usually close. One is Washington state, where Biden won by 19 percent in the 2020 election, and another is Montana, where Trump won by 16 percent. Those two states also show high correlations. Does Frank believe there was vote manipulation in those states? If there was manipulation, why?

- Some critics claim (with respect to Lindell as well as Frank) that their theories would involve massive and potentially unworkable collusive effort by hundreds of people. Changes in the electronic tabulation would require changes, potentially, to thousands of paper ballots.

9   "Dr. Douglas G. Frank's Election Analysis," accessed February 20, 2022, https://electionfraud20.org/dr-frank-reports/.

10   Ibid.

Frank disagrees, as do I. Once the electronic changes are made, one or two people can make the paper ballots conform to those changes by filling the mail boxes or drop boxes with hundreds or even thousands of paper ballots—assuming they have a supply of harvested ballots on hand.

14

PATRICK COLBECK AND HIS THEORY
OF THE ELECTION

Mr. Colbeck is a former aerospace engineer and former member of the Michigan State Senate. He believes that 2020 election fraud would have featured a combination of process and technology exploits, and would have been carried out in four stages: Preparation, Main attack, Back-up attack, and Defense of the attacks. He does not make these assertions as fact, but simply as an invitation for more investigation and analysis.[1]

PREPARATION
The ground work for electronic election fraud is the general weakening of election controls and standards, and it would probably take place over several years. It might include moving to same-day registration, no-excuse-needed absentee voting, mail-in ballots sent to everyone, puffing up registration lists, and the use of electronic voting systems.

MAIN ATTACK
The main attack phase features the stuffing of the ballot box with fraudulent mail-in ballots. Electronic voting systems are used to monitor the status of turnout so as to determine if a backup attack is necessary.

BACK-UP ATTACK
This stage is needed only if there is a miscalculation. Colbeck theorizes that Democrat

---

1   Patrick Colbeck, "Anatomy of the Steal," *Nemos News Network*, October 24, 2021, https://nemosnewsnetwork.com/anatomy-of-the-steal-the-four-phases-of-an-election-takeover-former-michigan-senator-patrick-colbeck/.

operatives thought the 2020 election would yield a total of 145 million votes. Instead, there were about 160 million votes. Because of that mistake, a riskier effort was needed, involving the use of digital controllers to directly modify voter databases. Once the election results were modified directly in the election databases, other election records had to be updated as well.[2]

DEFENSE STAGE

To prevent detection of the scheme, real audits must be blocked. This is particularly true if the audits include residential canvassing, signature matching, and examination of spunk logs and routers. The mainstream media does this job.

HELP FROM LADY DRAZA

As noted, the "Back-up attack" theory involves the direct alteration of the voter database by use of digital controllers. Colbeck obtained support for this notion from a cyber and electrical engineer named Draza Smith. (I understand that her friends call her "Lady Draza.") She had noticed something peculiar while reviewing 2020 election results: In some of the swing states the cumulative vote totals momentarily dropped to zero, and then jumped back up. Coincidentally, she had observed that behavior before, with a particular type of digital controller.

Armed with that information, Colbeck did some checking and found out that, indeed, digital controllers could be used with respect to election results. Further investigation convinced Mr. Colbeck that Michigan had all the ingredients necessary to carry out electronic election fraud by means of direct changes to voter databases.[3] Again, Colbeck asserts this as only a theory, but one that is supported by many facts.

---

2   Colbeck notes that the updates may have been implemented via the late night ballot drops that were observed at the Detroit TCF Center, and by means of last-minute poll book updates at the Wayne County Board of Canvassers.

3   Ibid.

15

AN ANALYSIS OF THESE THEORIES

IGNORE THE GOVERNMENT. HERE IS WHY.
Pardon me while I digress.

Ideally, we would simply ask our federal government: "Are Lindell, Frank, and Colbeck crazy? They claim or imply that there were cyber intrusions into our election. Is that credible?" The answer is clear, according to Chris Krebs, former head of CISA (Cybersecurity and Infrastructure Security Agency): It is "nonsense."

Political motivations
But in our new, "1984" world, the federal government does not have much credibility, especially in politically-charged controversies. If this sounds paranoid and political, so be it . . . because it is true. Recent events have taught us that there are, entrenched in the federal bureaucracy, workers with their own agendas. To wit:

- An FBI agent illegally altered an email printout so that the agency could get FISA warrants to use against the Trump campaign (Russia probe).[1]

- For nearly a year before the election, the FBI had Hunter Biden's laptop, and could trace all the emails to confirm their authenticity. FBI knew the emails were discovered on a laptop, and not from hacking. Nevertheless, just before the

---

1   Kyle Cheney and Josh Gerstein, "Former FBI attorney to plead guilty for altering email in Russia probe, *Politico*, August 14, 2020, https://www.politico.com/news/2020/08/14/fbi-attorney-guilty-email-russia-probe-395317.

2020 election, the Bureau used the Russia hacking angle, in conjunction with Twitter employees, to suppress the Hunter Biden story. See footnote.[2]

- Almost immediately after social media suppressed the Hunter laptop story, fifty-one former intelligence officials wrote that they were "deeply suspicious that the Russian government played a significant role in this case."[3] This letter, written by many Biden supporters, was based on absolutely nothing, and it obviously had political subtones.

- Christopher Krebs gave the impression that the 2020 election had no fraud, and he repeated that canard right up until the day he was grilled under oath at a Senate hearing. Then he clarified that he had no idea whatever if there was fraud. He had never considered that issue. See Christopher Krebs on page 271.

- In early 2021 the Intelligence Community's Analytic Ombudsman reported that IC analysts "appeared reluctant to have their analysis on China brought forward because they tend to disagree with the [Trump] administration's policies, saying in effect, I don't want our intelligence used to support those policies." In other words, the United States intelligence community altered its report in an effort to undermine Trump policies and hurt his re-election chances.[4]

- Of course, we should not forget the text messages of Peter Strzok and Lisa Page, and their mention of an "insurance policy." And, exactly what happened in the meetings with Andrew McCabe?

2   Twitter's head of Site Integrity, Yoel Roth, stated in a declaration to the FEC that, before the election. "Federal law enforcement agencies communicated that they expected 'hack-and-leak operations' by state actors might occur in the period shortly before the 2020 presidential election. . . . I also learned in these meetings that there were rumors that a hack-and-leak operation would involve Hunter Biden." Twitter used those warnings from federal law enforcement as justification for suppressing the Hunter Biden story.

3   Zack Budryk, "50 former intelligence officials warn New York Post story sounds like Russian disinformation," *The Hill*, October 20, 2020,https://thehill.com/homenews/campaign/521823-50-former-intelligence-officials-warn-ny-post-story-sounds-like-russian.

4   Marmee Rooke, "DNI John Ratcliffe Bombshell Report: China Interfered in the 2020 Federal Elections," *Federalist Papers*, January 18, 2021, https://thefederalistpapers.org/us/dni-john-ratcliffe-bombshell-report-china-interfered-2020-federal-elections.

Lack of government competence

Political motivations are just part of the problem. There is also a question of competence. When it comes to detection of cyber intrusions, the U.S. government does not have a good track record.

- Christopher Krebs said he was certain there were no cyber intrusions in the election. Shortly after making that sweeping statement we all learned about one of the most damaging cyber intrusions in history, the "Solar Winds" hack. It went undetected for more than a year, and even affected many federal government agencies while Krebs was head of CISA. It was finally discovered by a private company, after Krebs left CISA.[5]

- In November 2021 we learned of another hack—one directly targeting the 2020 election. "Iranians downloaded confidential voter data from 100,000 voters in an unnamed state in September and October 2020," according to prosecutors. They posed as "Proud Boys" (some sort of conservative group) in an apparent attempt to discredit Republicans. Again, Krebs and CISA were clueless.[6]

Government secrecy

There is one more reason that we can't expect an honest answer from the federal government regarding these cyber theories. According to Mary Fanning and Navid Keshavarz-Nia, the cyber system used in the 2020 election had its roots in U.S. intelligence agencies, and it is highly classified. If that is true, we can't expect anyone in government to confirm its existence.

For the above-stated reasons, we cannot assume there were no cyber intrusions into the election simply because our federal government says so. It is a sad situation, but the government has zero credibility in matters concerning the election.

MY TAKE ON THE LINDELL, FRANK, AND COLBECK THEORIES

There are six swing states analyzed in this book. In addition, there were a few other states in contention before the election. Those states are Florida, Ohio, North Carolina, and perhaps New Hampshire.

Lindell seems to say or imply that all or most of the fifty states were hacked, and

5   "The SolarWinds Cyber Attack," Republican Policy Committee of the U.S. Senate, accessed February 1, 2022, https://www.rpc.senate.gov/policy-papers/the-solarwinds-cyberattack.

6   Ben Feuerherd, "Iran hackers stole US voter data, posed as Proud Boys in effort to influence 2020 election: feds," *New York Post*, November 18, 2021, https://nypost.com/2021/11/18/iran-hackers-stole-us-voter-data-to-influence-2020-election-feds/.

voter databases were directly modified in many cases. To me, however, it does not seem likely that non-swing states would be targeted.[7]

On this matter, Dr. Frank is a bit more circumspect. He seems to believe that many or most elections were electronically monitored, but data changes were made only in critical swing states.

Colbeck also believes that there could have been hacking and direct voter database manipulation. Like Frank, he believes that direct changes to the voter database would not be required in normal circumstances. Those alterations to the database would occur only if an emergency "back-up attack" was needed, due to an exceedingly high voter turnout. The Colbeck/Draza theory of digital controllers makes the idea of direct database manipulation seem plausible, at least in the swing states.

After weighing the ideas of these very bright people, and considering the Mesa County cyber analysis produced by O'Donnell and Daugherity (page 261), I think it is possible that computers may have been used to monitor the ongoing election results and to find out where more ballots would be useful and feasible. If digital controllers were used to make last-minute changes to some of the voter databases, then those middle-of-the-night vote spikes appear sinister and troubling. Please read footnote.[8]

The fact that our federal government denies the possibility of hacking is not convincing to me. There have been too many lies.

Only extensive auditing, including full access to election machines, can tell us if these theories are credible. Until we have such auditing and such access, I rate these theories: POSSIBLE.

---

7   I can think of only two possible reasons to cheat in the non-swing states: for the sake of local elections and/or for long-term aspirations. ("Someday, we will turn California red!")

8   Note that O'Donnell and Daugherity add an alternate theory: That Dominion machines include a built-in algorithm that is pre-set to manipulate votes. In other words, hacking is not required.

PART V

ODDS AND ENDS

16

DON'T TRUST DOMINION'S "TRUSTED BUILD"

Dominion's installation of the Trusted Build update on the EMS in May of 2021 . . . destroyed all data on the EMS hard drive, including the batch and ballot records that evidenced the creation of new databases.[1,2]

—REPORT OF CYBER EXPERTS O'DONNELL AND DAUGHERITY

> *Question: Why would someone violate federal election law (apparently) by destroying "all data on the EMS hard drive" in Mesa County, Colorado?*

Answer: Perhaps that person did it to cover up something worse that was done on October 21, 2020, while people were in the process of voting for President of the United States.

Jeffrey O'Donnell and Dr. Walter C. Daugherity are two respected cyber experts who examined Mesa County's election database prior to and after Dominion's "Trusted Build" update in May 2021. They reported several alarming findings:

They discovered that critical files, including log files, had been destroyed during the Dominion update process. This destruction apparently violated federal record retention requirements.

More disturbing were the findings that arose from the examination of the pre-Dominion database files—the files that nobody was supposed to see:

---

1   "EMS" is the acronym for Election Management System.

2   Jeffrey O'Donnell and Dr. Walter C. Daugherity, "Mesa County Colorado Voting Systems Election Database and Data Process Analysis Report no. 3," March 19, 2022, 4, https://static1.squarespace.com/static/620c3af99f21b965e2cbef44/t/6 239f21179bda53621a515e2/1647964693221/mesa-forensic-report-3-signed+%281%29.pdf.

There was an unauthorized creation of new election databases during early voting in the 2020 General Election on October 21, 2020, followed by the digital reloading of 20,346 ballot records into the new election databases, making the original voter intent recorded from the ballots unknown. In addition, 5,567 ballots in 58 batches did not have their digital records copied to the new database, although the votes from the ballots in those batches were recorded in the Main election database.[3]

In other words, while people were voting, someone deleted the election database and installed a "new" database, minus 5,567 ballots. As a result of this activity, none of the original voter intent is known. According to the report of these experts, these changes had to occur in one of three ways:[4]

1. Direct action by Mesa County personnel

2. By some sort of remote trigger from, perhaps, a local network or the internet

3. By means of "a software algorithm running inside the DVS [Dominion] computer systems in Mesa County"

The report casts doubt on option one: "Our analysis shows manipulation, which was neither initiated nor authorized by Mesa County election clerks."[5] That leaves the other two options: triggered remotely or a built-in algorithm.

O'Donnell and Daugherity noticed something else that is troubling. The secure hash algorithm (.sha) files were missing, and this makes the authenticity of each ballot "impossible to verify."[6] This is very similar to the findings of VoterGA.org in Georgia. (See page 107.)

> *Another question: Since Dominion performs the "Trusted Build" operation throughout the country, why did the experts concentrate on Mesa County, Colorado?*

---

3   Ibid., 3.

4   Ibid., 12–13.

5   Ibid., 9.

6   Ibid., 4.

Answer: Mesa County is one of the few places—perhaps the only place—where a back-up copy of the database was made (secretly) before the "Trusted Build" operation, and that back-up copy was available for examination. The person who made the backup has been targeted by law enforcement. For all we know, there could have been database manipulations in many counties in the country.

A self-described whistleblower, named Tina Peters, was the elected County Clerk in Mesa. Peters initially assumed that the election process was entirely secure, but after some surprising results in a city election she heard of people questioning the election process.

As the County Clerk, Peters knew that Dominion workers would periodically show up to perform "maintenance" on the computer system. As a precaution, Peters decided to make a back-up copy of the election database before they arrived, which was near the end of May 2021.

Months later, images of voting system information appeared on the internet, and the Secretary of State assumed they came from Peters, and perhaps they did. After all, Peters regarded herself as a whistleblower who was pointing out serious potential problems with the Dominion upgrades.

The Democrat administration in Colorado and the Merrick Garland Justice Department didn't see Peters as a sympathetic whistleblower. Rather, she was a criminal who somehow distributed computer images to the public. Heavily-armed FBI agents conducted early-morning raids of the homes of Peters and three associates. In one case a battering ram was used to break in the door.

After the raids, Tina Peters received death threats, so pillow czar Mike Lindell provided her with security and housing for several weeks. Because of that act of kindness, Peters now faces an ethics probe (for receiving a gift valued over $65).[7] Also, she was arrested for allegedly taking pictures during the trial of one of her workers, and resisting the police when they attempted to seize her phone.[8] I hope she is flossing her teeth every day. Otherwise she might end up in solitary confinement.

Tina Peters has been through a lot, but the O'Donnell/Daugherity cyber report may provide sweet solace. It is a devastating report that will also be of great interest to Mike Lindell, Sidney Powell, and a few thousand others who are being sued by Dominion

7   Bente Birkeland, "FBI searches Mesa County clerk Tina Peters' home in election security breach investigation," *Colorado Public Radio News*, November 17, 2021, https://www.cpr.org/2021/11/17/tina-peters-mesa-county-fbi-raid/.

8   Bente Birkeland, Mesa County clerk Tina Peters arrested after allegedly recording court hearing," *Colorado Public Radio News*, February 8, 2022, https://www.cpr.org/2022/02/08/mesa-county-clerk-tina-peters-arrested-after-allegedly-recording-court-hearing/.

for spreading (alleged) lies about the company. The entire eighty-seven-page report is linked in the footnotes.[9]

FOLLOW-UP: IT HAPPENED AGAIN

According to O'Donnell, some people might believe that his report involved an isolated anomaly, like "some mouse ran over the keyboard." That notion was dispelled after a subsequent election, which was held in April 2021. Voting started in March, however . . .

> They were about 40 percent of the way through the election and this rogue process woke up. . . . Same unauthorized process occurred again. . . . The working theory is that there is an algorithm running inside these [Dominion] machines that knows what the desired results of the elections are in that county.

In other words, the "glitch" that took place during the November 2020 election took place again during the April 2021 election.

O'Donnell added that there are certain "fingerprints" in those elections that he has seen in several other counties in the nation. His recommendation—which is simple and affordable—is to eliminate the computers and go to in-person voting (where feasible), using paper ballots.[10]

> | *Final question: Is anyone in our federal government investigating this?*

Please watch O'Donnell's forty-six-minute video using the link in the footnotes. This is disturbing but vital information from a true cyber expert.

9   Jeffrey O'Donnell and Dr. Walter C. Daugherity, "Mesa County Colorado Voting Systems Election Database and Data Process Analysis Report no. 3," March 19, 2022, https://static1.squarespace.com/static/620c3af99f21b965e2cbef44/t/6 239f21179bda53621a515e2/1647964693221/mesa-forensic-report-3-signed+%281%29.pdf.

10   Jeffrey O'Donnell, "The Election Fraud Pattern Has Been Discovered, This Will Not End Well for [DS]," *X22 Report*, April 30, 2022, https://rumble.com/v1315c3-jeff-odonnell-the-election-fraud-pattern-has-been-discoveredthis-will-not-e. html.

17

THE DEBUNKERS (AKA THE MEDIA)

*A lie doesn't become truth, wrong doesn't become right, and evil doesn't become good just
because it's accepted by a majority*

—BOOKER T. WASHINGTON

You can't write a book about the 2020 election without reading the views of countless self-proclaimed fact checkers and debunkers. Often, these fact checkers are simply
political operatives who wish to add a sense of precision and factuality to their opinions.
Or maybe they just want to establish their creds with the boss.

As a public service I have attempted to shed light on these people by classifying
them within three categories. First, however, we must discuss . . .

THE DOG THAT DID NOT BARK

Mainstream media love to rush out fact checks, and there are often 2 or 3 within days
of the publication of election "disinformation." Sometimes, however, the media hounds
are silent. How strange! Here are a few powerful and disturbing reports of potential
election fraud that received little or no attention from the media. In most cases there
was complete radio silence. I wonder why!

- In Georgia, the election integrity organization, VoterGA.org and its team of
  cyber experts identified 524,000 ballots that were physically impossible or completely without authentication. For example, 4,000 were scanned at the same
  time—the same split second. No scanning machine on earth can go that fast!
  Others had no .sha (authentication) files, or the .sha files were added days later.
  Where are the fact checkers? (See page 107.)

- Dr. Shiva Ayyadurai identified numerous precincts in Pima County, Ariz. with impossibly high turnout percentages (close to 100%). Trump led other Republicans in Pima precincts with moderately high turnout, but he trailed badly in the precincts with the absurdly-high turnout rates. Could those precincts be where, according to an anonymous tip, 35,000 ballots were being added to Democrat candidates? This is significant evidence of fraud. Where are the fact checkers? (See page 71.)

- Cyber experts Jeffrey O'Donnell and Dr. Walter C. Daugherity examined the election database of Mesa County, Colorado both before and after Dominion implemented its "Trusted Build" update. They found that someone deleted the data base and installed a "new" database, minus thousands of ballots. Where are the fact checkers? (See page 261.)

- In early 2022, Dr. Shiva Ayyadurai conducted a test of the signatures on 499 early voting mail-in ballot envelopes in Maricopa Co., Arizona. Each signature was examined by six individual, including three forensic document examiners. With regard to 60 signatures (12 percent), the verdict was unanimous: The signatures did not match the signatures in verified records. If this test sample reflects the general voting population, we can estimate that there could have been as many as 204,000 phony votes in the 2020 election. Where are the fact checkers? (See page 97.)

Now, back to the three categories of debunkers:

LAZY
These are the very lazy debunkers who do little more than add a few overworked words and phrases to their writings, as you might sprinkle salt and pepper on your food. In two or three paragraphs they throw in words like these a couple of times each: baseless, unfounded, big lie, misinformation, bogus, far-fetched, and conspiracy theories. If they're more experienced they will also point out troubling associations. For example, "Senator Rightwing was once seen in a picture with the mother of a Qanon supporter."

A BIT MORE DILIGENT
The next category comprises debunkers who work a little harder—but just a little. They always support their debunkings with one or more of these four citations (just these, no other):

- "The November 3rd election was the most secure in American history." (Krebs)

- "[W]e have not seen fraud on a scale that could have effected a different outcome in the election." (Barr)

- "Trump and his allies have lost nearly 60 election fights in court." (Buzzfeed and countless others)

- "Hand recounts of paper ballots have confirmed election results." (USA Today and several others)

These arguments sound pretty good, but pick up each rock to see what is underneath. They cite Krebs, even though he was only referring to cyber security—not election fraud. And, with respect to his area of expertise (cyber security), we now know that he and his CISA agency missed one of the largest hacks in history and missed an Iranian hack designed to hurt Trump in the 2020 election. (See page 271.)

They cite William Barr, but we know that DOJ never conducted an investigation. And Barr's statement (about not seeing fraud) was made on December 1, 2020, so it didn't encompass revelations after that date.

They make reference to "60 election court losses" without mentioning that most of them were ended on the basis of procedure or process (standing, laches, mootness, jurisdiction). A review of ninety-two cases by the organization, Promoting American Election Integrity, shows that only thirty were decided on merit, and Trump and/or his supporters won twenty-two of those cases.[1] See "Court cases – substance versus process" on page 279.

Finally, they say that there was no fraud because the total of paper ballots matched the electronic vote total, as if no one can stuff a drop box with ballots harvested from the nearly 15 million unaccounted-for ballots mailed out during the 2020 election. This is a red herring that has been cited by lots of people who should know better, including Christopher Krebs, William Barr, and computer expert Alex Halderman.

> In reality, none of the standard four arguments means a thing. The "fact checkers" pushing these assertions are politically motivated, confused, or ill-informed.

[1] "2020 US Presidential Election Related Lawsuits," *Promoting American Election Integrity*, accessed February 21, 2022, https://election-integrity.info/2020_Election_Cases.htm.

PRECISION FACT CHECKERS

Once well-respected media outlets are now simply nothing more than propaganda outlets.

—FORMER MICHIGAN SENATOR PATRICK COLBECK

There are several organizations that incorporate into their names or stories the word fact. These organizations include Factcheck.org, PolitiFact, Lead Stories, and the *Washington Post* Fact Checker. To give a sense of precision to their opinions, they often use some sort of visual truth meter, as if they are measuring voltage from a car battery.

QUESTION TO CONSIDER: PLEASE READ THIS AND SELECT BEST ANSWER

Who is most likely to be knowledgeable and accurate when it comes to election related issues?

> A. A cyber expert
>
> B. An experienced election expert
>
> C. A CPA auditor
>
> D. Politifact.com

Obviously, the answer is D: Politifact.com. That organization utilizes those super accurate "Truth-O-Meters" that can gauge the precise amount of misinformation given to you by Fox News.

Sometimes these fact checkers make valid arguments, but often they resort to political smears. And they do whatever it takes to always end up debunking the viewpoint of their target—generally, a conservative.

To debunk that consistently, the precision fact checkers employ sleight-of-hand, such as this:

Refusing to recognize evidence for what it is
A "Fact Focus" was written by 12NEWs (NBC) about the canvass report of Liz Harris. Ms. Harris and her many volunteers knocked on thousands of doors in Maricopa County, Arizona, and elicited responses from over 4,500 people. By any measure, that was a huge survey, about which Harris wrote a report (accurate as far as I can tell). Incredibly, the Fact Focus said:

THE FACTS: The report doesn't provide evidence for these far-fetched claims, and the county's election results have been certified for months.[2]

This fact check is nonsensical because the Harris survey results are evidence (albeit, not the evidence the fact checker wanted to see). And the date of the election certification is completely irrelevant.

Splitting hairs
A Lead Stories fact check by Alan Duke reached heights of absurdity with this title line:

Fact Check: GOP observers did NOT swear in affidavits they were told to leave Fulton County, Georgia, vote count center on election night.[3]

However, buried in the article is this statement by same Alan Duke:

Their affidavits . . . said [that] a supervisor "yelled" to the election workers who were prepping ballots for scanning to "stop working" and return the next morning. The observers said they eventually followed those workers out.[4]

Technically, Duke is right: They did not swear that they were told to go home. The observers swore that election managers said there would be nothing else to observe for the rest of the night. No one made them leave, and they could have sat there all night, waiting in the dark for the work to resume in the morning. Is that what Mr. Duke would have done?

Getting the facts wrong
Sometimes, the fact check is just plain wrong. An AP fact check reported this:

---

2 Associated Press, "Arizona canvass report draws nonsensical conclusions," *12News.com*, September 9, 2021, https://www.12news.com/article/news/politics/elections/fact-focus-arizona-canvass-report-draws-nonsensical-conclusions/75-79325610-1aae-4831-a8f5-1629c9301add.

3 Alan Duke, "GOP observers did not swear in affidavits they were told to leave Fulton County, Georgia, vote count center on election night," LeadStories, December 5, 2020, https://leadstories.com/hoax-alert/2020/12/fact-check-trump-observers-did-not-swear-in-affidavits-they-were-told-to-leave-fulton-county-georgia-vote-center-election-night.html.

4 Ibid.

Trump persisted in misrepresenting developments at ballot-counting centers, falsely tweeting that campaign observers in Pennsylvania were blocked from seeing what was going on as Biden overtook him in the vote count.[5]

Well, if poll watchers have the eyes of eagles, then the fact check is correct and Trump is wrong. But, here are the facts: Democrats in Philadelphia kept GOP observers fifteen to eighteen feet away from processing tables, and the mostly Democrat Pennsylvania Supreme Court let them get away with that. Perhaps my eyes aren't so good, but I would have a very hard time verifying a signature, or anything else, from a distance of fifteen to eighteen feet.

Other sleight of hand

Some of the fact checkers claim to have debunked something when they have merely obtained another possible explanation. All possibilities are worth hearing, but citing other possibilities does not constitute a debunking.

Sometimes the fact checkers resort to citing the censorship of other media, as if that means something. For example, "Mr. Trumpster stated these claims in an article banned by Twitter." That might be persuasive were it not for the fact that half the country is banned by Twitter.

When all else fails, and the fact checkers are really hard up, they resort to fact checking some anonymous schmuck on Facebook, or some anonymous gal writing in the comments section of an article. How desperate can you get?!

5   Calvin Woodward, "Trump's vote falsehoods, into day of defeat," *AssociatedPress News*, November 7, 2020, https://apnews.com/article/election-2020-ap-fact-check-joe-biden-donald-trump-virus-outbreak-79c34b72633683af195ae945503883fe.

18

CHRISTOPHER KREBS AND CISA

The November 3rd election was the most secure in American history. . . . [W]e can assure you we have the utmost confidence in the security and integrity of our elections, and you should too.

—JOINT STATEMENT FROM CHRIS KREBS, CISA ET AL.[1]

On November 12, 2020, that statement was issued by Christopher Krebs, jointly with an assortment of other government employees, vendors, nonprofit organizations, and activists. It was a very misleading statement because Krebs, and the agency he headed (CISA)[2] had done absolutely nothing to verify:

- That mail-in ballot applications were fully completed in accordance with state regulations

- That signatures on ballot documents matched signatures on registrations

- That ballots were authentic and were submitted in a timely manner

- That the ballots received were from U.S. citizens

- That underage people were not voting

- That the people voting were alive

---

1   "Joint Statement," *Elections Infrastructure Government Coordinating Council*, November 12, 2020, https://www.cisa.gov/news/2020/11/12/joint-statement-elections-infrastructure-government-coordinating-council-election.

2   CISA is the acronym for Cybersecurity and Infrastructure Security Agency.

- That people were voting only once and in the proper jurisdiction

- That ballots were not being shredded

- That people from all political parties were allowed to observed the processing of ballots

Misleading or not, busloads of U.S. media debunkers were happy to use this statement to discredit every effort made to verify election integrity. And Krebs was equally happy to sit back and let them do it—until he no longer could.

KREBS IS PINNED TO THE MAT

Krebs was finally cornered by a tag team of Senators Rand Paul and Rob Portman. In a Senate hearing on election integrity held on December 16, 2020, Senator Paul made these remarks while interviewing Krebs:

> [I]f you're saying it's the safest election based on no dead people voted, no non-citizens voted, no people broke the absentee rules, I think that's false, and I think that's what upset a lot of people on our side. It's that they are taking your statement to mean, oh well, there was no problem in the election. I don't think you have examined any of the problems that we have heard here.[3]

To this, Krebs had no response. He stared silently with arms crossed while he ignored Senator Paul. After more than an hour went by, Ohio Senator Rob Portman forced the issue by repeating Senator Paul's question. Finally, Krebs made a rare confession:

> The focus of the statement, the joint statement, was security. . . . I think terms have been conflated here . . . alleging that we were speaking to the fraud aspect. *We absolutely were not* [emphasis added].[4]

---

3   "Election Security and Administration," U.S, Senate Homeland Security and Governmental Affairs Committee, December 16, 2020, https://www.c-span.org/video/?507292-1/senate-hearing-election-security-administration, @1:26:41.

4   Ibid., @2:30.

Krebs in Senate hearing, per C-Span video

So, more than a month after the joint statement claimed the election was the "most secure in American history," and more than an hour after being challenged by Senator Paul, Krebs was forced to state the truth: He admitted that he could not attest to the "integrity of our elections," as had been avowed (falsely) in the joint statement. And yet, at that very same Senate hearing, Krebs made this strange statement: "We're past the point where we need to be having conversations about the outcome of this election." How does that work? Krebs admits he knows nothing about "the fraud aspect," but it is time to move on and stop "having conversations" about the election.

In truth, Krebs was very happy to have many more conversations about the election, and he did so in several interviews conducted by adoring journalists. He cheerfully let those people use the discredited "joint statement" as proof of a fraud-free election. Krebs did not protest. He did not correct them. And no one asked him to.

KREBS NEEDS TO TAKE A COURSE IN AUDITING 101

After acknowledging in the Senate hearing that some election computers may have been connected to the internet on Election Day, Krebs expressed confidence (in a 60 Minutes interview) that votes were not altered with those computers.[5] How did he know? Because recounting of the paper ballots produced totals that agreed with the amounts on computer printouts. A simple analogy shows the folly of that argument: If you suspect that I gave you 10 counterfeit bills, would you feel better if I recount them?

When ballots or ballot applications are mailed to everyone in the state on the basis of out-of-date registration lists, millions of the ballots or applications go unused. Those

---

5   Scott Pelley "Interview of Christopher Krebs on 60 Minutes," *CBS News*, November 30, 2020, https://www.cbsnews.com/news/election-results-security-chris-krebs-60-minutes-2020-11-29/.

documents can be retrieved, filled out, and mailed to the election center to ensure that the paper ballot count matches the electronic count of ballots.

KREBS MISSED THE IRANIAN ELECTION HACK AND SOLAR WINDS FIASCO

Let's turn to the field of expertise that Krebs has mastered—supposedly. He was head of CISA (Cybersecurity and Infrastructure Security Agency), the U.S. agency that ensures our defenses against cyber-attacks from within and without. After Krebs expressed absolute confidence that the election was protected from cyber intrusions, it turns out that the election was not protected.

In a federal indictment, two Iranian hackers were charged with "successfully hacking into a state computer election system, stealing voter registration data and using it to carry out a cyber intimidation campaign that targeted GOP members of Congress, Trump campaign officials and Democrat voters in the November 2020 election."[6] The Iranians, who posed as "Proud Boys," managed to steal data for more than 100,000 voters. Krebs completely missed that hack.

Last, but not least, consider Solar Winds—the cyber assault that is considered to be one of the largest and potentially most harmful in history. This hack, which primarily targeted vendors in the global IT supply chain, probably originated in March 2020, according to experts. That is when Krebs headed CISA. The cyber intrusion remained undetected until December 2020, when a private company—not CISA—discovered it. You might think Krebs would temper his boastful reports concerning our most secure election in history, but he doesn't. He keeps peddling the old line to his journalist admirers.[7]

---

6   John Solomon, "Two Iranian hackers charged with stealing voter data, intimidating GOP lawmakers and Dem voters," *Just the News*, November 18, 2021, https://justthenews.com/politics-policy/elections/two-iranians-charged-cyber-intimidation-campaign-targeting-voters.

7   Pam Baker, "The SolarWinds hack timeline: Who knew what, and when?" *CSO United States*, June 4, 2021, https://www.csoonline.com/article/3613571/the-solarwinds-hack-timeline-who-knew-what-and-when.html.

19

ATTORNEY GENERAL WILLIAM BARR

People trying to change the rules to this, to this methodology—which, as a matter of logic, is very open to fraud and coercion—is reckless and dangerous and people are playing with fire.[1]

The words, above, were spoken by Attorney General William Barr in September 2020, just a couple of months before the 2020 election. He condemned the use of mail-in ballots, and feared the fraudulent voting that could result. But very soon after the election—way too soon—Barr and a department of very reluctant lawyers figured out that there was no significant fraud anywhere in the nation. It only took those sharpshooting attorneys about four days to figure it all out. Here is the timeline.

DOJ'S "REVIEW" LASTS JUST FOUR DAYS
On November 9, 2020, Barr issued a memo that, on its face, seems pretty reasonable. The Barr memo said, in part:

> [G]iven that voting in our current elections has now concluded, I authorize you to pursue substantial allegations of voting and vote tabulation irregularities prior to the certification of elections in your jurisdictions in certain cases. . . . Such inquiries and reviews may be conducted if there are clear and apparently credible allegations of irregularities that, if true, could potentially impact the outcome of a federal election in an individual state.[2]

---

1   Katelyn Polantz and Caroline Kelly, "Barr says voting by mail is 'playing with fire,'" *CNN News*, September 2, 2020, https://www.cnn.com/2020/09/02/politics/barr-mail-in-voting-playing-with-fire-situation-room/index.html.

2   Attorney General William Barr, "Memorandum for United States Attorneys," Office of the Attorney General, November 9, 2020, https://int.nyt.com/data/documenttools/barr-memo-elections-fraud/9bf5cac375012c4c/full.pdf.

To paraphrase Barr: If you hear of a substantial and credible allegation that could actually change the results of the election, you are authorized to pursue it.

No one was being ordered to start an investigation. They were simply being told to keep their ears and eyes open and use judgment. And consider this: Would you want a prosecutor to ignore substantial and credible allegations of fraud?

Barr's memo may sound reasonable to you and me, but we are not highly sophisticated and ethical DOJ attorneys. One such lawyer is Richard Pilger, who quit as director of the Election Crimes Branch of DOJ on the day Barr's memo was issued. Pilger explained his employment change this way:

> Having familiarized myself with the new policy and its ramifications, and in accord with the best tradition of the John C. Keeney Award for Exceptional Integrity and Professionalism (my most cherished Departmental recognition), I must regretfully resign from my role as Director of the Election Crimes Branch.[3]

Here are a few key points regarding the Pilger statement:

- First, he has a "cherished" award for Exceptional Integrity. Did you realize that?

- Second, while maintaining his exceptional integrity, he managed to avoid losing a dime of pay. (He merely transferred to another job in the department.)

- Finally: His little hissy fit must have earned him lots of points with the incoming Biden administration (and MSNBC?).

Eager to get in on the act, sixteen other federal prosecutors wrote to AG Barr to say they had found no evidence of "substantial allegations of voting and vote tabulation irregularities," so he should rescind his memo. When did they write that memo to Barr? They wrote it four days after Barr wrote his memo. Barr issued his memo on Monday, November 9, and the sixteen prosecutors responded on Friday, November 13. As you can see, they didn't wait long for the allegations to come rolling in.[4] They gave it four days.

---

3   Dartunorro Clark and Ken Dilanian, "Justice Department's election crimes chief resigns after Barr allows prosecutors to investigate voter fraud claims," *NBC News*, November 10, 2020, https://www.nbcnews.com/politics/2020-election/doj-s-election-crimes-chief-resigns-after-barr-directs-prosecutors-n1247220.

4   Katie Benner and Adam Goldman, "Federal Prosecutors Push Back on Barr Memo on Voter Fraud Claims," *New York Times*, November 13, 2020 and updated September 21, 2021, https://www.nytimes.com/2020/11/13/us/politics/justice-department-voter-fraud.html.

A couple weeks later, on December 1, 2020, William Barr declared: "To date, we have not seen fraud on a scale that could have effected a different outcome in the election."[5] The declaration was made after zero investigations were undertaken. But, for the self-proclaimed conspiracy debunkers in the media, Barr's statement, along with the "60 court cases" canard and the Krebs "most secure in American history" claim, would become the go-to proof of Biden's clean victory over Trump. To this very day, I still hear it used by lazy fact checkers.

Of course, Barr's December 1 statement infuriated President Trump, who excoriated the Attorney General in a meeting later that day. And before long, Barr tendered his resignation. Since then, Barr has become an election Einstein in the view of the adoring press.

ENTER ATTORNEY WILLIAM MCSWAIN

Months after the election, at a rally in Florida, Trump made a cryptic remark about "a U.S. attorney in Philadelphia that says he wasn't allowed to go and check Philadelphia." About a week later, Trump unleashed a potentially serious allegation against his former AG:

> I just a day ago received a statement from the U.S. attorney, highly respected, in Pennsylvania, that Bill Barr would not allow him to investigate voter fraud. Can you believe it? Now you have to understand, Philadelphia is the second most corrupt place, so I understand, okay? So, I understand, in the nation. . . . But the U.S. attorney was not allowed to investigate what . . . this just came out in a letter. . . . He was not allowed to do his job. And I saw that. He was all enthused, and then all of a sudden it was like he was turned off. And so were others.[6]

Barr was enraged by the allegation, and accused McSwain of writing his letter to Trump "in a very deceptive way that is intended to convey an impression, it's a false one, that he was restrained from looking into election fraud." McSwain countered that he received "various allegations" of irregularities but was told by Barr "not to make any public statements or put out any press releases." In addition, McSwain claimed that Barr wanted him to give any information regarding wrongdoing to Josh Shapiro, the Democrat Attorney General of Pennsylvania. As Shapiro was strongly anti-Trump, that would likely kill any investigation.[7]

---

5   Michael Balsamo (AP), "Barr says Justice Department found no evidence of fraud that would change election outcome," *The PBS News Hour*, December 1, 2020, https://www.pbs.org/newshour/politics/barr-says-justice-department-found-no-evidence-of-fraud-that-would-change-election-outcome.

6   Robert Farley, "Barr Disputes U.S. Attorney's Vote Fraud Claim," *FactCheck.Org*, July 14, 2021, https://www.factcheck.org/2021/07/barr-disputes-u-s-attorneys-vote-fraud-claim/.

7   Ibid.

I have a few observations about William Barr, and his understanding of election results. He has no understanding.

In an interview with Jonathan Karl, made months after the election, Barr said that election machine irregularities would be revealed when the paper ballots were recounted:

> It's a counting machine, and they save everything that was counted. So you just reconcile the two. There had been no discrepancy reported anywhere, and I'm still not aware of any discrepancy.[8]

Barr was making the same junior-level mistake made by Christopher Krebs, the former CISA head. See page 273. There was a time, a few years ago, when Barr's understanding of election fraud made some sense. That was when people actually voted in person. But now, with millions of mail-in ballots ready to be scooped up out of mail boxes, homeless shelters, nursing homes, etc., simple recounts are meaningless. It is now necessary to confirm that a ballot received from John R. Smith actually came from John R. Smith. And it is also necessary to establish that, if John R. Smith votes in Nevada, he actually lives in that state, and not in California.

IT'S NOT JUST FRAUD, MR. BARR

One more point: Barr's statement seems to limit election problems to "fraud," and, as Barr surely knows, fraud almost always requires intent. However, there can be plenty of election irregularities that do not require intent. For example, a county or precinct office may be violating election law without even realizing it. They may be inadequately training staff, using unsecure computers, violating chain of custody rules, ignoring time limits, etc. Those violations of rules and laws are probably not fraud, but they still count. For God's sake, doesn't Barr know that?

Interesting follow-up: There is a scandal in Pennsylvania, and it involves the destruction of key election documentation by officials in Delaware County. See page 183. Was McSwain referring to that? Or, was McSwain alluding to Jesse Morgan's missing trailer filled with hundreds of thousands of ballots? We still don't know what happened to it. See page 188.

8   Jonathan Karl, "Inside William Barr's Breakup With Trump," *The Atlantic*, June 27, 2021, https://www.theatlantic.com/politics/archive/2021/06/william-barrs-trump-administration-attorney-general/619298/.

20

COURT CASES BASED ON SUBSTANCE VS. PROCESS

How many times have you heard something like this: "State and federal judges dismissed more than 50 lawsuits presented by Donald Trump and his allies"?[1] Or this: "Trump and his allies have lost nearly 60 election fights in court"?[2]

Those claims are not wrong, but they are misleading to the point of being dishonest. Most of the election legal challenges were not decided on merit; rather, they were dismissed when a judge decided Trump or his allies lacked standing, the Trump team was late in filing (laches), the case was not within the jurisdiction of the court, or the case was moot. (Most of the damage had occurred already or the damage was minor.)

There may be some disagreement as to the number of cases that fall within each category of disposition. First, it depends on what you call a case. For example, if a case is tried in a federal district court, and later appealed, is that one case, or two? Also, some of the election related cases were filed in the name of Trump, and some cases were filed by others, but on his behalf.

One of the very best summations I have found is on a website called, **Promoting American Election Integrity** (https://election-integrity.info/). On that website, Ray Blehar and John Droz created a detailed table of court cases, including the nature of each claim and its final resolution (process or merit). As of June 10, 2022, there were

---

1   Reuters Staff, "Fact Check: Courts have dismissed multiple lawsuits of alleged electoral fraud presented by Trump campaign," *Reuters*, February 15, 2021, https://www.reuters.com/article/uk-factcheck-courts-election-idUSKBN2AF1G1.

2   Zoe Tillman, "Trump And His Allies Have Lost Nearly 60 Election Fights In Court (And Counting)," *BuzzFeed News*, December 14, 2020, https://www.buzzfeednews.com/article/zoetillman/trump-election-court-losses-electoral-college.

ninety-two election related cases listed in the table, and only thirty were decided on merit. According to Blehar and Droz, Trump and the GOP prevailed in twenty-two of those thirty cases.[3]

Of course, Trump was ultimately unsuccessful in his effort to get the courts to delay certification in any state. However, the "*Trump lost 50 or 60 court cases*" canard is phony and should not be used in assessing the validity of specific legal arguments.

3   "2020 US Presidential Election Related Lawsuits," *Promoting American Election Integrity*, accessed 2/28/2022, https://election-integrity.info/2020_Election_Cases.htm. [Author's note: This is an excellent information source for ideas to increase election integrity while making voting easier. This website has many useful reports and statistical analyses pertaining to every aspect of the 2020 election.]

21

WHAT DO THEY TEACH IN JOURNALISM SCHOOL?

College tuition is costly—and unnecessary. Just follow the guidance below and you will have the equivalent of a Journalism Ph.D.

- Give a partisan label to legislators from one political party and an authoritative label to legislators from the other. For example, House Republicans investigated Benghazi, but The House Select Committee is investigating the January 6th "insurrection."

- Set up straw-man narratives. If the target of your article referred to "irregularities," pretend he referred to "fraud," which is much harder for him to prove because it requires intent. If he claimed to have "evidence," pretend he claimed to have "proof." These little tricks make it easier to get the fact check "ruling" you want.

- By the way, when you issue your fact checks, try to add a visual aid, such as a picture of a pressure gauge or electric meter. That way the reader will know precisely how much misinformation was given to him/her/they.

- Use judicial dismissals as evidence of a baseless argument, even when the dismissals are based on standing, laches, mootness, or jurisdiction. Most readers don't even know what those things are!

- Pretend that censorship by other news outlets is evidence. For example, Ms. Congresswoman said something so false that she was banned by Twitter. That little trick should be useful for about half the population.

- Mix up tenses: past and present. For example, if a Congressman says he does not own Twitter stock, pretend he said he never owned Twitter stock. If Trump says he *does not* have a project in Russia, pretend he said he *did not* have a project in Russia. That way you can claim he lied, even if he did not. (Hats off to Jake Tapper for that little gem.)

- Completely ignore inconvenient stories. People don't need to hear about crime in America, the border crisis, Americans and allies still trapped in Afghanistan, shortages of baby formula, or Hunter Biden's possible crimes (drugs, gun registrations, taxes, money laundering, "the Big Guy," or violations of the Foreign Agents Registration Act).

- Pepper your writings with loaded language like recycled, debunked, baseless, peddled, conspiracy theory, groundless. Allusions to the Holocaust are particularly effective. That imagery can be achieved with the phrase "election denier."

- Claim a 3-hour riot is an "insurrection," even though rioters couldn't possibly take control of the government because no one remembered to bring weapons! (Trump supporters have lots of guns but, fortunately, they are not smart enough to remember them when it is insurrection time.)

- Use polls as evidence. For example, this Senator must not be telling the truth because 55 percent of people in our survey said so. By the way, always use polls of *Americans* rather than *registered voters*. That way, 10 to 15 percent of your sample will be noncitizens. (There is no reason to explain that to your readers.)

- Point out spelling and grammatical errors to discredit the target of your report. Here are a few you kan yous in this artikle.

- Identify troubling associations. For example, "The Senator's son has a friend whose mother was seen shopping in the vicinity of Washington, DC on January 6, 2021."

- Repress stories by calling them dangerous. For example, questions about the 2020 election are a danger to democracy. Come to think of it, this book is a danger to democracy!

- Encourage boycotts of people, businesses, and competing news sources until they stop covering cover stories you don't like. People don't need to hear that propaganda!

- When all else fails, play the "race" card. Remember, something that sounds innocuous could actually be a dog whistle for white supremacists. And be sure to warn your readers that, even people like Candace Owens and Larry Elder might be white supremacists.

If you master the issues listed above, you will be well on your way to a great job at MSNBC or even CNN. However, there is one more journalistic principle to discuss, and it is the most important of all. You must, at all costs, avoid retracting your stories. Your first impressions are usually best, so don't let them be compromised by changing facts.

A great illustration of this journalistic principle is the story of Officer Brian Sicknick. On January 6th, Sicknick had his head bashed in by Trump supporters wielding a fire extinguisher. Later, the coroner claimed that Sicknick died of natural causes and had no injuries. That medical report can mean only one thing: The coroner is a white supremacist and a Trump supporter. Experienced news people realized this, and that is why they did not change their original reporting.

APPENDIX A

SPECIAL AUDIT CONSIDERATIONS FOR ELECTIONS

The audit process and concepts outlined in Part I: The Audit Process, should not be confused with the type of "audit" typically held after an American election. Although they vary, post-election audits are generally no more than self-administered ballot recounts.

SAMPLE PROGRAM FOR ELECTIONS

To design a serious program for an election audit, we must consider certain unique issues. First, the auditor must respect the privacy of the voter. For this reason, it may not be possible to follow a specific transaction through the entire process. Second, there is usually very little time between the election and the certification process. The auditor has to work quickly and efficiently. (Legislation and/or a constitutional amendment to extend the timeframe should be considered.)

In December of 2008, the Maryland State Board of Elections, in conjunction with Pew Charitable Trusts, issued a "Pilot Election Audit Program" that may be a good starting point for any county's election audit. The program can be found here: Sample Election Audit Program.[1] It is necessarily general, since every jurisdiction has its own election laws and regulations. Also, the program is a bit out-of-date in a couple ways: (1) At the time of the report's issuance, absentee and provisional ballots comprised a much smaller share of the vote, and (2) In recent years, the accounting profession has improved audit efficiency with an increased emphasis on the process of "risk assessment."

---

1   The Maryland State Board of Elections, "Development of a Pilot Election Audit Program," *Pew Charitable Trusts*, December 3, 2008, https://elections.maryland.gov/press_room/documents/Maryland_Pilot%20Election%20Audit_12-3-2008.pdf.

Here are the key areas of focus for the Maryland Pilot Program. (More detail is found at the link, above.)

1. Verification of the voting system software

2. Chain of custody of the voting system's memory cards

3. Chain of custody of the touch screen and optical scan voting units

4. Pre-election preparation of touch screen and optical scan voting units

5. Pre-election preparation of the election management system

6. Preparation of the precinct register

7. Accurate absentee and provisional ballot canvasses

8. Proper accounting for paper ballots

9. Polling place reconciliation

10. Allocation and deployment of Election Day equipment and supplies

11. Poll worker performance.

To appropriately modify this program, I recommend that the audit should start with a careful assessment of internal control risk. A district with mostly in-person voting has much less risk than one with widespread mail-in ballots. Other risk factors would include:

- Is there automatic registration with a drivers license?

- Can applicants be asked to document citizenship? (Presently, federal law prohibits this, but it is being challenged.)

- Can people register online?

- Is there same-day registration?

- Is the registration list kept up-to-date?

- Do people have to request a ballot, or is it mailed automatically?

- Do people need an excuse to mail absentee, or is no reason needed?

- Do people have to submit identification with a mail-in ballot?

- Is voter ID required for in-person voting?

- Is there a signature requirement, and are signatures matched to signatures on file? (For the 2020 election, signatures matching standards were weak in several swing states.)

- What are the residency requirements (ten days, thirty days, longer)?

For certain key states, some of these risk factors are shown in Table 12, below.

INDEPENDENCE IS MANDATORY

These risk factors will dictate the amount and type of auditing to be performed in each jurisdiction. However, one audit concept is universal: All auditing must be performed by people completely independent from election staff and from county and state administrators. A nonpartisan and independent team of auditors should be formed, in advance of each election, and they should commence audit work immediately after every close election. As noted, it may be necessary to enact legislation to extend the timeframe between the election and certification of the results.

Finally . . .

- If you are concerned about election integrity,

- If most people vote via mail,

- If identification is no more than a signature,

. . . then I strongly recommend post-election, door-to-door, in-person canvassing of a statistically significant sample of registered voters. They should not be asked for whom they voted: Rather, they should be surveyed to determine if they voted, and by what means —in person or by mail-in ballot. These responses should be compared to the election department's records and, if there are significant differences, the canvassing efforts should be expanded.

If government officials will not authorize independent canvassing of voters, the losing side (be it Republican or Democrat) should consider hiring an independent team of door-to-door canvassers, supervised by CPAs, attorneys, scientists, and other professionals. The team should be independent and beyond ethical and professional reproach. They should issue a comprehensive canvassing report, to be used as evidence in any legal challenge to the election results. A significant error rate might convince a court that there is need for an expanded audit or even for a new election.

APPENDIX B

VOTER LAWS FOR KEY STATES (EFFECTIVE 1-1-22)[1]

TABLE 12: KEY VOTER LAWS[2][3][4]

State	Auto register?	Online register?	Same day register?	Residency requirement?	Request ballot?	Excuse needed?	ID required? In person	Via mail
Arizona	No	Yes	No	In state 30 days	Yes	No	Yes	Need ID 1st time
Florida	No	Yes	No	Yes	Yes	No	Yes	ID when requesting
Georgia	Via DMV	Yes	No	Yes	Yes	No	Yes	ID required
Iowa	No	Yes	Yes	Yes	Yes	No	Yes	No
Michigan	Yes, via DMV	Yes	Yes	In county or township 30 days	Yes	No	Yes	No
Minnesota	No	Yes	Yes	In state 20 days	Yes	No	1ST Time need ID	No
Nevada	Yes, via DMV	Yes	Yes	In state 30 days	No	No	1STTime need ID	No
Ohio	No	Yes	No	In state 30 days	Yes	No	Yes	ID required
Pennsylvania	No	Yes	No	In state 30 days	Yes	No	1ST Time	ID when requesting
Texas	No	No	No	Must reside in county	Yes	Yes	Yes	No
Wisconsin	No	Yes	Yes	In precinct 10 days	Yes	No	Yes	ID when requesting

---

1   In the 2020 election, these rules were temporarily modified in some states. All information is subject to change. In some cases new legislation is pending.

2   Information per *Ballotpedia* (https://ballotpedia.org/Main_Page), accessed on April 17, 2022.

3   Voter ID information is per *Voteriders.org* (https://www.voteriders.org/), accessed April 17, 2022; and per Vote.org (https://www.vote.org/voter-id-laws/), accessed April 17, 2022.

4   All of these states have signature requirements; however, in Pennsylvania and Wisconsin the signatures are not necessarily used, due to administrative or judicial decisions.

APPENDIX C

USEFUL REFERENCES

- Dr. Shiva Ayyadurai's Election Integrity website, https://vashiva.com/election-integrity/. .... Many interesting articles on the website of this well-known scientist and engineer.

- Ballotpedia, https://ballotpedia.org/Main_Page. ... A very comprehensive collection of statistics related to every aspect of state and federal elections.

- Benford's Law, https://towardsdatascience.com/benfords-law-a-simple-explanation-341e17abbe75. .... A Simple Explanation by Robert A. Gonsalves.

- Election Integrity Force, https://electionintegrityforce.com/. .... A Michigan-based nonprofit organization that has trained hundreds of poll challengers, issued dozens of election-related FOIA requests, and has participated in national efforts to bring transparency to election integrity issues.

- Dr. Douglas G. Frank's Election Analysis... https://electionfraud20.org/dr-frank-reports/. .... A large collection of election-related articles and studies, including Dr. Frank's "6th order polynomial" analyses of various state elections in 2020.

- The Legitimacy and Effect of Private Funding in Federal and State Electoral Processes, https://americanvotersalliance.org/wp-content/uploads/2021/06/2.-The-Legitimacy-and-Effect-of-Private-Funding-in-Federal-and-State-Electoral-Processes.pdf. ....A report from the Amistad Project of the Thomas More Society, regarding the impact of big nonprofit funding of elections.

- Let's Fix Stuff (Website of Patrick Colbeck), https://letsfixstuff.org/. .....Probing articles on election irregularities and other topics. A very interesting website.

- The Maryland State Board of Elections, https://elections.maryland.gov/press_room/documents/Maryland_Pilot%20Election%20Audit_12-3-2008.pdf. ..... "Development of a Pilot Election Audit Program," Pew Charitable Trusts, December 3, 2008.

- The Navarro Report, https://electionfraud20.org/navarro-election-report/. .... A report on irregularities in the 2020 election.

- Promoting American Election Integrity, https://election-integrity.info/. ..... An excellent information source for ideas to increase election integrity while making voting easier. This website has many useful reports and statistical analyses pertaining to every aspect of the 2020 election.

- U.S, Election Assistance Commission, https://www.eac.gov/election-officials/chain-custody-best-practices. ..... Recommended chain-of-custody procedures.

- United States Election Project, http://www.electproject.org/home. ..... An information source for the United States electoral system.

- Vote.org, https://www.vote.org/voter-id-laws/. .....State voter ID laws.

- Voter Registration Trends (Seth Keshel), https://www.scribd.com/document/498212060/Voter-Registration-Trends-Seth-Keshel. ...... Analysis of voter registration trends in key battleground states.

- Vote Reference, https://voteref.com/. ...... Provides public access to government documents.

- VoterGA.org, https://voterga.org/..... "Voters organized for trusted election results in Georgia." A website that chronicles the legal battles of VoterGA.org and its leader, Garland Favorito, concerning the 2020 Georgia election, and election reform generally.

- Voteriders, https://www.voteriders.org/. ..... Provides assistance with state election ID laws.

- The What, Why and How of Election Audits, https://www.ncsl.org/research/elections-and-campaigns/the-what-why-and-how-of-election-audits-magazine2021.aspx ..... National Conference of State Legislatures.

INDEX